ABOUT THE AUTHOR

With over 20 years of dedicated experience in the field of education, Rita Bateson is a distinguished consultant specialising in bespoke educational solutions tailored to the International Baccalaureate (IB) framework. Rita's extensive background includes roles as a book author, curriculum developer, teacher and educational leader across various prestigious institutions and organisations.

Rita has a rich professional history, teaching mathematics and physics at the highest level in the UK, Switzerland, Bermuda and Germany, working as head of departments while simultaneously an IB examiner in mathematics. Rita's expertise was further honed during her tenure as the Senior Curriculum Manager for Mathematics and Sciences at the International Baccalaureate in their Global Headquarters in The Hague where she oversaw global support.

Rita authored the official MYP mathematics textbooks, *MYP: By Concept* for the IB with Hachette Learning. As the Founding Head of Secondary at Nord Anglia International School Dublin, Rita successfully led the school through rapid expansion and achieved IB authorisation for both the Middle Years and Diploma Programme, earning high commendations and bringing IB Continuum to Ireland for the first time. In 2024 she founded an educational consultancy Eblana Learning, supporting the IB and schools globally in their curriculum and AI development.

ACKNOWLEDGEMENTS

To my inspirational mentors, family, friends, editors, collaborators and partners in fun and good craic!

A special thank you to So-Shan, Meena, Robert, Irina, Rachel, Andrew C, Shannon and so many more.

And to Andy and Ellie, for everything. Always.

CONTENTS

PREFACE

The location is a sunlit, bustling piazza in Rome. A handsome, slightly balding man sits at a table in an outdoor café, sipping a cappuccino. He wears an achingly trendy white suit, looking cool despite the sun. He appears to be reading a newspaper printed on pink paper. Placing the newspaper down, he makes direct eye contact with me. I lean forward. He speaks of the majesty of Paul Gascoigne and of Faustino Asprilla's latest goal celebrations. I cannot tear my eyes away. I am spellbound!

I am 14 years old and the man on the TV is James Richardson, the presenter of *Football Italia* – a British TV show from the 1990s. Interested as I was in this golden age of Italian football, my attention was gripped by this unfamiliar lifestyle. Here was this non-Italian somehow mimicking their 'vibe' – sitting in a café, looking effortlessly sophisticated and cool. My fate was sealed. I would live in Italy ... But how would I get there? I needed a way to travel, my only goal in life to find, and then taste, a cappuccino. Not easy in Dublin at the time.

These dreams were in stark contrast to my actual surroundings, living a suburban adolescence in the grey Ireland of the 1980s. Little did any of us know that we were about to enter a period of intense, and uncharacteristic, optimism in Ireland. Peace was coming to the island and the diaspora grew in confidence around the globe. Being Irish was a little bit cool for the first time in our history, and the Irish went straight out to exploit it!

With the intensity of a teenager, I vowed travel would be my life. But not teaching. Never teaching! There were at least four generations of teachers just before me, and a suspicion that our Viking ancestors came to Ireland not to pillage but to lecture. And so I wanted to forge my own path and direction. But life has its own intentions, and teaching came for me anyway.

After university in Dublin, I prepared to travel, but a broken jaw delayed it. My parents insisted that not being able to speak was not a disadvantage as 'there was nothing wrong with my ears', and I could listen and learn while recuperating. The list of one-year courses was limited, so the teacher qualification seemed to mollify them.

The problem was that from my first moment in front of a class I adored it. I even ignored the classic 'Don't smile til Christmas' advice, as I could not hide my glee. I loved teaching then and I adore it still. I am annoyingly more enthusiastic about it now than I was more than 25 years ago when I began. And this was a transferable skill, an opportunity to pack up my qualifications and carry them lightly with me all over the world.

Once qualified, the first international school I applied to in Italy advised me to get UK experience, so I immediately moved to Leeds to find a job. The recruitment cycle was unfamiliar to me, so I had no idea that a school still looking at the end of August was a red flag. Neither did I understand what they meant when they told me that, as a school, they were at about 11%. I smiled politely and happily took the job offered. Later it became clear that they meant approximately 11% of their students achieved five GCSEs each!

It was a baptism of fire, as the last teacher in was given the least desirable classes – as a rite of passage, I presume. I was given all the 'bottom sets'. My favourite and most challenging was a Year 11 set 9, who had very little interest in the beauty of mathematics but did derive great joy from creating new nicknames for me as their first order of business daily.

This resistant audience aside, I found myself impressed by the teaching methods in England. Unlike the extremely traditional, and change resistant, Irish system at the time, the UK was experiencing massive investment under 'New Labour'. My mind was blown by assessment for learning (AFL) and skills achievement, and anything at all that diverged from memorisation and mastery. Resources were 'adapted', teachers defined 'expectations' for students and gave detailed feedback on learning how to learn. Brain Gym and whiteboards were all the rage. What an enlightened and progressive system, I thought …

But the wanderlust persisted. Once I'd met, and married, my new English husband we headed onwards to Switzerland, where we first encountered the International Baccalaureate (IB), in the form of the Diploma Programme (DP). This was an epiphany for me! A revelation! Here was something truly revolutionary, thought I. What I had thought was true pedagogic love for the English system had been but a passing whim. Here was a system that valued the whole person, more than results or league tables. But I was a fickle follower, it appeared, because discovering the Middle Years Programme (MYP) in Bermuda several years later, it supplanted the DP in my heart almost instantly too.

In the years, and various schools, that followed, we encountered diverse backgrounds and attitudes to education and behaviour. Whether there was extreme wealth or poverty, affluence or physical neglect, privilege or deprivation,

I always found that the kids themselves had good hearts and great minds, and wanted to understand and be understood. No matter the context, each year had its joys, and I feel fortunate to have had the opportunity to be a positive influence in their lives.

It has to be acknowledged that the IB has an intense learning curve – I often felt that I needed to learn and unlearn in equal measure. But, thanks to our initial IB experience and training, we as a teaching couple could access new opportunities and advancements. And so we forged onwards to Bermuda, the Netherlands, the US, Germany and Ireland. With each new role I became increasingly submerged within the world of the IB. Teaching has been a wonderful way to develop my career, see the world and do a meaningful, rewarding job at the same time.

None of these systems are perfect of course, just as there is no perfect school. I have been through periods of awe, overload, comfort, ease, disillusionment and influence. I find myself now in an era of radical acceptance of the IB's strengths and occasional contradictions. You can be truly converted to the worldview of the IB while simultaneously understanding the frustrations it can bring forth. You also need to be self-aware enough to know when you start to sound like you're in some kind of cult.

I understand now that I have also been extremely privileged and the role that plays in everything. I had no idea how lucky I was to speak English, to have a recognisable and well-regarded education, and the freedom of movement globally that so many are denied. The IB philosophy has a way of reminding you of that privilege, and your responsibility to acknowledge it and change it for others where you can.

Fortunate as I was in this, we were doubly blessed to have made most of our mistakes in teaching in an era before the parent email or the social media record. Today, the job itself is vastly different to when I started. Expectations are also different. Nowadays you wouldn't hear of a 'hangover cabinet' for furtive napping. As teachers, we were virtually inaccessible to parents for months, and as a result things were neither discussed nor addressed. The situation is much better now, in terms of safeguarding and higher standards and expectations, but mistakes are so much more visible, and this can make the risk of experimentation less appealing.

One day, my husband, Andrew, saw a job advert that he described as 'short of saying the candidate must have green eyes and hate fish, it could be describing you perfectly'. The position was for a passionate educator to become curriculum and assessment manager for the ivory tower of the IB itself, in The Hague. I reluctantly left the classroom but relished the opportunity to actually craft what was going to be taught in classes around the world. This was the most formative part of my journey so far.

My motivation in authoring this book is to share the most successful practices I have observed in schools globally. It was a dream job, working with incredible mentors and thinkers. No one rolled their eyes when I got excited about research, or laughed when I proposed something new to try. I was encouraged to challenge ideas, but more importantly to make abstract ideas in education work at the school level and in a variety of contexts. My mentor, and professional hero, Robert Harrison consistently assured me that, while I missed the classroom, I was instead in thousands of classrooms every day with my work. That helped my homesickness for teaching, at least in the short term.

So, I have lived the IB for years now and done almost every single role within and without it – writing the curriculum, publishing the official textbooks, opening up a greenfield site for the MYP and DP, examining, leading workshops, etc. It became clear to me that this unique bird's eye view allowed me to help those who are struggling, curious or simply hungry to improve. This book is for anyone interested in the past, present and future of curriculum development in MYP Mathematics, and I hope it has practical transfers for other subjects too.

The book is also designed as a resource for those who might feel overwhelmed, tired or change resistant. They may wish to live the IB philosophy and pedagogy but in the most efficient way possible, as many teachers are tired and overburdened. Every day I see posts on social media and in WhatsApp groups clamouring for help and guidance, and I try to help where I can. But it's unsustainable in that format. These teachers are often confused or panicked, but they crave reassurance through genuine assistance and I hope they find it in these pages.

CHAPTER 1
THE IB MISSION

This book is written to support MYP mathematics teachers, to enable and empower them to function as successful curriculum designers and exemplary practitioners.

Key thinking points

In this chapter, there are explanations/discussions of:

- the IB and its guiding mission statement
- the history of the IB
- the development of the Middle Years Programme (MYP)
- the key features you'll find throughout this book.

Where should we start?

Let us begin. Each of the chapters that follow will be framed by a learner profile attribute and linked to the ideas within. However, as this is the introductory chapter, we will begin with the International Baccalaureate (IB) itself, where it has come from and what it is for. Our considerations begin with the IB's mission statement. This mission statement underpins the entire philosophy of the organisation and will help to ground our deliberations within the aims of the IB.

You've probably worked in many places that have mission statements. You may even feel that they all sound the same. Certainly, there are commonalities between schools' mission statements seen online. None say they wish to provide a substandard education or that their students will be anything other than world-class. I've never read one that I disagreed with, as they all feature honourable intentions and ambitions. Who wouldn't want that?

So we need to look at the IB's mission statement with fresh eyes, as if for the first time. Before The Hague, I have to confess that I hadn't read it particularly thoroughly. In fact, I'm not sure I read it at all. It was always at the front of the guides, on the pages I flipped past to get to what I thought was most important – the syllabus. Years later, when it was part of my job, I finally did just that. I read it slowly, and determined how much of it I understood and agreed with. Also, did any of it actually impact my teaching practice?

What are the key features?

Throughout this book, as we move through the different stages of curriculum development, I will indicate different features that can support your understanding. These key features include resource signposts, information about influential researchers and educators in the field, AI prompt suggestions and recommendations for further reading.

What is the IB mission statement?

> The International Baccalaureate aims to develop inquiring, knowledgeable and caring young people who help to create a better and more peaceful world through intercultural understanding and respect.
>
> To this end the organization works with schools, governments and international organizations to develop challenging programmes of international education and rigorous **assessment**.
>
> These programmes encourage students across the world to become active, compassionate and lifelong learners who understand that other people, with their differences, can also be right.
>
> International Baccalaureate Organization

I find nothing to object to in this statement. These are lofty, excellent goals and truly the purpose of education, but there is something special for me about the last phrase 'other people, with their differences, can also be right'. In literature, there is a practice of reading called *florilegia*, where extracts are brought together, like a 'best of' or curated group. The word comes from Latin and refers to the gathering or collecting of flowers. The idea is that the reader waits for something to blossom on the page and then gathers it, to savour and enjoy later. The modern equivalent, I believe, is when we see something on our phones that we like and we take a screenshot to remember it later.

For me, this last line of the mission statement blooms when I read it. It sparkles. It glows and clamours for my attention. I cannot think of any greater goal for myself and for the conflict in the world than the idea that other people can also be right. It implies that I have to sometimes accept that I am, on very rare occasions, wrong myself. This lesson in humility, and prompt for compassion and peace, is the most powerful for me. It is something I have never seen in any other statement of a mission.

In one particularly stressful phase of a curriculum rollout, all the curriculum managers had been attending seminars and conferences, trying our best to help stressed and anxious teachers accept that the changes were for the better. We were emotionally and intellectually exhausted, and some of us felt a little jaded from travel and from what we perceived as an ungrateful audience to all our hard work. It was not a good look for me and I will admit I am now quite ashamed of it.

I was facilitating a session one day when I had two educators from the same region of conflict ask for advice on some rather different assessment challenges. The first, a Palestinian teacher, explained that it was not unusual for them to have to climb over rubble in the morning to get into school, and what were my recommendations for criterion assessments when this happened? By coincidence there was an Israeli teacher present, and she echoed these concerns from her school's side: 'What should I do when a Criterion B assessment is interrupted for a bomb siren and the students might reveal the pattern?'

Key feature: Anecdotal evidence

As we proceed through the world of curriculum development, learner profile attribute by learner profile attribute, I will share insights from the thousands of schools I have worked with and from my own personal experience. These examples and counterexamples may resonate with something you have experienced or align with your view of the MYP. Alternatively, they might also serve as a warning of what not to do!

These questions baffled me. I sputtered out something along the lines of, 'I think you guys have more important things to consider than MYP grading in that case.' Wow, was I ever wrong!

Both teachers disagreed with me instantly, in the most strident terms. They explained that this education was precisely what they valued and were hoping to instil in the next generation, that the IB gave them a language to talk about tolerance and acceptance when conflict was at its most harmful. It genuinely had never occurred to me that anything we did could ever be this important. They were living the mission statement in trying to create a better and more peaceful world. It humbled me, and I remembered those two teachers every time I made a curriculum change, resource or recommendation, asking myself how it might impact schools like theirs.

On a practical note, it is really important to make students aware of this mission statement. Assemblies are great for this, but a physical reminder in the form of a classroom poster can frame conversations. It is something to refer to regularly, especially useful in conflict resolution or restorative conversations: 'You two seem to be having a disagreement, but can we both accept that ...', 'Our goal in this school is to be a community and to understand each other ...'.

Later, when I was head of school for a brand new MYP and DP school in Dublin, we made sure that we had large mission statement posters in every classroom and working space before authorisation. Of course, this was intended to impress visitors, but it also served as a subliminal reminder for every day. We placed the school's own learning vision alongside too – it helped us live and breathe the IB ideals as a community. If you don't have one in your classroom or office, go and print one right now. Or ask your coordinator – it might inspire them to share with all.

Where did it all come from?

So where did the IB come from? If you are reading this book, then I have to assume that you are relatively new to the IB and certainly weren't involved in its inception. So you may only be familiar with the modern and current version of the IB, vast, global and influential. But it wasn't always thus ...

The IB was born of two extremely specific needs, one of which was very practical and the other much more idealistic. The two goals were symbiotic but not in an immediately obvious way, born of the coincidence of post-war liberalism and rising globalism. From a practical perspective, there was a growing need for a portable or transferable education for international families. These families were highly mobile, increasing in number as the globalism began to have an effect. Families of diplomats and multinational executives understood the dangers of moving their children repeatedly, in and out of very disparate national systems, often to their detriment when applying to colleges.

The second goal was much more progressive in its thinking – there were calls for a different type of education, one that would help young people engage with the complexities of the world and a desire to make it a better place for all humanity. This was heavily influenced by the culture of post-war liberalism that also lay behind the establishment of other institutions of international order, such as the United Nations, among others. This motivation also fitted well in the worldview of these diplomatic families, who were for the most part also internationally minded and motivated to preserve peace and harmony. The issues in education crossed disciplinary, geographical and cultural borders, just as these families would.

To meet both these goals, a teacher-led initiative began, with its origins in Geneva as well as several established international schools, and drawing on substantial grants from Unesco and other supporting governments. Its remit was to develop an internationally recognised educational programme that would be validated for university entry. The Diploma Programme was the priority, and following a prolonged period of development, was established in 1968. It remained the priority of the IB for far decades afterwards. There had been some preliminary work done on similar primary school provision, but little progress had been made in this area due to lack of funding. The middle years were overlooked as it was felt that the British system's qualifications at the time provided sufficient support, albeit without a shared philosophy.

Before long, the IB Diploma was recognised and highly attractive to others besides the jet-setting diplomats and executive multinational families. It was desirable as a philosophy in schools beyond the private, international and self-considered Tier 1 scene. Cynics might say it also became a respected brand and quality mark, which gave schools credibility and recognition if they had sufficient resources.

Another concern of schools and teachers when interacting with the IB is often the associated cost. These are expensive programmes to get authorised and to sustain. One member of the Heads Council described it me as 'reassuringly expensive', which was an opinion I hadn't really considered before. His position was that, to maintain such a high standard and **pedagogy** required a commitment that kept half-hearted, opportunistic enterprises at bay.

My time at the IB coincided with a period of massive transition from small educational organisation to behemoth, and there were teething problems from such rapid expansion. Perhaps it can appear austere, authoritative or confusing, but in the not-too-distant past the IB was a very tight-knit community of educators. Many of the older IB Educators (often called IBEN) would bemoan the changes, feeling the lack of the connection present in the early days. Talking to the original author of the Primary Years Programme (PYP), Ann Hickey, recently, it was clear that it was an organisation for teachers, run by teachers.

Others believed that the organisation was elitist, out of reach of so many who could benefit from this philosophy. There had been a feeling that the focus was palpably white, western facing, overly British and of the old-world order. The IB was certainly responsive to this criticism, and I saw many advances in this over the years. One colleague, David Jones, was particularly vocal on this matter. In my interview he grilled me intensely on how I would support under-resourced and under-recognised schools in Africa, for example. It was a regular refrain in discussions, often to positive effect.

Lastly, the rapid expansion gave rise to another problem. There was a question of principles and moral authority, which continues in certain circles online to this day. I was involved in many heated debates between colleagues regarding our investment or expansion into cultures that didn't always fully subscribe to the same beliefs. There were those who felt that it showed us to be over-adapting and compromising too far, while others felt that the IB's presence in any environment where it could encourage peace and intercultural understanding warranted some flexibility. I was often in the first camp, but passionate educators from schools in those regions utterly changed my mind. Theirs were the voices to be respected.

It cannot be understated how influential the IB philosophy and approach has been on other educational systems. This is rather disgustingly referred to in the organisation as 'positive backwash', and it is true that many other systems have made incremental changes towards it. It is the very manifestation of a rising tide lifting all boats. Some openly reference the ideas, others more obliquely, but the impact is clear. It is hard to imagine, as we view the global influence it has, that the IB only recently celebrated its 50th birthday!

The three other programmes came later, in the form of the aforementioned Primary Years Programme (PYP), a Middle Years Programme and a Career-related Programme (CP), giving the IB a full continuum of strong, stand-alone programmes. These were all designed to be 'broad, balanced, conceptual and connected', with a range of academic studies and learning experiences. The table below shows a comparison of the four programmes. We will discuss the development of the MYP in the next section.

Programme	Unique characteristics	Curriculum (content)	Assessment (certification)	Common threads throughout
Primary Years Programme (PYP), 1997	In the PYP, learning aims to transcend traditional boundaries between subject areas, using six transdisciplinary themes of global significance.	There are sample scope and sequence documents provided, but curriculums must be developed by schools.	Assessment guidance is neither defined nor prescribed by the PYP, and so these are school-based decisions.	Common threads between all four programmes: – international mindedness – developing the attributes of the IB learner profile – approaches to learning. All four IB programmes also require completion of a culminating project: the PYP exhibition; the MYP personal project or community project; the DP extended essay; the CP reflective project. These are a showcase for knowledge, understanding and skills. They are a culminating celebration of learning.
Middle Years Programme (MYP), 1994	In the MYP, students explore six global contexts that are developed from, and extend, the PYP transdisciplinary themes.	While there is no defined curriculum content, there is a great deal of guidance in the guise of a framework. The exact content can be determined by the school, although there is an expected exit point, 'Prior Learning', for the DP.	Assessment is defined but not prescribed in the MYP. External assessment is available in the form of eAssessment, but it is by no means taken up by the majority of schools. It remains the only route to a validated MYP Certificate.	
Diploma Programme (DP), 1968	In the DP, the curriculum consists of six subject groups and the three elements of the DP core, as well as the theory of knowledge (TOK) course, which encourages students to become more aware of their own perspectives and assumptions.	There are individual detailed subject guides and specifications in each subject offered in the DP.	It is the only programme to have clearly defined curriculum and assessment outcomes, and fully externally validated grades.	
Career-related Programme (CP), 2012	In the CP, students combine the study of DP courses with career-related studies and the four elements of the CP core, to prepare them for personal and professional situations.	The CP curriculum is a subset of the Diploma Programme where students engage with a number of DP subjects as well as additional requirements.	Assessment follows Diploma Programme protocols, with adaptations allowed.	

These programmes have developed organically over time and in response to real demand but weren't always developed in reference to one another. It is also fair to say that each review does look for opportunities to bring them iteratively closer to one another.

Interfacing, or communicating, with the IB can sometimes feel frustrating. You might face inconclusive answers or find that educators interpret details differently, leading to certain interpretations becoming 'the gospel'. There have been strides in the past decade: an improved IB Answers service, more school services teams and a revamped exchange platform on My IB are products of this drive to improve access.

Education is an act of hope in the face of an always-uncertain future. An IB education calls forth the absolute best in students and educators alike. The IB believes that together we can help to prepare students for living and working in a complex, highly interconnected world.

Source: 'What is an IB education?', My IB

Key feature: Further reading

Although most of us are trying to figure out the most efficient ways to balance everything, occasionally we get some time to read and further our craft. Many of us even enjoy reading about mathematics for pleasure, or we might need some recommendations for uber-keen parents or students. When it is relevant, I will highlight some academic research or current writings that fit within the scope of our discussions. In the appendix you will find a list of books that would make the ultimate MYP Mathematics library, should you be blessed with an infinite budget.

What about the MYP?

In this section let's dive further into the MYP in particular, and its own unique features and history.

Why did the MYP develop, and how?

The MYP sprang from an initiative by groups of teachers and administrators who wanted to develop a curriculum for the middle years of schooling. It was intended that this curriculum would share much of the same philosophy as the DP and would prepare students for success in that programme. It would also provide academic challenge while concerning itself with the development of young people and their personal, social and emotional wellbeing.

Key feature: Resources signpost

Throughout this book you will find directions to resources which will help you implement the advice given. They can also help you elevate your practice or understand the programmes better. These resources might be online, games, manipulatives, groups or companies to add to your repertoire.

It could be said that this is the last chance for students to play with learning before the high-stakes, controlled environment of the DP and CP. The first draft of the MYP curriculum was produced in 1987, and the IB authorised the first 15 MYP schools in 1994. It often surprises me how much later the MYP arrived than the DP. I was almost in university myself when the first MYP schools were authorised.

One of the most significant steps in trying to start to articulate the three programmes was adopting the PYP student profile and renaming it the IB learner profile, describing the attributes of an IB educated learner. Presented by the head of programme development, Judith Fabian (and built on the inspirational work of Kevin Bartlett and others), the learner profile gave a common language across the programmes and strengthened their connections. Judith was a formidable head of programme development, in the best way. She was cool and calm, with an effortless authority, in the style of Mary Robinson. I was in awe of her and tried to learn as much as I could before she retired.

Details of other key individuals, groups and research influences behind the development from 1980 to 2010 can be found in *History of the Middle Years Programme* (Nicolson, 2010). For those interested in the granular detail of who, when and what was decided, this document is a treasure trove of detail and long-forgotten conversations. To make sure I fully understood the nuances, I also interviewed the author, Malcolm Nicolson, who was also the head of MYP development at that time.

The history of the MYP document details an uncertain period, due to a lack of strategic planning, when the future might have been hugely different for MYP. It may be because the Diploma Programme was increasing exponentially and curriculum development in that programme was rolling out so they were stretched to the limit. As an account it is highly personal, sometimes indulgent, but rich in detail. Speaking to Malcolm added colour to that detail, including the fact that the origin of the document was a drunken warning from one of the programme's founders that 'everyone who knew everything was dead or dying and this knowledge hasn't been captured'. I found this fascinating.

Reading Malcolm's history of the MYP made me realise that the people behind the curriculum had names and faces, and that these were humans who were thinking about the classroom and the examinations and more. As a result, it made me determined that this book would hopefully do the same – give insight into the 'behind the scenes' conversations that happen in the meetings that decide our fates in schools. Malcolm's document ends just before the most significant phase of the MYP development: the 'Next Chapter'.

In 2010, the IB began this major review of the programme, leading to the publication of a new *From Principles into Practice* (FPIP) and new guides for all subject groups in 2014 (IBO, 2014). Malcolm and his team achieved a huge amount in a very short time, and the review was financially very successful and conceptually progressive. He was most proud of the changes they made to the concepts, and felt that if they could do it all again there would more of a focus on design thinking. He also indicated a wish that the next review would have been done sooner.

We discussed the shame that no similar document exists for development since 2010. Without the institutional memory, who is to know or to care that there were at one point 97 key concepts in Arts and only 4 in Sciences, and that they ended up at 16 because 'it felt about right', or how the global contexts came to be, thanks to a timely intervention from a PYP colleague.

Every academic staff member must join at a certain point in the review cycles, and some are luckier than others. I initially felt that I was unlucky to have arrived just after the launch of a hugely significant review into the entire programme: the aforementioned Next Chapter. It felt like I had arrived at the end of this particular party, feeling like the lights has just been switched on and I was a little too late for all the fun. For example, after Next Chapter further changes were off the table to allow for bedding in. Robert Harrison (my mentor) was in a similar position, having taken over not long before my arrival. I was his first hire in his new role. There were limitations to what we could change post-review, but it was a very exciting time as he brought a vision and thoroughness to the review changes.

Before long I felt very fortunate to be there to support its rollout, find mistakes and correct them, and add detail and understanding where I could. Following this, I authored further guidance, a new MYP Mathematics framework and supported the eAssessment development. Our lot in life became advancing the cause, promoting the ideals and picking up any loose threads of the review that might have remained. I literally slept with the curriculum guide under my pillow and the pages of *From Principles into Practice* taped to my bathroom walls.

Meanwhile, my husband's plight was to temporarily remain in Bermuda, playing golf and receiving 'We're sorry your wife left you' pity cakes.

Now we are at a point in time where many in the community have no idea of the world before then, or even recognise the change. Funnily enough, most people I meet now have no memory of the MYP before the Next Chapter, and fewer still remember the days of *Homo faber.*

The Next Chapter review addressed concerns of the community and countered the critical nicknames: 'Many Years of Projects', the 'muddle in the middle', the 'forgotten middle child'. Some concerns remain.

Often the pressure in the Diploma can drift downwards and be visited upon the MYP. This comes in the form of 'they need to be ready for Diploma' or 'they need to know x and y and we don't have time for the concepts stuff'. Running counter to these claims is the evidence of iterative change in the DP. In the last DP review, the curriculum manager, Deb Sutch, was very open to embedding and increasing the conceptual understanding, thereby moving the DP incrementally closer to the MYP.

But still there is this backward-mapping pressure. It is fairly commonplace to have the MYP 1 to 3 curriculum (or grades 6 to 8), a very inquiry-based, joyful curriculum, and then have MYP 4 to 5 as ostensibly a pre-DP curriculum. The separation of standard and extended certainly reinforces this idea, and we have to remind ourselves that it is not a 'mini DP', that it must remain its own programme.

By all means, please prepare them for Diploma Programme success, but not at the expense of the MYP's own unique identity. Too much in one direction and they are only good 'knowers', who don't seem to think for themselves, too much in the other direction and they are fantastic 'thinkers' but don't seem to know anything. The sweet spot in the middle is where the MYP functions at its best. But this takes thoughtful planning and careful execution of that plan to give students the best experience. Don't allow it to become the forgotten middle child if you are fortunate enough to work in a continuum school.

The next phase of curriculum development is upon us now, and the 'Enhancing the MYP' project will no doubt visit all these aspects of the MYP. I feel confident that they will retain the benefits, **rigour** and innovation of the programme, while increasing flexibility and assistance for schools. As always, good teaching and learning will remain, and it is in the very capable hands of an experienced curriculum manager, for whom I have a great deal of respect.

How do I bring all this together?

Now that we have a detailed knowledge of the 'who', 'how' and 'when', we should think about the 'what' of putting together a strong MYP Mathematics curriculum. There are many layers of moving parts to an IB education. This section is intended for those of you brand new to the curriculum, but I hope it will also prove useful to those who are familiar with, but not fluent in, IB terminology.

It can be such a shock to the system when first confronted with the IB lingo. After a while you forget how many of the terms and ideas you take for granted. A colleague called David Hunt joined the IB around the same time as me. He was not an educator and had never encountered the IB prior to his appointment. I hope he will forgive me that I can't remember what his specific job title was, but it was definitely business-facing. One day in conversation he took me by surprise when he stopped me mid-rant with, 'You people all are talking in a language that you think is English and sounds like English, but it really isn't!' I was intrigued as well as defensive.

He challenged my viewpoint in a very helpful way. I had always taken for granted that the onus was on the receiving end – they would simply have to 'learn it and get with the programme', literally. David helped me to understand that: 'You want people to come to the product, you want it to be user friendly, to increase its reach,' he explained.

This was something from the business world that I did not comprehend. 'You're dealing with teachers,' I would say. 'They will learn it.' To which he would counter, 'They are also people, and these particular people are often time-poor, under pressure or working in a non-native language.' He also was keen to stress that the education world was populated by non-teachers too, and that clarity was a form of kindness to them.

With this in mind, take a look at the MYP Programme Model circle on the IB website which illustrates everything we must bring together. This single image shows all the elements of the programme in concentric circles, placing the learner profile at the centre. This can help us to collate the ideas. It does not, however, give us an elaboration of relative importance for us as curriculum planners.

The following chapters will provide a deep dive into each part of this programme model in turn. We discuss concepts in chapter 1, for example, action and service in chapter 7, and projects in chapter 8. There is inevitably so much more to think about than what is contained in the circle that represents the IB Middle Years Programme.

Let's break these ideas down first and then reassemble them into a gold-standard, world-leading curriculum! Thinking of Dave Hunt and his frustration with too much jargon, here is an analogy to explain how the optimal curriculum should work, without overly relying on the definitions:

MYP conceptualised as baking delicious treats

- Concept-based education – The concepts are the big ideas within the programme, those things that are important, transferable and ever present. These are the base ingredients of baking – the flour, sugar and eggs. They form the basis of everything that we do and provide the structure and substance. We will discuss concept-based learning in the next chapter too.
- Subject groups – Each subject group (Languages, Individuals and Societies, Sciences, Mathematics, The Arts ...) adds a unique flavour, like different ingredients (cocoa, vanilla, fruits, nuts) that you choose based on the type of cake (or educational experience) you want.
- Learner profile – The IB learner profile attributes (Thinkers, Communicators, Risk-takers, etc.) are like different baking techniques. They shape how students approach learning and personal development, much like how kneading, mixing or creaming affect a cake's texture and consistency.
- Assessment criteria – Just as following a recipe correctly and giving the right amount of time and attention ensures a successful cake, adhering to IB assessment criteria and guidelines ensures students meet the **objectives** and achieve academic success. For further discussion of assessment, turn to chapter 3.
- International-mindedness – Adding spice, flavouring, colouring or extracts. Adding depth and perspective to give flavours. Unique flavouring is the special ingredient, like a unique spice or extract, which gives an IB education its distinctive global perspective and flavour.
- **Approaches to learning** (ATLs) – These are the methods, tools and technique that teachers use, akin to mixers, ovens and baking pans. They facilitate the learning process, ensuring that the 'ingredients' are combined

effectively to produce a well-rounded education. You will see these in all programmes, and we discuss them in chapter 4 in some depth.

- Branches of reasoning – There are categories of baked goods such as buns, breads, cakes and cookies. All share a family resemblance but are sufficiently different to keep things connected yet interesting.
- Inquiry – This is like a baker experimenting with different recipes and ingredients to create something new or improve upon an existing recipe. It's about asking questions, exploring and being creative in the learning process. We encourage curiosity and innovation in students' approach, and in the questions they ask and answer.
- Service – In the IB, service learning is about applying what you've learned to help and enrich the community. Students use the skills, knowledge and understanding they've gained to make a positive impact on others, just as sharing a cake can bring joy and benefit to those who receive it. We discuss the role of service within the mathematics curriculum in chapter 8.
- Reflection – Just as bakers taste the cake they have made and decorate it, continuous reflection and improvement in the IB ensures that the educational experience is both effective and appealing, by adjusting the ingredients or method accordingly. In the IB, reflection is a critical part of the learning process, continuous and deeply personal. Just as with baking, we are testing, tasting, adjusting and then savouring our success.

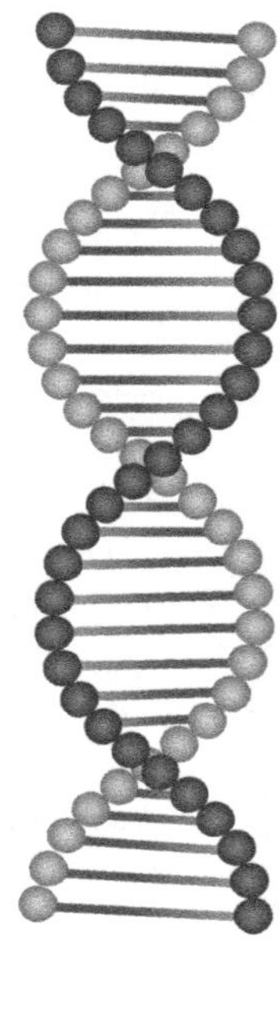

You could also look at the complex and beautiful structure of DNA as another analogy to illustrate the interconnected nature of the programme components. You could say that one of these is close to my heart and one is close to my head! One represents the creative and playful side of mathematics. The other speaks to the part of the mathematics teaching identity that craves completion, order and connections.

The structure of the DNA double helix can be visualised as the MYP programme if we assign different parts of the curriculum within. I like to imagine each of the strands of the double helix as ribbons of contents and concepts, existing relatively independently of one another. The elegance of the MYP programme is that we connect them using 'meaning-making connectors'.

The nucleotide base pairs that connect them can be imagined as different pairings via approaches to learning, global contexts, inquiry and learner profile attributes. These connections allow these ideas to interact harmoniously and remain intimately linked. The molecules that make up parts of the backbone are a good representation of reflection, action and service, and just as DNA carries the genetic information necessary for life, so does the MYP equip students with everything they need to thrive.

Key feature: Further reading

Eugenia Cheng

The model of thinking about the IB requirements as baking must have been influenced by the writings of Eugenia Cheng. She is a mathematics communicator and writer, who seems to have the power to make all mathematics delicious.

The idea of baking a cake reminds me of the holistic and dynamic nature of an IB education, where learning is not only about acquiring knowledge but also about reflecting, inquiring and using that knowledge to contribute positively to the world. It is like a carefully balanced recipe. Remember, it is always important to check the expiry dates on your ingredients. Are you serving up the same thing every year without checking if it has gone stale?

As an experiment, I asked ChatGPT to develop this metaphor of the MYP curriculum as a cake for me. First it congratulated me on my idea – 'What a creative analogy' – which I adored. I knew the praise was entirely hollow, but I love compliments! Next, it served me up a word soup instead of a pleasing cake. It had simply taken every aspect of the IB it could scrape from the large language model and made most ideas a flavour or taste. It made a reasonable attempt at connecting some of the bigger ideas.

Why not try to develop your own analogy using ChatGPT, to test your comfort levels with this emerging technology? There will be lots of opportunities for us to discuss the use of generative AI throughout this book, for those interested in this world.

I like the idea of a very fluffy and emotionally laden image contrasting with one that is more clinical, appealing to different aspects of my own nature and in recognition that students will react differently to different comparatives.

At the end of each chapter, you will see the following radial chart. This is a self-assessment tool for you to track your growth in understanding the most important elements of MYP curriculum development. Starting from the centre, shade your level of familiarity from beginning to expert. Over time we will see growth in each sector, as we progress through the chapters and learner profile attributes.

Self-assessment

Complete the reflection:

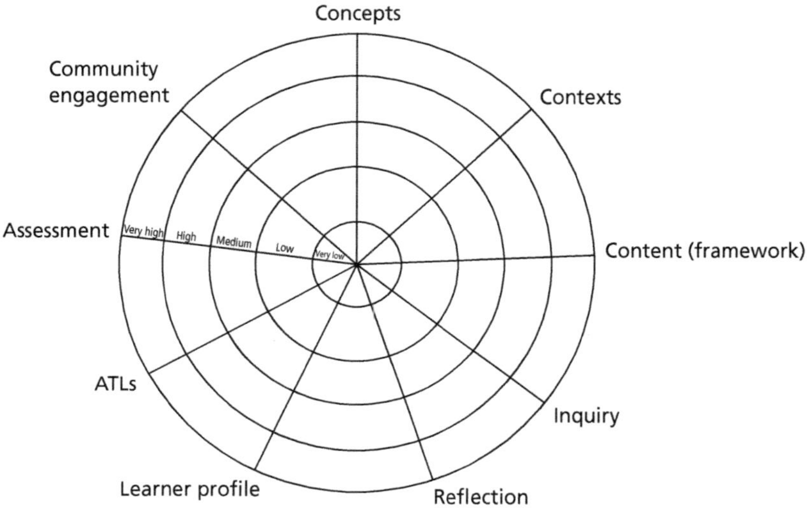

Shade in your knowledge level from low to high as you feel your comfort level lies.

> **Key feature: Reflection**
>
> What analogy would you create for a complex interrelated structure such as the MYP? Would it be two-dimensional or three-dimensional?

Glossary

Approaches to learning Refers to a range of skills that help students guide, support and structure learning.

Assessment The collection of evidence in order to make judgements about teaching and learning.

Curriculum An overall plan for learning that is broad, balanced and coherent. It describes the entire learning experience in a school.

Objective One of a set of statements describing the skills, knowledge and understanding that will be assessed.

Pedagogy The art and science of teaching (young people) as a professional practice.

Rigour A thorough and robust understanding of subjects that prepares students for further education and lifelong learning.*

* *Not an official IB definition.*

CHAPTER 2
REFLECTIVE

We thoughtfully consider the world and our own ideas and experience. We work to understand our strengths and weaknesses in order to support our learning and personal development.

Key thinking points

In this chapter, there are explanations/discussions of:

- why Reflective is an appropriate starting learner profile attribute when thinking about curriculum development
- the purpose of this book and how to use it
- what the 10 learner profile attributes are
- why the learner profile attributes give richness to our curriculum design
- the nature of mathematics (meditations)
- the key differences between MYP Mathematics and other systems.

'... we work to understand our strengths and weaknesses ...'

Why choose Reflective as the learner profile attribute for this chapter?

When we embark on any curriculum development, it is important to reflect. We reflect as a matter of course throughout each MYP unit of inquiry, encouraged by the IB to do so. This is facilitated by the inclusion of **reflection** in the unit planning process and then, even more explicitly, by the reflection prompts before, during and after each unit in the unit planner. To have fidelity with this process, we will reflect on where your strengths, weaknesses and needs might be. In this chapter we will consider why you have chosen this book and how you could use it most effectively. It is not designed in a way that insists on linear reading (although you can read it like that if you prefer). Take time to reflect on your needs. How will they be best served, given the demands on your time and attention?

How should you use this book?

'... to support our learning and personal development ...'

Honestly, use it in any way that you find it helpful. These chapters were designed for you, wherever you are on the journey. Maybe you're a newbie or it's your first time in an IB school. Or perhaps you're a PHE or sciences teacher who has had to pick up some mathematics classes and you just need some direction. I hope this book will support more people than those who are new to the system – more experienced educators and coordinators should also find it a nudge to revisit and elevate their practice. Within each chapter, you will discover findings and suggestions, reflection opportunities and anecdotal examples to inspire or forewarn, and all of them delivered in an inquiry-based approach.

Picture the book as a digital image on a computer screen in the old dial-up days, or sometimes on Instagram with a bad Wi-Fi signal. Imagine that your understanding is an image loading on a computer, one that doesn't have the bandwidth to download all at once. First you will get broad brushstrokes, vaguely recognisable shapes, then gradually more detail will come into focus. The image gets sharper, finally the resolution is fully loaded, and the picture (and understanding) is crystal clear!

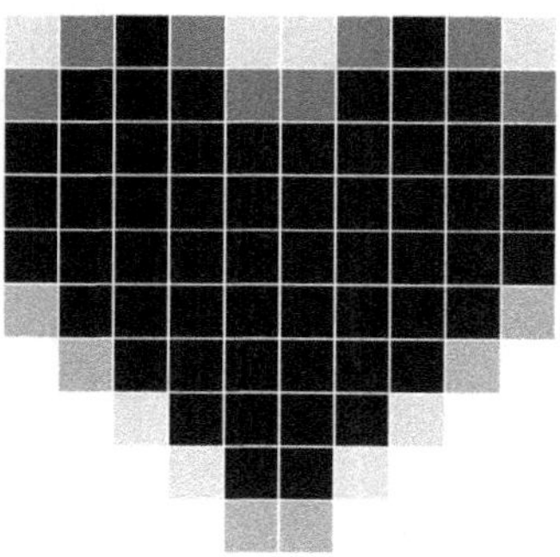

@1 x resolution
(10px x 10px)

@2 x resolution
(20px x 20px)

Let's look at some of the ways you could use this book ...

Linearly

As a mathematician, you may find it logical to read the entire tome linearly, chapter by chapter. In this case you will progress seamlessly through the initial, foundational pieces into a deeper understanding. This is reminiscent of how we scaffold the branches of reasoning and content for our students, spiralling throughout the years, visiting and revisiting the most important ideas:

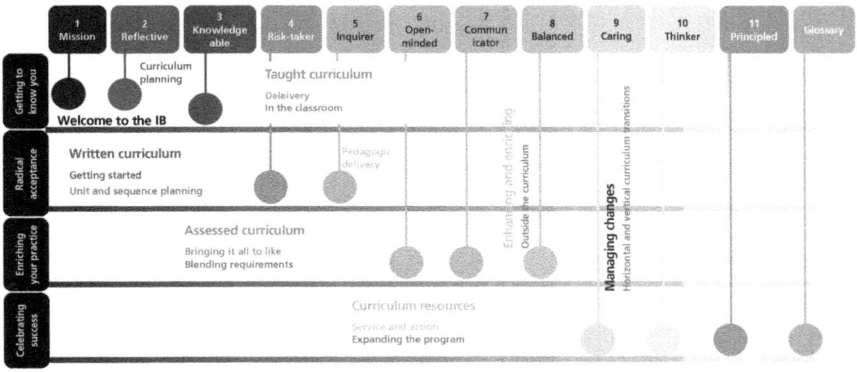

If a linear reading of the book is your preferred style, take time to reflect on the parallels of the structure with the unit planning process. We begin with our aims and goals in sight, and end with assessment as a summative activity. We can reflect on our increased knowledge and **skills**, and celebrate achievements with certain performance of understanding. Consider now your criteria for success once you have finished engaging with these ideas. Reflect on the changes you would like to see, the questions answered and other possible encouragements you might find useful.

When time permits

In the busy life of a teacher, we often have to snatch pieces of time for professional development during the school day. If you are reading the book in this way, then I suggest you pick a chapter, choose one inquiry question within and read it while invigilating outside the next examination room.

Make sure to have something to write with, to capture your thoughts, and give yourself space and time to engage with the reflection questions honestly. Each inquiry section has been designed to have a reading time of about 8 to 12 minutes (each chapter is made up of several inquiry sections, each of which starts under a new main subheading). Refer to the workbook for more structured and practical exercises.

Some of the chapters work well as stand-alone experiences. I would suggest one of the following:

- Chapter 5 – Inquirers. This chapter focuses on the role of inquiry-based learning and how we can blend it with assessment for a rigorous curriculum.
- Chapter 7 – Communicators. Here we will consider the taught curriculum, how we communicate mathematically in a multimodal way.
- Chapter 10 – Thinkers. For educators who have a little space or time in their curriculum and are looking for a creativity boost, this chapter will work well as an example of 'nano-learning'. Here we discuss enriching and extending the curriculum beyond our classroom walls.
- Chapter 11 – Principled. For quick, action-driven changes that you could make tomorrow, this chapter is worth giving a free period or exam invigilation to.

With others

I was introduced to professional reading circles by Robert Harrison, my mentor, who had had some experience of these in previous schools. He would laugh at me when I sent him my reading wish list as it was always crazy long. At a recent professional reading circle, most colleagues hadn't had a chance to read the selected book, so we agreed to spend the time quietly reading together. After 20 minutes of quiet page-turning and the occasional nod or smile, we turned our attention to a discussion of the contents.

Two things were very noticeable. First, people loved the chance to read uninterrupted! They commented on the satisfaction and rejuvenating effect of simply reading together. Second, their comments were instantaneous, and that made everyone more open to the perspectives of others. The lack of reflection time had the opposite effect to that I'd expected: it made people more willing to listen and accept that other opinions were valid and worth considering. You can consider the level of reflection you might integrate, either before or after reading, to elevate your thinking.

Collaborative time, coupled with reflection, is such a critical component to a successful IB school, and reading this book, in sections, could be a productive use of that time in departmental or cross-departmental meetings.

The accompanying image shows some suggested focus areas for collaborative planning time, if you are reading these chapters with colleagues.

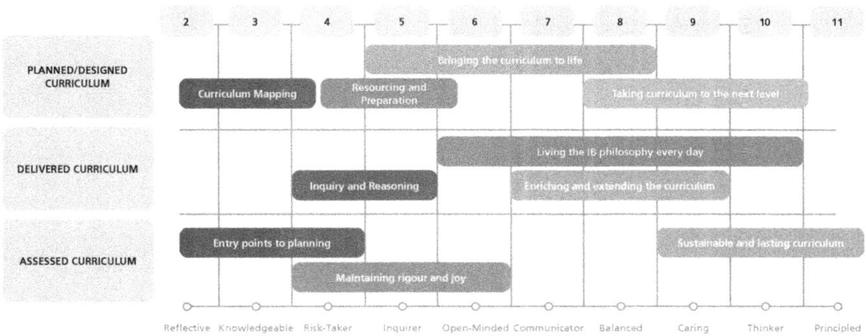

By immediate need

When you are reflecting on your curriculum needs, it may be that there are immediate areas for intervention. For example, you might be a candidate school having challenges with curriculum alignment. You may be in an established school and have been asked to lead a session for parents on approaches to learning (ATLs) in mathematics. Maybe your school is undergoing an accreditation and part of the self-evaluation requires articulation of curriculum thinking. Certain chapters lend themselves well to different, typical school-wide initiatives, such as equity and access or data-driven assessment.

If you already have initial training or insight into the programme basics, then dive into a chapter that suits your current needs or levels.

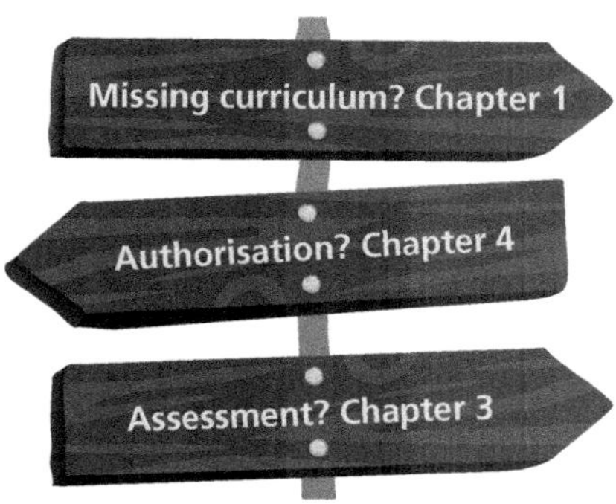

Whatever order or time you choose to read it in, whomever you read it with, commit to a process of honest exploration and reflection.

What is the IB learner profile?

I chose to start this book with the mission statement and then subsequently take you on a journey, using the IB learner profile attributes as our guide for each chapter. Each learner profile attribute will frame the contents of the chapter and holds space for the inquiry questions within, each deeply rooted in the definition.

Why did I opt for the learner profile attributes as my chosen framing for curriculum development?

- To increase your familiarity with the learner profile attributes and to engage at a deeper level with their definitions. The sole purpose of the learner profile is character formation through attitudes, and we are forming our MYP curriculum character/attitudes throughout this book.
- To use the attributes to bring together a variety of ideas of curriculum under a suitable umbrella. I chose it as a new way to think of these ideas in terms of holistic curriculum development.
- I really love the learner profile! It is hard to believe it is less than 20 years old. I consider it one of the most enduring legacies of the IB and its most influential contribution. I have transferred and applied it to so many different situations:
    - as a celebration and recognition process in assemblies
    - wall displays
    - mission statements
    - essential agreements and class manifestos
    - on reports, in comments and references
    - on school greetings cards
    - stickers, T-shirts, wristbands
    - professional development requests
    - as a lesson observation protocol
    - as a frame for our Covid-19 protocols and rules.

When I was at the IB, there was an extensive, and expensive, review of both the mission statement and the learner profile. Both of which included a variety of panels and focus groups, hosting internationally and in person. The review concluded that no change was needed. The cost and time spent seemed to me to be an utter waste, and I moaned at my boss, Robert, about it. His response was typical of his insight: 'No, this is extremely important. It ensures that they are fit for purpose so we can test and renew our ideals.'

This layering of these ideas will guide us through all the aspects of an IB education, giving you everything you will need in your MYP toolkit. The inquiry questions may be factual, conceptual or debateable, and will give structure to each chapter. The point of the book is how best to teach mathematics in an MYP classroom, what language to use, how to encourage and inspire students. Simultaneously, by this modelling, we will expand your repertoire by repeated exposure and absorption. The chapters scaffold to create a comprehensive understanding of all aspects of MYP Mathematics and to advance your **mastery**.

Some things will work for you, others can be considered or ignored, but all are provided with intention and thoughtfulness, grounded in experience. Some might not survive contact with the classroom for you!

This book is a labour of love, the sum total of all I have learned from the IB world, which has made me a passionate advocate of the IB. More than that, though, it is an insight into the journey of someone who deeply loves teaching mathematics and, despite how embarrassing it is to write, has been told she is an exceptional teacher. It is the distillation of the 'magic' I bring to the classroom and an effort to share that magic with you. It is the book I would have appreciated when I was starting out as a teacher, and the one I didn't know I needed. I must have been subconsciously writing it all along, with every mistake I made and each success I had. I hope it helps you move from lost to found, from surviving to thriving.

What is mathematics exactly?

Now that we understand the bigger picture of the MYP landscape, we must consider our place within this complex ecosystem – our subject group of mathematics. Initially, we should revisit what mathematics is, why we enjoy it (and I presume we do at least a little or we wouldn't be teaching it) and what difficulties we encounter as teachers of mathematics.

A side note on terminology

Using the abbreviation 'math' versus 'maths' can be controversial in international school circles. In writing, using one or the other gives a certain bias or accent, and may jar with the reader if they use the other form. And so, I will stick with my decision at the IB to only ever use 'mathematics' in full, however cumbersome that might be. I've tried the compromise of using a single term 'math(s)' but found it too distracting.

Why the study of mathematics? Why do we regard it as important and why do we value it sufficiently to insist that everyone must study it, in every school system, around the world? What does it bring our students? In my research for this book, I have read literally hundreds of books on mathematics. The finest description I have seen was where mathematics was described quite simply as 'an urge'. I've seen it variously described as:

- the urge to quantify
- the urge to find patterns
- the urge to compare
- the urge to control
- the urge to create
- the urge to solve.

While I appreciate the idea that it is a subject of urgency, I prefer to consider mathematics as an invitation or desire. In my wider definition, mathematics can be:

- an invitation to expand
- an invitation to find truth
- a desire to extract usefulness from a special case to be used again
- a desire to bring order and clarity to a situation or problem
- a constant struggle between simplification and complex beauty.

This list is not exhaustive, and I invite you to add some examples of your own. When we teach mathematics, we invite students to engage with the subject without these bigger motivations. We assume that wisdom is obvious. It is easier to proceed under the premise that the subject is important 'because you need it' and with the 'you have to pass your exam' side of the argument, when the truth is so much richer.

'We thoughtfully consider the world …'

It is quite simply a beautiful subject. The danger is that we don't often get the time or tools to transmit this love fully to our students. I certainly didn't have that experience in school. My joy in the subject, I realise now, came from the positive feedback I received because I could observe three examples, replicate the exact algorithm on the next 15 to 20 questions in class, and then again in the exam, frequently and with ease. My pride was misplaced. There was never a mention that different approaches or interpretations existed in mathematics until I saw them much later. None of this is to disparage my own teacher, Mrs Solan, who worked effectively in precisely the way required. She taught us mastery (or mistressy?) and did it so thoroughly that I use all her techniques to this day.

I strive to give that understanding of approach to my students, without allowing it to overwhelm them with possibility and uncertainty. When we teach mathematics, we are still teaching for mastery, which doesn't always sit well with joyful learning or inquiry. Mathematical beauty is a less accessible form of beauty, which is rewarded by experience and therefore sadly unattainable – without striving and determination that is. The hope is that, with the help of this book, more and more of your students will experience and appreciate this.

Our process with students must be as follows: presence in a problem; then acknowledging their discomfort; processing what is required; and moving through comfort and into confidence. Frequent returns and retrievals may be necessary to make meaningful, lasting progress. It is a difficult journey but highly successful in reprogramming their concerns. Mathematics anxiety is a recurring theme, in chapters 7 and 8 in particular.

Daniel Pearcy, in his book *Mathematical Beauty* (2020), makes an excellent defence of what mathematical beauty is and how to communicate this to others, in a way that I could never quite articulate. His premise is that teachers engage with their subject for love, and often outside their classroom, and that this is unremarkable for the art teacher or the music teacher but not so for the teacher of mathematics. Another great writer on the joy and fun of mathematics is Matt Parker, who has a variety of books, videos and resources online.

I was such a fan of Matt's work that I contrived an invitation for him to the IB Symposium one year, where he seemed baffled to be there and referred to himself in a self-deprecating manner as the 'light relief'! I was enchanted that he addressed all books to their new owners by signing their name in binary. It does not take much to delight us mathematics nerds.

Key feature: Reflection

- When have you encountered a different attitude to mathematics than other subjects? Who held that attitudinal difference?
- Why do we value mathematics – is it a utility subject, a state of mind, a sacred truth?
- Can you argue that it is the most important subject?
- Formulate an argument to support why mathematics is the most important subject.
- Consider why society holds mathematics both in reverence and avoidance.

The true mathematics teachers, who live and breathe their subject and play with it for fun, would tell you that it is a universal truth through space and time. As a subject, it has historically attracted a certain type of learner, one who craves order, logic and correctness. It has become a synonym or identifier of intelligence, and has created stronger feelings than most subjects, both in its fans and its detractors. 'Mathematics anxiety' has been well studied and discussed, but when I searched online for 'Geography anxiety' or 'Design phobia' I strangely could find no results!

So, what is the nature of the challenges when teaching mathematics? First, this tendency to overstate the importance of mathematics relative to other subjects is a real concern for us. Mathematics evokes a different attitude in people than other subjects, both negatively as well as positively. On the positive side, the overvalue placed on it by parents and schools can often empower teachers of mathematics beyond the level other subjects might.

What will students actively be using regularly in five to ten years' time? How does that impact what and how you teach? Note your ideas in the table below.

	Important to learn	**Less important to learn**
Enjoyable to teach		
Less enjoyable to teach		

One of the challenges of teaching this subject is the range of what is needed. You must have subject matter expertise, be familiar with a wide range of content and approaches, and possess the inherent confidence to communicate rigour and competence to students. Meaning in mathematics is cumulative, so learners must experience it in a variety of ways and contexts over time, without losing interest. They must accumulate knowledge and new situations to strengthen their connections and begin to transfer their understanding. You probably will also inherit students who have their own, very strong feelings about the subject and may not be predisposed to repeated exposure.

There are also specific challenges in international schools when teaching mathematics to a diverse student body. Often, there is a high turnover of students and staff, and there may be significant gaps in their knowledge of the curriculum. More than that, though, one of my least favourite ideas of mathematics is that it is a universal language. So many international teachers will tell you this is simply not the case. There are definite similarities in how schools teach mathematics around the world, but quite honestly there are massive differences too, and you never know what you don't know! Decimals and commas are a common usage difference, methods can also vary even to the simplest manipulation of algebraic equations (inversing versus balancing operations). It shocked me to my core that Japanese students circled right answers and ticked wrong ones.

To illuminate this, I often show a page taken from an Irish-language textbook, safe in the assumption that no one present will speak Irish. I explain the entire example in my native, incomprehensible, language to the consternation and confusion of the audience. While they can recognise the calculation as familiar, it is incomprehensible. Just because the symbols are the same, the methods and meanings may differ vastly, and they cannot access or replicate it.

Whatever the reason, it is fair to say that the subject itself, the curriculum and the teachers come under a great deal of scrutiny. As a former headteacher and consulting with others I heard this as a familiar refrain. More emails are written about mathematics, more reports are fretted about and more tutoring sought in mathematics than almost every other subject. Why should this be? Parent education and support is discussed throughout the book.

Sometimes those in leadership carry their own relationship with mathematics with them to this day. It may frame how they make mathematically relevant decisions. I've seen 'mathematically anxious' administrators accept blindly whatever mathematics departments suggest, to avoid engaging with it. For whatever reason, I haven't met many school leaders who were mathematicians by trade or loved discussing the subject. It felt sometimes like the difficult family member you are obliged to invite to a party.

Key feature: Anecdotal counterexample

I have been guilty of using data-driven arguments to my advantage. Too often I heard 'I'll have to take your word for it on the numbers' from decision-makers who might not have had a high level of mathematical comfort. I began to lean in to this to give me a better chance of being convincing. You might be tempted to use your mathematical understanding to the same ends, but be careful!

I found myself in such a situation where I was advocating on behalf of my school with a regulatory body and had done an in-depth statistical analysis to show that certain students were being disproportionately disadvantaged. I was in full flow about 'parity', 'statistical significance' and 'confidence intervals' when one of the external visitors started to push back on the numbers with gentle but insightful questioning.

Never having experienced this type of interrogation before, I was taken aback. Little did I know that within months this man, Professor Philip Nolan, would be responsible for the mathematical modelling for the pandemic for the whole of Ireland. So he certainly knew his stuff and I was glad I had done my homework properly, but was reminded every time he appeared in Covid-19 press conferences on television, to practise a little more humility in this regard!

What makes MYP Mathematics different?

What is mathematics in the MYP specifically? In the IB, mathematics holds an important place – the course content gives credibility and rigour. This is useful when defending the often-heard accusation that it is a very humanities-driven set of programmes. The MYP Mathematics course aims to add relevant context to mathematics, where students can construct meaning from authentic examples. It is intended to support inquiry and allow students to become competent users (and confident consumers) of mathematics. All four criteria aim to capture these important skills.

Marcus du Sautoy, the Oxford professor, spoke at an IB conference several years ago and made a passionate plea to educators to embrace what he called the 'true power of mathematics'. He described how patterns, with their beauty and abstraction, were one of the most crucial contributions that mathematics could make to the world, and crucial to students' understanding of the subject. The MYP teachers in the room practically levitated with pride and excitement; we beamed at one another like the nerds that we are. Here was proof that we were on the right track – already understanding what was important and making up 25% of our assessments.

Mathematics has been an anomaly in the MYP for a long time, as it has always been the only subject with content detail provided in the form of a framework. No other subject had this level of detail and direction. In fact, when we designed topic lists for the first time in other subjects it was highly controversial, except for the mathematicians. It is also the only subject group that encourages streaming or acceleration in MYP 4 and 5 in the form of standard and extended.

A downside can be that if you are in an international school the challenge may be upon entry. You know that what students will have experienced before your class will be broadly the same across the world and across systems – for example, you know they will have seen fractions, division, bar charts, mean, mode and median before. Your challenge is that you don't know when, how and if it was done well or perfunctorily, nervously or creatively! They will all have had different experiences, and your job is to encourage or course-correct as needed.

It may be that you have more than one set of rigorous demands being placed upon your school. I spoke to a teacher this week who was really tearing her hair out marrying the MYP philosophy with a very prescribed and strict national curriculum. She had many questions about the difference between the 'musts' and 'shoulds' so she could do justice to both systems. Other teachers reaching out for help describe feelings of a lack of direction or support. These are questions that ChatGPT or other AI models cannot always assist with, without a good deal of specificity.

Key feature: AI prompts

Speaking of ChatGPT, we cannot deny the impact that generative AI such as ChatGPT and other large language models (LLMs) are having on the classroom and assessments spaces already. Those of us of a certain age also hate change, or might be effort-sensitive in this regard. To make this journey easier I will give some ideas for engineering prompts to help you get familiar with these environments and to give you enough generated output for you to assess how you feel about these developments. These prompts can be used as an experiment, a content generator, or a way to try to keep up with the students in your class or other teachers in your department. The best way to learn something is to have to teach it yourself. Naturally, as the LLMs develop and become more ubiquitous, we will see the outputs changing and attitudes probably hardening in different directions. But now is the time to inquire and play!

The upside is that having to consider this point of realistic and relevant mathematics has changed how I view the world, seeing mathematics everywhere. Many new concepts or formal ideas in MYP are honestly not readily experienced in everyday life and this forces you into a more creative space, in the hunt for relevant and realistic connections. We want to make the learning relevant and lifeworthy. It is definitely more time-consuming initially than teaching from the book. And teaching from the book is definitely easier. But the enjoyment and engagement you get in MYP classrooms is different to anything I have experienced in any other classroom. It is refreshing never to be asked 'Why do I have to learn this?' or 'Miss? When will we ever use this again?' This frequently happened to me in other systems, and I do not miss it.

Key feature: Progression and self-assessment

We are on a path of lifelong learning and we model this for our students. At the end of each chapter, you will find a radial bar chart like the one below where you can mark your current understanding of each of the most important components of the DNA/cake-making/IB process.

An excellent mathematics teacher, nationally or internationally, will make their lessons fun, include rigour in their choices, ensure students are well prepared for later assessment, and explain complex ideas in a way that inspires and includes their students. In the MYP we are expected to do all this and more!

Self-assessment

Complete the reflection:

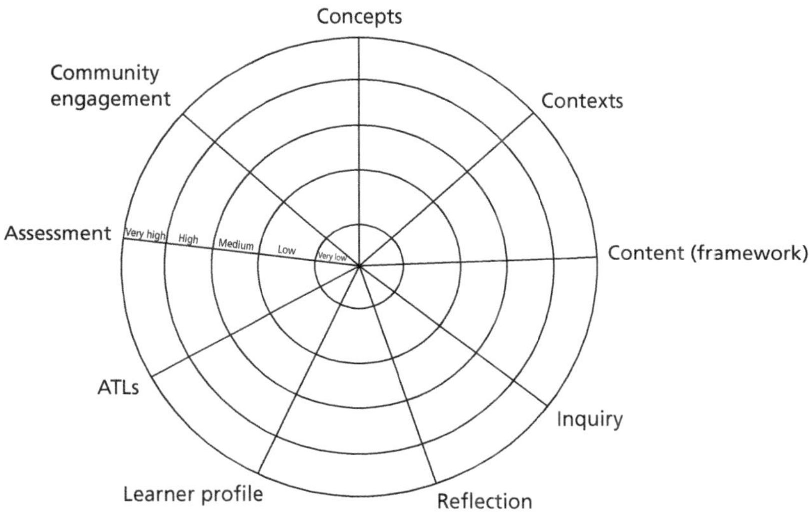

Shade in your knowledge level from low to high as you feel your comfort level lies.

Glossary

Assessed curriculum MYP assessment gives teachers and students reliable and valid information on student learning. Integrated with the designed/planned curriculum and delivered curriculum, the assessed curriculum is considered throughout the processes involved in planning for learning.

Delivered curriculum The construction of meaning so that students' learning will be purposeful in class. Previously called the taught curriculum.

Mastery Deep understanding and proficient application of knowledge and skills in a subject area.*

Planned/designed curriculum A formal, comprehensive, school-wide set of documents written by the school, which describes what will be delivered in each subject to each age group. Previously called the written curriculum.

Reflection A cognitive act that considers past experiences in order to improve, modify and plan for the future.

Skills The abilities we use to guide, support and structure learning.

** Not an official IB definition.*

CHAPTER 3
KNOWLEDGEABLE

> We develop and use conceptual understanding, exploring knowledge across a range of disciplines. We engage with issues and ideas that have local and global significance.

Key thinking points

In this chapter, there are explanations/discussions of:

- the chosen learner profile attribute, Knowledgeable, and how it relates to our curriculum development
- a strengths-based approach to curriculum review
- comparing and determining/a discussion of different needs and profiles in the MYP community
- how the IB operates curriculum review as a model for schools
- the philosophy of concept-based education (reflection)
- the application of a concept-driven approach in the IB, specifically in the MYP, and how this manifests in mathematics.

Why choose Knowledgeable as the learner profile attribute for this chapter?

In every chapter we will approach all aspects of curriculum development through a learner profile attribute. For this, the first chapter on creating a planned or designed curriculum, it seemed obvious to me that this should be considered through the learner profile attribute Knowledgeable. In fact, it was the easiest match of any chapter!

Our goal is always to bring our students to a better understanding of the world. Curriculum starts with knowledge and ends with understanding, as they say.

Disciplines, subjects, subject groups are all heroic attempts to organise humanity's accumulated wisdom. Our best judgement must be used to decide what is the worthiest, and most efficient, learning for these fresh minds to carry forward.

Using this definition as a starting point makes clear that knowledge without context is left lacking. We must explore knowledge, but this engagement should be significant. The learner profile definition of Knowledgeable specifically references **conceptual understanding**, and much of chapter 4 will be an exploration of the MYP's concept-based approach. It also refers to exploring knowledge across a range of disciplines and, as one of the main connectors for MYP disciplines and subjects, to the **concepts** that link and transfer across the programme. The present chapter will consider what the IB values in knowledge acquisition and what is thought to be best way to earn, and hold, that knowledge. We will also consider the need for change, and when and how this can be successfully achieved in your school context. You will have multiple opportunities throughout to reflect candidly on your educational values and principles.

How does the IB review its own curriculum?

Before we begin to work through your specific profile or curriculum needs, let us take the opportunity to understand how curriculum is reviewed at the International Baccalaureate itself. This can help frame our own development and changes. This valuable insight can influence how we can align with, or prepare for, future changes in the IB requirements. We can use the IB's review processes as a macrocosm of what should happen in schools, if time and resources allowed.

So how does the IB review its curriculums, and why? It is important to the organisation that it is a thought leader, that it lives up to its own ideals of reflection and action, but also that the integrity of the programmes remains in place. The perception of the IB is often that it is the gold standard, and it is important to maintain this organisationally. It may not always be known for its alacrity, but it certainly is thoughtful and thorough in its considerations.

With regards to the MYP, there is a very clear exit point, if we assume that the natural progression is on to the Diploma Programme (DP). The entry points for students into the MYP are often less clear. We cannot assume that all MYP students have experienced the PYP, for example. Another complication is that, while the DP stands alone as an offer, the MYP is often integrated with other systems or curriculums in a myriad of ways. There is also the added complication that this five-year programme is not always offered in its entirety, so schools may offer only two or three years of the MYP. It has always been my firm belief that it takes students at least a year to get familiar with the language or the grading by criteria, etc. By the second year they are more comfortable and trust the process, and so it is a shame that this might be all that some students get.

'We engage with issues ...'

The curriculum must remain fit for purpose, innovative and practical for schools to implement. What might first appear to be completely parameter free, and an opportunity ripe for creativity, is soon discovered to be in fact complex and nuanced. How and why are certain areas of mathematics assumed appropriate for the ages of approximately 11 to 16? What will be useful to them beyond DP? What do we value them knowing, as learners but also as lifelong consumers of mathematics? How can we bring more joy? How has technology impacted what is important and less important? What urgent issues are there in this field? What is the most recent research indicating?

Here are some questions that apply to schools even more than to the IB itself. When we are planning for change, before the change:

- What is your immediate need for this change or review?
- What might be changed that might have to be undone? (Here we must consider the 'law of unintended consequences'.)
- How will it be impacted by the inevitable churn of people? Or ideas?

How these questions are answered, how the knowledge is identified and how this is all imparted are the true processes of curriculum development. These are the questions you should ask yourself and your team when reviewing in any form.

As I mentioned earlier, the last whole-programme curriculum review of the MYP was well underway when I arrived at the IB. It was being launched with schools, issues were emerging and a vast amount of support was required. Other subjects and other programmes were at different stages of development, so I saw the review cycle from several vantage points in time and progression. Later, I was tasked with reviewing the mathematics **framework** in isolation, the logic being that schools still needed time to bed in the 'Next Chapter' changes. The framework needed a thorough audit and refresh, so I will talk about this mini-process as it may relate to your school.

The review cycle at the IB is highly collaborative, inviting schools, teachers and experts to contribute at various points of the review. These contributors are naturally self-selecting as these are the people either connected to the IB or regularly up to date on the various communication channels. They are passionate and often opinionated, in a good way, and a good curriculum manager will ensure they have a cross-section of differing and sometimes clashing opinions. From this diversity of thought often come very productive disagreements. Robert was always excellent at reminding me that the most important voices may be among those who did not have the time or awareness to apply to be part of the review, that they were who we truly needed to hear from.

Malcolm Nicolson echoed this sentiment when I interviewed him. He explained that he better understands now how disconnected we were from the classroom, and those teachers we did hear from were those whose opinions may have been the loudest or who had the best access. Those schools with the resources to attend and the confidence to present their critiques may not always be representative of the whole population. We often labour this point as mathematics teachers teaching statistical literacy, and the IB is not immune to this problem. If this is something you might be interested in learning more about, take a look at the IB's media channels – call-outs are frequently seen on LinkedIn, in coordinators' notes and on social media channels.

There is a risk of groupthink if too many educators come from the same types of schools or languages. I experienced this phenomenon in action, followed by an immediate flip, thanks to the interjection of one of the teachers. I was hosting a CRM (curriculum review meeting) at the global headquarters and there were a dozen teachers, professors and examiners present. One educator had the most valuable contribution when, in pedagogic excitement, we were adding ever more potential topics. She begged us to pause, exclaiming that she had a 40% drop-out rate, and overburdening teachers in her school with aspiration was deeply unhelpful, not to mention irresponsible. Enrichment opportunities were then discussed, which then appeared in the final framework, thereby allowing but not mandating teachers to go further with their students if they could.

Curriculum development is not a dark art, but it is a sort of alchemy (and, as they say, alchemy became chemistry once people started sharing results!). It is crucial to understand that it is almost always a work in progress, even for the IB. For schools it can be an acknowledged work in progress, but not indefinitely – this work must be closer to completed than to emerging. Too many schools say it is a work in progress year after year.

Key feature: Who to follow

In the MYP curriculum department in The Hague, there was an authentic team who welcomed debate, held contrasting views and wore their wisdom lightly. Many of them are prolific online and worth a follow: Andy Mayes, Margareth Harris and Danielle Veilleux. If there were an updated History of the MYP this group would feature prominently. In a later iteration of the team, Dr Sumaya Alyusuf taught me much more than many of my college professors combined and I am fortunate to call her a friend to this day.

This culture of debate, or 'rush to slow judgement, not no judgement', as TOK manager Jenny Gillett would often say, has reframed how I approach professional situations. Now it is very typical for me to ask, 'Who are you reading professionally?' in an interview. Likewise, I will ask students or staff, 'What would a critic of this argue against you right now?' Perhaps this is just another instance where we practise our humility, in that other people with their different positions can also be right ...

The official review process is illustrated in a diagram by the IB on their website, but here is a brief overview of the main stages of how I saw curriculum review being carried out by different teams. Initially the manager must ensure they are completely familiar with the current and previous versions of the guides. This helps to identify shifts in elements that have disappeared and/or reappeared over the years. This is also where I learned that the word 'elements' is used in the IB when you don't know what to call a group of disparate ideas. Next, or concurrently, it is imperative to be up to date on all research and trends within that subject's teaching. Special care must be taken not to be fooled into thinking that the only research that matters is that which has been published in English. It is harder to source but well worth seeing what other research language barriers are preventing you from considering. This is something that I would not recommend to a teacher in a school setting, as there would never be enough time for this!

Next in my case I had to accumulate and anonymise all the problems, queries, complaints and clarifications I had been sent, including raw data from questions sent to IB Answers. These questions make their way through various chains to whoever is best placed to answer, so I recommend using this as a service when you can't get a straight answer or technical support. It was frustrating, given how many of these we answered daily, to hear the academic team in The Hague referred to as 'The Vague' in workshops, but it was a great reminder to me to avoid ambiguous answers wherever possible. I learned quickly that teachers and coordinators require clarity in responses. My least favourite responses were those I was compelled to give, in cases where the MYP did not have a direct answer available. These 'That is a school-based decision' answers made me feel like Father Jack in the comedy series *Father Ted*, spouting 'That would be an ecumenical matter!'

Once the research is completed, a process of standardising and benchmarking curriculums globally is essential to prove the robustness of our decisions and changes. (I also found learning to say *curriculums* instead of *curricula* to be frustrating.) Any curriculum changes must be shared with schools, sometimes piloted, and differing opinions sought too. The Assessment division has a particular role in the approval of the 'content horizon', as students can only be reliably and fairly assessed if they know exactly what is to be expected of them. Their input in the lower years is less crucial, due to the nature of the flexibility of the MYP.

There is always a recognised tension between curriculum and assessment, to ensure that the needs of both are met and that one does not dominate the other. I have seen these dynamics play out both constructively and destructively, depending on the interpersonal dynamics of the managers in the two different locations. Academic colleagues might resent assessment-driven decision-making, while assessment colleagues might bemoan the navel-gazing woolly-headed thinking of the other side! Luckily, I had incredible counterparts who wanted to ensure the introduction of eAssessment remained as true to the MYP philosophy as they could, given the limits of our, then new, on-screen testing environment.

It is true that curriculum developments are always ongoing in the IB, as nothing should remain immutable. A review is somewhat overdue, so there will be more changes coming. Although no book can be entirely future-proofed, I have taken the position that though the curriculum itself and the expectations may change, it is unlikely that the basis of the most important mathematics needed at specific ages will vary greatly or that the underpinnings of the programme will vary – and that good teaching will remain good teaching, and good learning is all that matters.

What are the different stages of curriculum development?

So much about your curriculum development will come from your particular entry point or context. Some of the most common profiles that might undertake this work include:

- a brand-new school introducing IB programmes year by year and creating new curriculum from scratch
- an established school adopting the MYP for the first time in place of another system
- a school that implements the MYP alongside another requirement, for example a national curriculum or another examination-based syllabus
- a coordinator who wants to learn more about each subject and how they interact together to make a successful programme
- a long-established DP school introducing the MYP for the first time, with a reticent or anxious teaching body

- an MYP school in need of a refresh of a stagnant or unchanged curriculum
- many other profiles that span or blend the above, or have a myriad of pressure points.

In this chapter we will discuss how and when curriculum development should take place for these profiles and many more. Each of these different contexts requires a high level of self-awareness, knowledge and humility.

Each also needs to embrace change, when change is truly valuable. There is no need to change for change's sake. We can categorise these needs and motivations into different stages, or types, of curriculum management, as shown in the accompanying image.

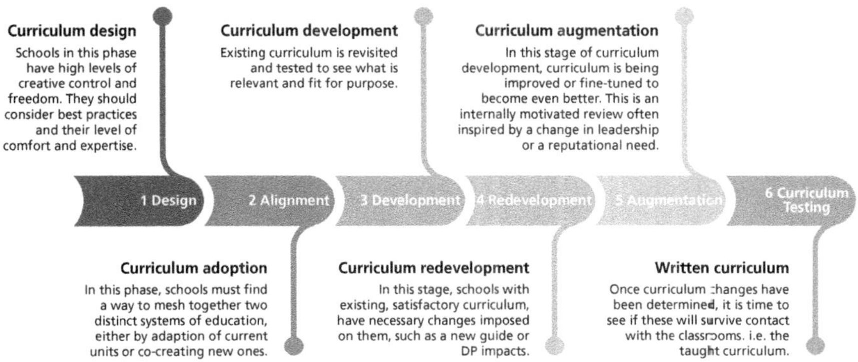

The stages of curriculum management

First let's look about who might be at these different stages of curriculum management.

1. Curriculum design or creation:
    - start-up or 'greenfield' schools
    - introducing an IB stream or parallel offering
    - existing schools but with bespoke and malleable curriculum.
2. Curriculum adoption/alignment:
    - introducing the MYP within an existing curriculum
    - existing school that has a different fixed curriculum and is now embedding the MYP as well
    - second curriculum changes and the MYP must flex around those changes

- existing schools that are already MYP but have another expectation introduced, e.g. NGSS, state curriculum introduced, UDL school push (curriculum alignment).

3. Curriculum development:
    - established school changing systems from one to another in entirety
    - leaving iGCSE or bespoke curriculum to MYP
    - government requirements
    - pre-authorisation.
4. Curriculum redevelopment:
    - changes to the MYP curriculum (redevelopment with a possibility to augment)
    - changes to DP curriculum with MYP impacts
    - schools with certification/accreditation looming – NEASC, ECIS, COIS, etc.
    - pre-evaluation.
5. Curriculum augmentation:
    - new leadership, new vision
    - time for change/refresh
    - paradigm shifts such as the pandemic, AI, on-screen assessments
    - experienced staff but curious about the mechanics of curriculum review, coordinator aspirational.

Now let's look in more detail at each of these stages, to better equip you for the task at hand.

1. Curriculum design

In this phase of curriculum development, you are in the enviable position of creating from scratch. You have no national curriculum and no legacy or historical factors to consider. This freedom and flexibility can feel daunting. What feels like wide open freedom to some feels like operating in a vacuum for others. Many schools look at this blank canvas, assess the time and needs, and instead start to search for an 'off-the-shelf' curriculum. Who could blame them, if time is of the essence? Others relish the chance to bring ideas and experience to bear on what they might consider the perfect curriculum.

We had exactly this scenario in our start-up school for Nord Anglia in Dublin. They called it a greenfield site, which I found the perfect metaphor. We were permitted to build whatever we wanted on this field, but it relied so heavily on the confidence and expertise of our educators. Many were examiners or curriculum experts and so created an interconnected, passionate curriculum within four to five months. This curriculum was then road-tested and modified throughout. Without experience and competence, this phase can be highly challenging. If this is your current situation, a better phase to start with is the next one we cover: curriculum adoption or alignment.

If you are in this stage of purest curriculum design, make sure to give yourself sufficient thinking and research time. You will need to determine your goals, your pathways to those goals and whether there are invisible expectations to consider. These might include the parent population or the needs of students once they reach the DP version of mathematics.

Ask yourself:

- Can you create a truly new and innovative practice?
- What backward mapping is needed?
- Do you have time constraints that mean you should start with an off-the-shelf model?
- What is your confidence level in your staff to deliver?
- How much support will be required?

This is purest curriculum design, the most creative but also the most overwhelming entry point. I have had the chance to do this twice in my career, and once it was for the IB itself. It is naturally very exciting, but there are fewer freedoms than you would expect. You must watch out for scope creep (where your vision far outpaces what you are able to deliver), and manage the weight of many expectations and needs.

2. Curriculum adoption, alignment or harmonisation

In this phase of curriculum development, you find yourself in a structure, sometimes more than one, where you need the MYP to operate harmoniously with another system. It may be that one of the two systems is more established and has greater buy-in from the staff. There may be resistance to the new entrant, which in a school is often the MYP.

When you are trying to align two different systems, it is crucial to establish the difference in level of flexibility and to identify any potential conflicts.

Key feature: AI prompts

Consider how generative AI might help you maximise your efficiency in mapping these two sets of requirements. Create a persona of a teacher who is experienced in both MYP and 'Other system'. Ask AI to identify similarities and differences between the two systems.

Alternatively, ask it to perform a gap analysis. Where problems or gaps exist, ask AI to identify a number of steps to bridge the gap. These suggestions may not be useful, but they may spark ideas of your own. If nothing else, they may lessen concerns about the potential workload.

What are the demands of both systems?

- Will there be different reporting expectations (e.g. percentages or GPA versus levels)?
- Are they mutually exclusive expectations?
- What can we keep?
- What work has already been done on aligning these systems?

This last point is particularly important, as many have had these kinds of headaches before. I was frequently asked for a crosswalk between MYP Mathematics and the AERO standards, for example. Likewise, I see educators on Facebook groups or similar sharing how to align with Common Core or German curriculum or AISSE, so never reinvent the wheel. One of my most challenging, and interesting, tasks was to work with Achieve in Washington, DC, to find common ground between the IB programmes and the Next Generation Science Standards in the US. This was a fertile working group and we managed to mesh the two different requirements very successfully.

The benefit is that the MYP often has fewer 'musts' than other programmes. If you are meeting the requirements for each strand of every criterion at least twice per year, and if you are teaching through inquiry, using statements of inquiry (SOIs), then you are likely to be meeting many of the demands of the MYP. In this case, you can allow the content of the second system to form the basis of the curriculum and use MYP delivery to engage your students.

In the process of aligning or adopting two different curriculums, determine the scope of work first. Are you starting units from scratch? Revisiting past units of your own? **Evaluating** someone else's work? Writing new units to fit a specific need? Are you collaborating with a partner on a unit? It is good to revisit units first to test their robustness in the face of the change ahead. Make sure to filter for great ideas and proven resources as the firmament for your new MYP-aligned curriculum.

3. Curriculum development, changing systems

Wherever possible, I would advocate giving a unit a chance before you discard it. There may be merit in it, and that could be a time-saver. It is better to retain and explain where possible. Some units may have to be archived to get a second chance another time around, like curriculum choices themselves. Maybe there are investigations worth keeping that suit both needs, which can be revamped or updated. Recycle and reuse to reduce the cognitive and planning load!

One of the major benefits of this stage of curriculum management is the enthusiasm and motivation of colleagues, if they are supportive of the change in system. If this is the case, start a reading group right now and have them follow the advice in this book. Capitalise on this momentum and make sure to protect collaborative working time as much as possible. Even better would be a retreat or day off-timetable to make huge strides as a group. These are like gold dust and just as valuable.

Key feature: Anecdotal counterexample

I once arrived at a new department to find staff set against the MYP. When I investigated further, fully convinced of the merits of the IB in all its forms, I was met with resistance, fatigue and in some cases outright hostility. It only became clear much later, when I discovered lots of archived investigations that looked really interesting and valuable to me, that they had been instructed to trash all their old units when the MYP was introduced. Their previous work had had a lot of time and energy invested, but they had been told 'it wasn't MYP enough' and they had to start over. The staff had internalised this criticism and turned their wrath on the MYP rather than this personal interpretation of one individual IB consultant.

4. Curriculum redevelopment

This level of curriculum scrutiny is highly reactive. It is often driven by a changing external need, such as changes in the MYP or DP. More often than not, it is also time sensitive, such as planning for a new curriculum in the coming school year or preparing for changes coming down the line in the DP. Naturally we want to give our students the best possible preparation, but often we feel that detail is scarce or that there is not enough information provided. This can feel very frustrating: 'How can they expect us to be ready when they've only released one specimen paper?' The reason behind this is often related to the piloting process and the translation requirements of the IB. Sometimes the material sent by schools was unusable or could not be translated. Perhaps there were authenticity concerns or copyright issues.

When there are changes to IB curriculum this is usually communicated well in advance of these changes, and both interim guides and final guides are produced in the hope that this will give schools enough time to prepare. But we know that schools never have enough time, so what is the best way to proceed here?

Start with a change analysis. What is new? What has been replaced? Is there a rationale provided for it? I wrote this type of document in 2019, and schools found it reassuring to see the reasons behind the change and not have to speculate about it. It saved them time and reduced (justifiable) grumbling significantly.

Again, the advice is similar to that for development: do not throw the baby out with the bathwater. Likewise, check the archives: 'Didn't we used to have a great matrices/vectors/discrete maths unit?' I chose these three examples as they are some of the things that have appeared, disappeared and reappeared in various guises over the years.

5. Curriculum augmentation or adaptation

This type of curriculum change is often motivated internally and with very good intentions. There may have been a recent change in leadership or staffing. There may be a particularly ambitious set of stakeholders involved, who want to improve for improvement's sake. Sometimes I have seen this in the form of an enthusiastic head of department who is bringing the whole team along in their ambitious wake. Other times it can be driven by a desire to recover from a hit to reputation or a reduced status or results.

We have also seen this happen quickly in response to external factors, such as during the pandemic or in the face of AI. This stage of curriculum change must be characterised by a deep understanding of the challenge, and a calm and measured approach. There is a need to avoid knee-jerk reactions, as the changes here must be future-proofed as far as possible. Overreacting to the stimulus here can result in burnout in teachers and change fatigue in students, some of which we are still offsetting and repairing from Covid with our younger years. We all changed our instructional practices so rapidly during various lockdowns, and I wonder how many people changed their teaching and learning permanently as a result.

In this phase of curriculum design, you are invited into a space of creative flexibility. Assessments can be retired, put on hold or archived. Remember the importance of backing up and keeping an offline copy for the future. Too often teachers leave and take their resources with them. This leads to a loss of institutional memory, and impoverishes the experience of the students and the school.

You'll notice from the descriptions above that the IB is almost always moving between stages 1–4 and back again, with occasional detours to stage 5.

What is meant by strengths-based planning?

First off, let us remember to stay calm and focused. Nothing is ever completely new and therefore nothing can be wasted. At all of the stages outlined previously, an honest reflection at the beginning of the process will help immensely. Listed below are some reflection questions that should help your planning at every stage.

Goals:

- Who or what is driving this change?
- Is everyone aware of the needs and goals of the curriculum development?
- Do they understand the motivating factors?
- Do they appreciate the limitations and challenges?
- Are there different versions of acceptable?
- Is it possible to identify what your ideal curriculum would look like at the end?

Time:

- Are you developing at speed?
- Is there a fixed time for development?
- Are there deadlines and deliverables?
- Does everyone understand these parameters?

Staff:

- How many people are involved in this change?
- Is there an overreliance on one person? (Watch out for 'hero head' syndrome.)
- Is it clear who is responsible/accountable/consulted/informed?
- How can we manage resistance or inertia?
- How enthusiastic are they?
- Are they working from a solid knowledge base?
- How experienced are they?

These last two are subtly different. We have all known teachers who are extremely experienced but may not be knowledgeable in the more modern pedagogies. Likewise, there are clearly very talented younger teachers who demonstrate that inner talent you know will make them excellent practitioners given the right circumstances and support, but who are still prone to making mistakes.

Resources:

- Is there a time or financial budget to support these changes?
- Will external support be required?
- How informed are senior leadership?
- How supportive are they?
- What factors might work against this curriculum change?

Where you do have really great resources and units, consider the effort involved to ensure they may be reconfigured. It's hard to tell unenthusiastic staff to be more ambitious. It can be even harder to dampen down naive enthusiasm with hard-earned wisdom and icy-cold reality. If you are a leader with curriculum responsibility, it may feel like you are saving their future selves from themselves. It is a worthwhile goal to monitor and maintain that work is reasonable and valuable. Make time for discussions about resourcing in terms of books, workbooks, online resources and **differentiating** for diverse needs.

When using strengths-based planning for curriculum development we aim to consider personality and the personal strengths of individual teachers, but also to utilise the department's strengths and culture. It can be that certain teachers have differing favourite parts of the curriculum. Irina, my co-author on our Hachette Learning textbooks, always loved teaching statistics and found algebra tedious. Another superstar colleague, Shannon, loves the problem-solving, making it an integral driver of her units, and her classroom hums with student-directed learning as a result.

How do you make best use of your current skills but more importantly the divergence of personalities in your department? While an interests-led curriculum may not be a desirable long-term goal, it can be really helpful in sharing out responsibility and ensuring a high level of buy-in. Allow teachers to follow their passions and expertise, and their contributions will be more valuable. It also gives us the opportunity to discuss, and remind ourselves about, our joys and pet peeves in the subject. It can be a bonding or cathartic experience. If you are in a team of one, ask yourself what kind of teacher you are. Explore where you can go it alone, and where you might need inspiration and support.

Key feature: Anecdotal evidence

We have an idea that most schools are operating within a reasonable context and have a sensible understanding of what is meant by an appropriate curriculum. During my time at the IB many of the questions I received reminded me that this is not always the case. Often a question would help me understand the limitations of my worldview and experience. 'If we march symmetrically or in patterns, could our marching band requirement qualify as the mathematics course?' These types of question reminded me never to take knowledge level for granted.

Other queries had very different impacts. 'Does the IB have any suggestions to help an MYP coordinator that has over 300 Personal Projects to supervise, mark, moderate and upload?' or 'Would it be OK if a school couldn't do experiments in science this year as it has no budget for supplies or no specialised teachers left in that district?' These questions grounded our expectations and motivated us to make the MYP as flexible, accessible and supportive for schools as it could be.

Considering the costs of curriculum review, it is an excellent exercise in prioritising resources – both time and money. It is possible to do on a shoestring, but in the longer term it is impossible to keep it going, or enrich it, without financial commitments and planning.

Remember that the MYP is a framework, designed to be flexible and modified to suit a variety of contexts. The danger in this is that it is only as good as its implementation. A poor version of the programme will indeed deserve the moniker 'muddle in the middle'. Unfortunately, anyone who has experience of a poorly run programme will associate the negatives with the programme itself and not the version of it they have seen. But a well-executed version of the MYP will be effervescent and impressive. We set up the MYP in Dublin in this way, taking full advantage of the blank canvas gifted to us.

What do I need to make this happen?

Whether creating, aligning or redeveloping curriculum you should use all of the assets at your disposal to make the process as user-friendly and robust as possible. The pace of school life can be intense, and change often needs to happen quickly. We remind ourselves that we are entering a cycle at any point and there will be changes to come. Once you have completed a self-assessment, such as a gap analysis or a SWOT or SOAR analysis, a good next step would be to establish where your subject is in the review cycle. Will it be a year or six before changes come? There should be clear signposting of this in the various fora that the IB provides, such as My IB, and on LinkedIn and X (Twitter). Make sure to use IB Answers, and reach out to other schools and experts online. Many in the community are very happy to assist where they can. There will be differing opinions and interpretations, so choose which advice you follow wisely.

The IB publishes curriculum review reports, the purpose of which is to lay the ground and show the direction of travel of a review. These will identify trends and patterns, and serve to justify the time and budget spent. Recently, more and more webinars are hosted by expert practitioners on behalf of the IB, outlining how changes can be implemented or introduced, and these webinars are often published as recordings afterwards (see IB Exchange for more information).

Given all this soul-searching and analysis, you may decide you need to start with a ready-made curriculum or a supportive curriculum mapping tool. When it comes to curriculum capture, we have been spoiled for choice over the past few years. Two of the most popular IB curriculum mapping tools are ManageBac and Toddle. These have pre-formatted blank unit planners into which you can input your curriculum specifics, or choose from a range of drop-down or clickable boxes. This has simplified the process considerably and there has also been a great deal of investment into embedding AI to streamline these processes even further. ManageBac was a game changer when it entered the market, originally as a CAS (Community Action Service) tracking tool.

Recently, Toddle has demonstrated a very high level of investment and responsiveness to customer needs. Try out both Toddle and ManageBac to see which you prefer; other players may also enter the market, but remember that paper sketching or mapping out can help your thinking too, in a different way, as they allow you to see everything at once.

In Hamburg I found it really useful for my team to see all the units displayed by year. It was a large department, so this allowed us to discuss units, who was where, and when joint assessments or challenges might happen. In Dublin we went a step further and had a curriculum wall (pictured here) in the staffroom for all subjects, arranged by year, which allowed us to build up a network of interconnected units. Having a digital archive of your units in one place and with the ability to generate all the curriculum documents that might be required by various stakeholders, visitors and evaluators (inspectors) is also extremely helpful.

Before we move to one of the cornerstones of IB curriculum development, let us consider how curriculum development enriches and nourishes you as a teacher. From a practical perspective it will help build your expertise and enrich your practice. It will increase your ability to discern between excellent practices and what lacks depth or rigour. This skill set will be so important in ensuring we avoid becoming obsolete in the face of AI.

Now that we have identified the various needs and phases of curriculum development, let us turn to the nuts and bolts of what these curriculum changes must have.

Key feature: Resources signpost

Do you still need ready-made units? Naturally I would recommend InThinking as an online repository of exemplary units, or start with the official MYP textbooks from Hachette Learning. Full disclosure: I authored both! This will give you a range of more than 50 units that have been tried and tested and offer a strong starting point. Using these as your initial foundation, you can modify and adapt them to your own context, teaching, school or student strengths.

The concept-based curriculum – what is it and why?

'... exploring knowledge across a range of disciplines ...'

Concepts are nothing new in education. Ideas are the very currency we trade in, but as one teacher at an IB workshop expressed it to me, 'These are the ideas I do love about mathematics, but I'd forgotten that over time and under pressure.' I thought he perfectly encapsulated why we must remember that how we gain and use knowledge is much more important than factual recall.

When Lynn Erickson gave the keynote speech at the IB Symposium in The Hague in October 2011, I wonder if she knew how much her ideas would impact the whole programme review, or that these ideas would still be firmly in place more than a decade later? Her presentation to the assembled group outlined her hierarchy within the structure of knowledge, laid out like this:

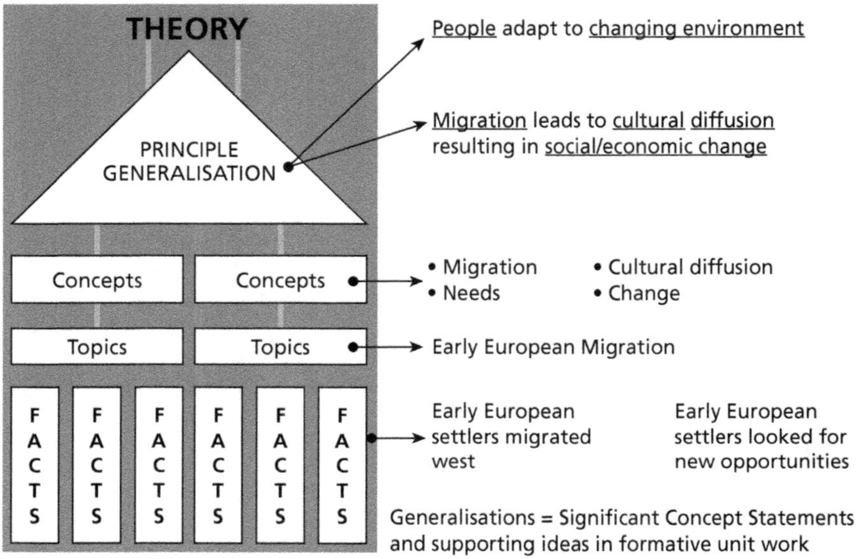

The structure of knowledge – MYP. Source: Erickson (2011)

Facts formed the foundation and could be divided into lesser **topics**. These topics had overarching concepts leading to significant concept statements. You can see the genesis of much of what we hold dear in the unit planning process already. In fact, much of the foundational work was laid in the PYP development earlier still.

When Lynn Erickson presented her concept-based learning approach at the IB Symposium, her influential keynote speech was entitled '**Synergistic thinking** and conceptual understanding in the IB programmes' (Erickson, 2011). Synergy has certainly fallen out of favour as a buzzword, but her thoughts have had lasting impact on the MYP, and later across the programmes. Her concepts of macro and micro concepts morphed into **key concepts** and **related concepts** as powerful tools for helping students develop their intellectual curiosity.

Her steer was to encourage concepts as the means to deliver depth in both thinking and understanding over topic-based models. She argued that topics and fact-based models failed to engage the intellect and were inefficient. Erickson went on to suggest 10 key concepts for science, for example, a number of which were later adopted in the *MYP Sciences Guide*. As far as I was told, she did not recommend any in the mathematics group!

At that time, education was in a phase where simply googling information had already had a disruptive effect, but there was so much more to come. Data richness and availability made some of these older approaches defunct. Topics alone, Erickson argued, failed to allow the brain to see patterns or make connections. This was a barrier to the higher-order, desirable skill of transferring information, a valued skill in the IB world in particular. None of this was new to the MYP, but it was formalised in a different package, which schools had to get used to.

The IB then defined this commitment to concept-based education in *From Principles into Practice* (IBO, 2014), with the definition 'a concept is a "big idea" – a principle or notion that is enduring, the significance of which goes beyond particular origins, subject matter or a place in time (Wiggins and McTighe, 1998). Concepts represent the vehicle for students' inquiry into the issues and ideas of personal, local and global significance, providing the means by which they can explore the essence of a subject.'

Big ideas in mathematics should have high relevance to the study of this field. These ideas, or concepts, should form the basis of what we learn and how this significance and relevance transcends time and place. Big ideas or concepts should encourage reflection processes. In mathematics we are blessed with a variety of concepts to choose from, including things like representations, proof, ideas of infinity, classification, ordering and formalising, but this is not an exhaustive list. There are fundamental ideas that occur throughout history. They recur or spiral at different levels. They may be anchored in everyday activities with a human dimension, but they don't have to be.

While we are thinking deeply about the concepts within mathematics, this is an excellent time to ask ourselves what we value most in the subject. Do we value fluency over understanding? Which methods can be seen as more successful? Can students learn to transfer ideas and broaden understanding without the use of concepts as abstract, powerful ideas? Can learners gain expertise without experience of the deeper, underpinning ideas? Looking back, it is probably fair to say that my own national mathematical education valued fluency and mastery over understanding and transfer, and that I feel fortunate that I had the chance to learn this alongside my first few cohorts of students.

You may hear teachers (or yourself) say, 'How can I do all this when I don't even have enough time for the content?' Reassure them that excellence in teaching and learning is still the only goal. We aim to teach the same mathematical knowledge but in a different way. You may well find that much of the philosophy chimes with your practice already, you just might not have articulated it in precisely the same way. There is a learning curve, but the incremental changes are worth it.

What does concept-based learning look like in MYP Mathematics?

In this image above, we can see Erickson's initial suggestions for a potential taxonomy involving mathematical understanding. We see now how this developed into a well-defined structure of inquiry, using key and related concepts in place of concepts and generalisation.

Key concepts

The MYP identifies 16 key concepts to be explored across the curriculum, which all represent understandings that reach across and beyond subject groups (the three key concepts for MYP Mathematics are in bold):

Aesthetics	Change	Communication	Communities
Connections	Creativity	Culture	Development
Form	Global interactions	Identity	**Logic**
Perspective	**Relationships**	Time, place and space	Systems

Source: IBO (2014)

The curriculum development process requires a commitment to using key concepts to plan disciplinary and interdisciplinary units of work. Teachers identify one key concept that drives the unit's development and can either be connected to, or arises from, the learning within, whether content, assessment or context.

Key feature: Reflection

- Which key concepts would you have chosen for mathematics?
- Can you identify why the three key concepts highlighted in the table made the final cut?
- Of the others, which would you say is the next most appropriate for MYP Mathematics?

These concepts are not only 'key' in the sense of being important; they also provide a key – a way into a body of knowledge through structured and sustained inquiry.

Source: IBO (2014)

It is important that these concepts are sufficiently important and accessible to students at every level from MYP 1 to MYP 5.

One of my very first outings as a curriculum manager was to attend a subject-specific workshop in Melbourne, Australia. A clearly very experienced teacher – I think his name might have been Graham – shared his thoughts. I braced myself for a critique, as his demeanour seemed to suggest that he might be hard to please. He said, 'I'd been watching the info coming out from the IB about the move to more concept-based. Huh, I thought to myself, I wonder what nonsense concepts they will come up with. I bet they'll be overly humanities! What fudge will they try to serve us now? How on earth could anyone reduce mathematics to a few buzzwords?'

Well, this type of teacher is destined to induce panic at workshops – they already distrust the IB and are supremely confident in the correctness of their every opinion. They are often to be seen reclining in their chairs with their arms crossed. Imagine my shock, then, when he continued, 'I saw them and thought, ah actually they're pretty good. Fair play. I even asked myself could I have identified three better ones, and I had to admit I could only come up with similar.'

'... develop and use conceptual understanding ...'

My relief must have been palpable to the room, there was such a shift in the anxiety levels among the teachers and the workshop leader, not to mention myself. He went on to expand on this, saying that the changes reminded him why he loved mathematics deep down, the epic form and beauty. It was my regular reminder that the IB has such a positive effect on our educators, as well as a reminder of how powerful the right teaching voice can be, given the opportune moment or platform.

Given that MYP Mathematics requires the use of these three key concepts, it can be a productive discussion whether others from the list might also apply? It is permissible to draw from other key concepts. It is also worth recalling that there were Post-its with hundreds of potential concepts plastered all over the working rooms at the IB, so a similar process can generate good debates in a department's collaborative planning time.

As noted a little earlier, three key concepts are identified for MYP Mathematics, with a further 12 related concepts to add depth and breadth to our curriculum development and inquiry. In chapter 4 we will discuss related concepts in more detail. For the moment, it is enough to understand that these concepts can be chosen first, and the content and inquiry can come from these choices. Alternatively, the content choices or assessment demands can be taken as the starting points and the appropriate concepts chosen to fit.

- **Form** is the shape and underlying structure of an entity or piece of work, including its organisation, essential nature and external appearance.

- **Logic** is a method of reasoning and a system of principles used to build arguments and reach conclusions.
- **Relationships** are the connections and associations between properties, objects, people and ideas – including the human community's connections with the world in which we live. Any change in relationship brings consequences, some of which may occur on a small scale, while others may be far-reaching, affecting large networks and systems such as human societies and the planetary ecosystem.

Here is a thought experiment. You have a unit on probability and reasoning about risk. There will be a quantitative as well as qualitative handling of data, and a lot of discussion of students and their personal risk profiles. They will be assessing risk and their comfort level with it. What is the best key concept here? Is it logic? Form? Relationships? Could you argue it differently for each?

I find this type of mental acrobatics really helpful in expanding my thinking about the various aspects of teaching mathematics in different ways. It drives my creativity and increases my mastery of a particular topic or idea.

There are some expectations for the use of key concepts (KCs) in MYP Mathematics, as in all subject groups, including:

- The choice and use of the KCs must be authentic and meaningful.
- Each KC must feature at least once over the course of the MYP, although multiple opportunities are clearly better.
- They should be introduced to the students while in a unit of inquiry and should demonstrate increasing levels of sophistication over the years of the programme.

There are lots of suggestions to match branches of reasoning or topics to concepts in the *MYP Mathematics Guide* (IBO, 2020, pp. 19, 20). I invite you now to try some out without their influence. Looking at the topics below, which concept would you choose for each and why? Would one of the others be possible too?

Geometric transformations	Logic/Relationships/Form
Systems of equations/simultaneous equations	Logic/Relationships/Form
Network paths, edges and vertices	Logic/Relationships/Form
Simple and compound interest	Logic/Relationships/Form
Voronoi diagrams	Logic/Relationships/Form

Key feature: Reflection

Consider, are there natural fits for each key concept to a certain area of mathematics? MYP Mathematics gives some suggestions as to suitable branches, but you may wish to develop your own.

- Will algebra always be Logic?
- Would reasoning with models always be the best match with Relationships?
- Or do you require greater flexibility of perspective?

The inclusion of Voronoi diagrams was intentional here as it opens up the dialogue to consider the positive influence these changes at the MYP have had on the DP. There is a greater emphasis now on concepts in the DP as a result. We will learn more about these granular details in chapter 6, Open-minded.

> Remember that in shifting to a concept-based curriculum, or improving the one you already have, you can only achieve as much as you can sustain. Fast food, fast fashion, fast forgotten. It is the same for superficial or non-meaningful change in curriculum. Ensure that changes are appropriate and sustainable wherever you can.

These concepts give our units of inquiry a focus, helping us to identify the knowledge that is transferable to new situations. This inquiry is another central idea in IB approaches to teaching and learning. Within the IB world we interpret inquiry as a process of curious investigation, often student-led and always student-focused, to progress understanding. We discuss this in much more detail in chapter 5, Inquirers.

As the key concepts capture the big ideas in mathematics, we need a vehicle to go deeper and broader within it. Many of the concepts that were considered for key concepts had to be rejected as their meaning was perhaps too mathematics specific and wouldn't resonate with other subjects, which is a key characteristic of the programme design. These concepts may have been too narrow or specific to operate at the key concept level, but they had value and authenticity to the study of mathematics. These formed the basis of the related concepts part of the unit planning process, which we will discuss in the next chapter.

Self-assessment

Complete the reflection:

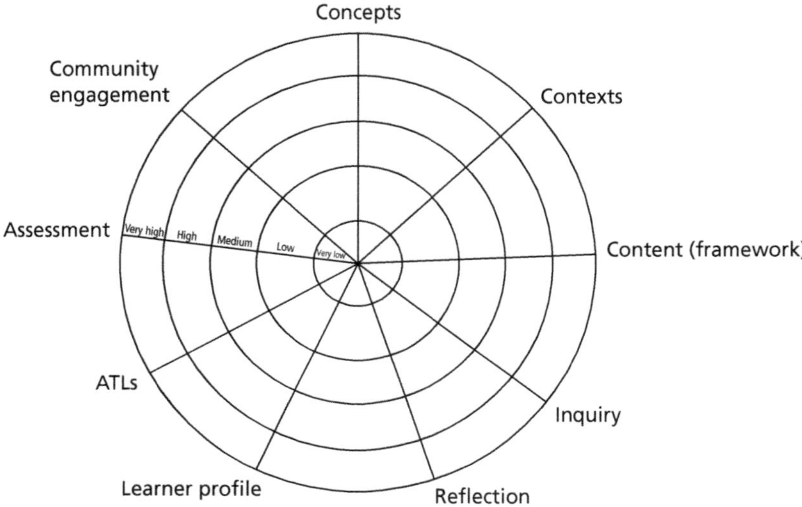

Shade in your knowledge level from low to high as you feel your comfort level lies.

Glossary

Concept Conceptual learning focuses on powerful organising ideas that have relevance within and across subject groups.

Conceptual understanding When concepts are used to formulate the understandings that students should retain in the future; they become principles and generalisations that students can use to understand the world, and to succeed in further study and in life beyond school.

Differentiating Modifying teaching strategies to meet the needs of diverse learners, through varied content, process and products.

Evaluating Making an appraisal by weighing up the strengths and limitations.

Form 'The shape and underlying structure of an entity or piece of work, including its organisation, essential nature and external appearance. Form in MYP Mathematics refers to the understanding that the underlying structure and shape of an entity is distinguished by its properties. Form provides opportunities for students to appreciate the aesthetic nature of the constructs used in a discipline' (IBO, 2020).

Framework The MYP framework provides a structure for organising parts of a curriculum and the relationships between them.

Key concepts Broad, organising, powerful ideas that have relevance within and across subjects and disciplines, providing connections that can transfer across time and culture.

Logic A method of reasoning and a system of principles used to build arguments and reach conclusions. Logic in MYP Mathematics is used as a process in making decisions about numbers, shapes and variables. This system of reasoning provides students with a method for explaining the validity of their conclusions.

Related concepts Concepts that are grounded in specific disciplines and explore key concepts in greater detail, providing depth to the programme.

Relationships In MYP Mathematics this refers to the connections between quantities, properties or concepts, and these connections may be expressed as models, rules or statements. Relationships provide opportunities for students to explore patterns in the world around them. Connections between the student and mathematics in the real world are important in developing deeper understanding.

Synergistic thinking The interplay between factual and conceptual thinking.

Topic For the purpose of external assessment, the MYP identifies a range of subject-specific topics that constitute one of the variables that authors consider when they create on-screen examinations.

CHAPTER 4
RISK-TAKERS

We approach uncertainty with forethought and determination, we work independently and cooperatively to explore new ideas and innovative strategies. We are resourceful and resilient in the face of challenges and change.

Key thinking points

In this chapter, there are explanations/discussions of:

- the reasons for choosing Risk-takers as the learner profile attribute for this chapter
- the importance of understanding various sections of the unit planner tool
- clarification of the unit planning process
- construals of a risk profile, appetite or budget when developing a planned curriculum
- related concepts, global contexts and an understanding of their genesis
- the risks and benefits of concept-based education
- development of the vertical and horizontal articulations of curriculum planning with cohesion
- the creation of statements of inquiry and their role in the unit planning process (elucidations).

Why choose Risk-takers as the learner profile attribute for this chapter?

This chapter will focus on developing the planned, or designed, curriculum through the learner profile attribute of 'Risk-takers'. Risk-takers seemed an appropriate fit for this chapter as it reminds us that when we start planning individual **units**, whether from scratch or not, we cannot predict how successful they might be. We build those units into a fully articulated curriculum, the alignment of which can also be risky: Do the units work well together? Do they give challenge and support where needed? Is there anything left out? Are the units resourceful, i.e. creative, and resilient – will they stand the test of time?

This chapter is designed for anyone who may be writing or revisiting units, wishing to make them as strong as they can possibly be. It is suitable for beginners as well as the content-confident, with a focus on moving your curriculum development from emerging to expertise. It is a highly suitable chapter for those who are preparing for an IB visit, either authorisation or verification, to ensure their units are as robust as possible.

The content is also useful for those schools that are processing feedback from a consultant or may have had recommendations or Matters to be Addressed (MTBAs) for an IB visiting team, regarding their units. The advice in this chapter will assist you in refining and improving the units to bring them closer to the IB philosophy and expectations.

The process of leading learning by inquiry can be a scary thought for the risk-averse, a headache for the risk-weary or exhilarating for the risk-takers. We acknowledge also that these changes, while fraught with the possibility of risk, don't always reach the extremes of pure success or disaster. So there is no need to panic, and we can allow ourselves a certain amount of risk and experimentation.

As we get further into curriculum planning, we find ourselves at a good moment to look at how the IB categorises distinct parts of the curriculum as planned, delivered and assessed. It identifies these in its usual preferred cyclical style (see image). We will cover all aspects of this cycle in the coming chapters.

The MYP's coherent curriculum comprises three interrelated components:

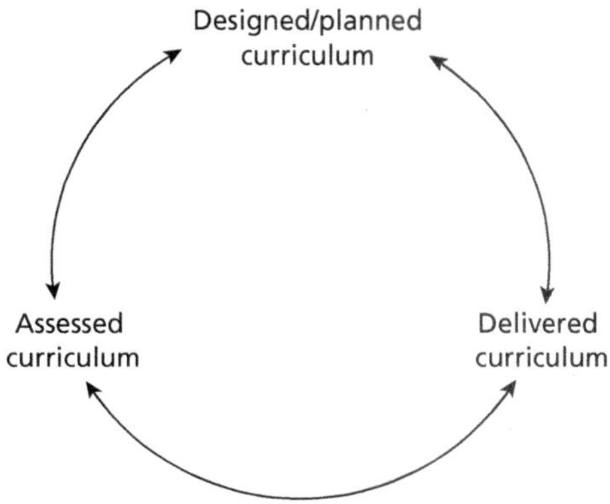

The MYP curriculum model

The MYP curriculum model comprises three sections, each connected by a bidirectional arrow and of equal weight and importance. The arrows indicate that the school's planned, delivered and assessed curriculums are in an integrated process of development and in constant motion or evolution. We can enter from any of the three stages and progress through the others in any direction that suits our school's needs. Due care and attention must be given to a process of continual monitoring and development so that the curriculum remains fresh.

What is a risk-taking budget?

Listening to a politics podcast recently I heard the presenters discussing the upcoming elections and how the electorate might respond to the political parties on offer. One particularly intriguing idea they discussed was the concept that the voting public has a 'risk budget' when voting. The presenters posited that many voters subconsciously consider, 'Should we continue with the current politicians or give others a chance?' This risk budget rises and falls in the minds of the voters, depending on various factors, such as the economy and national services. The voters, the experts contended, are making continual adjustments regarding how much discretionary risk there is and how much they can live without, and making judgements based on how to 'spend' or allocate that risk, all subconsciously. These adjustments determine how much risk of governance they feel the country can take on.

This idea appealed to me in that it relates to curriculum planning in general. Do we have a risk budget when we plan our curriculum? Does it change over time? Are there 'fixed costs' in our budget – risks we cannot avoid, such as external assessments? It is interesting to consider discretionary risks, and when you have some 'cash' left over to consider change such as new curriculum or pedagogy.

This interpretation of risk reminds me of how we used the idea of 'Risk-takers' during the various levels of Covid protocols in school. For us, as with many, enforcement of rules was a constant headache, as you probably remember all too well. One strategy we found particularly effective was to frame the conversation in terms of risk-taking and caring. Yes, we admit, we support risk-taking but it must be a sensible and desirable risk, and we must be caring with regard to the different risk profiles of others. By this, we meant that some are more cautious and it behoves us to meet their needs too. Just because you feel comfortable taking off your mask, against guidance, this does not show sufficient care or respect for others or their personal feelings of risk. This proved highly effective in classroom discussions, and reframed it from an argument about individual rights to collective care for one another.

Beginning as we have done with the IB's commitment to a concept-based curriculum, our initial thoughts were of the key concepts; now we turn our attention to the other parts of the unit-planning process and how to ensure that each unit is meticulously planned and aligned. Our goal is still to have vibrant units that are simultaneously rigorous and engaging, to meet the IB expectations.

'... with forethought and determination ...'

And so we enter the arena of risk, where we design or redesign units in line with the MYP expectations and requirements with forethought and determination.

Many of the early 2000s MYP publications were fixated on a 'gap', with publication titles ranging from *Mind the Gap* to *Bridging the Gap*. These began to address the apparent gap between the MYP and the DP as was felt at that time. It connotes a certain Anglocentricity to me, as 'mind the gap' is a phrase in my mind that I associate only with announcements on the London Underground.

It makes us question, is a gap a good thing or a bad thing? In the case of MYP to DP transitions, it is clearly thought to have been a bad thing at the time. Curriculum development can also be viewed as very gap-centric. Students may have a knowledge or skills gap; a department may be struggling with a reputation gap from where they feel they are and where they want to be. Perhaps the deeper problem is a confidence or motivation gap in students.

The first task of the curriculum developer is to figure out the nature of that gap in order to address it. A gap can grow into a dangerous chasm over time, if unaddressed. Each of these gaps may generate a different need and risk in your curriculum development. The danger is over-correcting or being reactionary.

And not all gaps are negative. In the inquiry chapter (chapter 5) we will discuss how gaps in skills or knowledge can open our curiosity and inspire creativity.

It can be helpful to recall why we invite this risk, beyond the obvious reasons. We had a traditional model, based on rote learning and direct instruction, which managed to transfer a great deal of mathematical understanding in a contiguous chain over hundreds of years. Why the need to change things? Is change really necessary?

Quite simply the answer is yes, but it can help to remind ourselves of the reasons. We must remind ourselves that all students who come to our MYP classrooms already have a relationship with mathematics. These relationships include interactions that are relentlessly personal and can be emotionally exhausting, resulting in a mathematics class where students are confronted, and must deal with success, failure, authority, identity, security, praise, power, competition, and both rational and irrational emotions. All this on top of their altered circadian rhythms, hormonal development and socioemotional development! If it can be proven that inquiry and concept-based education has a benefit in all this maelstrom then it must be worth the attempt. This is becoming more urgent as AI changes the parameters of education for us all. This must be a powerful call to action for us to take these risks.

If we consider ourselves to have a certain risk budget, which we want to spend wisely, we must consider what the priorities are for each unit. These can vary by unit, where some establish good habits and routines at the start of the year, but others must be flexible at the end of the year, when trips and exam season cause inevitable disruption. We ask ourselves honestly what the chief focus of this time of year is: making academic or social progress, consolidation or preparation for a transition? Once you have known your student body, population and individual classes for some time, you will know their needs better. What are the non-negotiables? For instance, if there is an external assessment, such as eAssessment or iGCSE or other national requirement, then the priority will always be exam success.

When we are planning, and analysing the risk, a useful prioritisation tool is the Eisenhower matrix seen here. This can be adapted for change management, in order to differentiate between urgent and important changes. It can help to determine when to start or stop experimenting with your curriculum. If students are included in the process of experimentation or development it can increase their agency and the quality of feedback. It can help students in their approaches to learning (ATL) skills – particularly their reflection and thinking skills – to be an active part of the experimentation. We know, too, that it can have an observer effect. We will discuss this more in the Communicators chapter (chapter 7).

The Eisenhower decision matrix

The Eisenhower decision matrix

One note of caution – make sure the parent education piece is in place whenever you make changes. In a school with academic pressure, often coupled with fees and parental expectations, the appetite for risk is often very low. Stakeholders – including parents, students and management – must understand clearly what is changing and why. Those making the change will be spending some of their reputational capital with the families. It is an easier feat to bring them along with you when you have a gravitas or credibility already established.

Curriculum changes can also be disruptive, and there is an often overlooked idea that our students are not human guinea pigs. If we are carrying out these changes with the best of intentions, and not publishing our results, or implementing them with certain groups only, we are unlikely to fall foul of the IB's policy on human experimentation, but it deserves consideration anyway. Reflect on when change needs to be radical or iterative. We can learn a lot from our MYP Design colleagues here. They talk about risk-taking in terms of a process of refinement. My husband introduced me to the design thinking approach of 'Innovating the adjacent possible', where we innovate by steps and iterations to get to our goal. Do what we can now and don't let the perfect be the enemy of the good.

What is a unit planner?

'We approach uncertainty ...'

The unit planner provided by the IB is blank template or pro forma to be completed by schools as they develop their units. It aims to capture all aspects of the planned curriculum that teachers should consider as the unit unfurls. It is not technically mandated or compulsory, and you can make changes, but it is essentially ubiquitous. All curriculum software that is IB aligned will have some version of the following.

There are signposts in each box of the unit planner to the chapter that supports this requirement.

MYP unit planner

Teacher(s)		Subject group and discipline			
Unit title		MYP year		Unit duration (hrs)	

Inquiry: Establishing the purpose of the unit

Key concept	Related concept(s)	Global contexts
Chapter 2	Chapter 3	Chapter 3
Statement of inquiry		
Chapter 3		
Inquiry questions		
Factual— **Conceptual—** Chapter 4 **Debatable—**		

Objectives	Summative assessment	
Chapter 4	Outline of summative assessment task(s) including assessment criteria: Chapter 4	Relationship between summative assessment task(s) and statement of inquiry: Chapter 5

Approaches to learning (ATL)
Chapter 5

Action: Teaching and learning through inquiry

<table>
<tr><th>Content</th><th>Learning process</th></tr>
<tr><td rowspan="3">Chapter 5 and 7</td><td>Learning experiences and teaching strategies
Chapter 6</td></tr>
<tr><td>Formative assessment
Chapter 7 and 4</td></tr>
<tr><td>Differentiation
Chapter 7</td></tr>
<tr><th colspan="2">Resources</th></tr>
<tr><td colspan="2">Chapter 7</td></tr>
</table>

Reflection has both a sequential and cyclical nature, as mentioned in chapter 2.

After the last curriculum review for the MYP, workshop leaders and schools were provided with a prepopulated planner that had guidance and steers in each box within the unit planning structure. I can't remember how it got its name, but we always referred to it as the 'bubble planner'. It still has value and can be a useful resource when conducting internal PD for teachers, especially novices to the MYP. Over time, this document has been absorbed into the curriculum guidance, through workshops and via prompts in ManageBac or Toddle and the like.

One of the funniest things at 'IB headquarters' was the strength of passion that could be aroused by something like a graphic organiser. There was ongoing disagreement about it – whether the correct term for a completed unit of inquiry (UOI) was unit plan or unit planner. One camp contended that the unit planner was provided by the IB, while the unit plans had to be developed. The opposing side used unit planner as the only name needed.

It was a heated debate! Looking back, I wonder why we were so passionate on both sides. It is true that it is probably a distinction without being a difference. Nevertheless a good curriculum manager knows that they will be challenged and questioned on it, so it is best to be ready for questions like this, which you think no one cares about – because someone will!

In the end, I think the internal battle was resolved with the decision that a unit planner was a tool, a unit plan was the goal. This never fully reached the community, which can be seen in particular in the subjects that have a PCUP for ePortfolio. These Partially Completed Unit Planners (PCUPs) are published every exam season as a starting point for schools to develop, not as an end product.

Discussions like these may seem like a storm in a teacup, and that's probably true. In our defence, I would say that if these things are not sufficiently thought through then there are reputational risks, and it may make the IB seem disjointed or ill-informed. A similar level of obsessive minutiae occurred when I became completely overwrought by an image used on the IB website. It was the landing page of the Online Curriculum Centre (OCC), now called the Programme Resource Centre (PRC), and I complained endlessly to the head of MYP, Robert Harrison, about it. It seemed to me to be the worst possible choice of image: the teacher was performing a demonstration; she had her safety goggles on top of her head and her hair was down. The students also had no safety equipment, hair everywhere and some of them looking uninterested. Robert humoured me and got the image changed, while feigning frustration at my collation of #badmathematics and #badscience examples.

Why are there different concepts?

'... to explore new ideas ...'

In the previous chapter, our discussion of concept-based learning included one of the biggest parts of setting up a curriculum in this way, namely identifying the big ideas in each subject to give breadth and connection to our choices of units. To introduce more and more detail, and to go deeper with these mathematical concepts, we turn to the younger sibling: related concepts. If you happen to be reading the chapters non-consecutively or non-linearly, you will find a discussion of the genesis of the IB's particular brand of concept-based learning in chapter 3.

What are these related concepts, and why do we need them?

One of the popular trends in schools in recent years has been the phenomenon of autonomous sensory meridian response (ASMR) videos on YouTube. I first realised quite how popular these were when I saw students in study hall playing old Bob Ross videos as their background noise while studying or working on assignments. I remember watching this US artist on television myself as a child. He would start with a blank canvas and patiently, quietly, calmly teach the audience to paint with oils. His style was impressive and he was immensely popular, and seemingly continues to be so. Bob would add large patches of colour before slowly building a scene with detailed mixing and brushstrokes. We were always amazed at what he could achieve. Forward to more recent times, I was surprised to learn how beloved he still was. At the risk of adding a third analogy, here is a perfect exemplification of this stage of the process: the key concepts provide a broad patch of colour, mountains or water, and the related concepts give us more detail and depth in the form of trees and foliage.

To this end, each MYP subject has a given set of related concepts, which are more closely designed to capture the relevant ideas within the subject group. During the last curriculum review, just as with the choice of key concepts, the process of identifying the related concepts was a creative and contentious one, but they were well received once published. I had occasion to change only two of them in the subsequent review, but more on that later. Unlike the key concepts, where I agree wholeheartedly with those chosen, it would have been a delight to have been there to argue for the inclusion of even more related concepts such as (mathematical) intransience, abstraction or identity.

Related concepts and their definitions are found in each MYP subject group guide, along with examples of how they are used to develop MYP units.

There should be at least one related concept in every unit, and they should:

- aim to promote deeper learning in the subject and be clearly discipline specific
- support the choice of key concept
- increase in complexity in their use over the years of the MYP
- be addressed in a cognitive and age-appropriate way throughout those years
- similarly, have different levels of abstraction.

They can be used by different subjects, if appropriate and relevant to the units of inquiry.

The following is a glossary of these related concepts for mathematics, as published in the *MYP Mathematics Guide:*

Related concept	Definition
Approximation	A quantity or a representation that is nearly but not exactly correct.
Change	A variation in size, amount or behaviour.
Equivalence	The state of being identically equal or interchangeable, applied to statements, quantities or expressions.
Generalization	A general statement made on the basis of specific examples.

Related concept	Definition
Models	Depictions of real-life events using expressions, equations or graphs.
Patterns	Sets of numbers or objects that follow a specific order or rule.
Quantity	An amount or number.
Representation	The manner in which something is presented.
Simplification	The process of reducing to a less complicated form.
Space	The frame of geometrical dimensions describing an entity.
Systems	Groups of interrelated elements.
Validity	Using well-founded, logical mathematics to come to a true and accurate conclusion or a reasonable interpretation of results.

Source: IBO (2020)

As I have already mentioned, two related concepts were changed in the last guide and this was done in service of greater alignment of the IB continuum. During one set of curriculum review meetings for the new DP Mathematics courses, which would go on to become A&A and A&I, there was a clear focus and emphasis on concepts. The changes from 'Justification' and 'Measurement' to 'Approximation' and 'Validity' helped us make the transition to DP Mathematics even clearer.

Can you use other related concepts? Yes. But, honestly, most find it enough to choose from, and cover, the ones already provided. This could form the basis of a good departmental discussion for a quiet time though. Additional concepts could be developed from these debates, but proceed with the use of any new concepts under caution and advisement.

At certain points of the curriculum review, and even post-publication, it became common to use the following formulation:

Key concept + Related concept = Conceptual understanding

Key feature: Resources signpost

You will find suggested related concepts in the MYP Mathematics Guide, at the beginning of each branch of reasoning. Why not try out the same thought process now?

Exercise

You are designing a unit on ratios, with a focus on gender balance and equality. Which two related concepts would you choose?

The purpose of this conceptual understanding stage was to ensure that there was a crystal-clear focus on the ideas featured in the unit. It was intended to familiarise teachers, and students, with the newly introduced concepts at both levels of detail. It was seen as a stepping stone before adding the **global context** to make a **statement of inquiry**. Over time it became clear that this step should be optional and it has gradually faded. I was pleased by this development as, without the relevance given by the global context choice, I found it cumbersome and far too often treated as a wordsmithing exercise.

Why do we need global contexts?

'... to explore ... innovative strategies ...'

According to *From Principles into Practice* (IBO, 2014), the global contexts are a crucial component of the unit planning process in that they give a purpose and a relevance to every unit. There are six to choose from and it is technically possible to develop your own. Every unit must have one attached to it and reflected in the statement of inquiry. The purpose of these six global contexts is to:

- allow students to develop their understanding of mathematics through inquiry, action and reflection
- connect academic knowing to real-world understanding and meaning
- clarify why we should learn what we are learning
- foster positive attitudes and outlook to global challenges, not to cause despair about the challenges we face.

Key feature: Further reading

Related concepts textbook

A textbook of activities by concept, IB Skills: Mathematics – A Practical Guide, was produced by the IBO with Hachette Learning in 2014, along with a supporting teacher guide. The book is laid out by concept and within each has three examples of sub-topics. It has some nice ideas to emphasise certain related concepts if you feel your curriculum is lacking in one or two specific related concepts. The authors, Talei Kunkel, Palmira Mariz Seiler, Marlene Torres-Skoumal and David Weber, are all exemplary practitioners and worth a follow online too.

A note of caution, though: this book deals with the old related concepts, before I changed the aforementioned related concepts to align with DP choices. I reached out to one of the authors, Palmira Mariz Seiler, to ask her about the experience of writing such a concept-based text given the little information available at the time. She commented: 'I am certainly proud of the work we did as by then we had no references – concepts in the MYP were something new and we could not even agree on their definitions. Meanwhile, the idea of concepts has evolved and now everything is clearer. ... As teachers can add to the list of concepts, I would have included an extra chapter guiding this extra concept (symmetry).'

Meet the global contexts:

- Personal and Cultural Expression
- Scientific and Technical Innovation
- Identities and Relationships
- Fairness and Development
- Orientation in Space and Time
- Globalization and Sustainability.

You can find full descriptions of these six global contexts in *From Principles into Practice* (IBO, 2014). It is important to note that they are very closely connected to the PYP transdisciplinary themes, in an age-appropriate way.

PYP transdisciplinary theme	MYP global context
Who we are →	Identities and relationships
Where we are in place and time →	Orientation in space and time
Forms of expression →	Personal and cultural expression
How the world works →	Scientific and technical innovation
How we organise ourselves →	Globalisation and sustainability
Sharing the planet →	Fairness and development

MYP global contexts are the IB's opportunity to support the mission statement by showing clearly what it means to be internationally minded, promotes multilingualism, intercultural understanding and global engagement.

Source: IBO (2014)

The global contexts connect the planned and the delivered curriculum by creating meaning or relevance. They should inspire explorations of our common humanity and shared guardianship of the planet.

When curriculum developers select a global context for learning, they should aim to answer all the following questions:

- Why is inquiry important in this area?
- Why are these concepts relevant and important to my students?
- Why should we/they care about this unit?
- Have I used, or overused, this global context before?
- Is there a better global context fit or a more relevant application for this body of mathematics?
- Is this the best global context match for the reasoning skills embedded in this unit?

First, identify one global context that establishes a focus for meaningful teaching and learning. As a subject group we are not compelled to have all six global contexts in every year, or even across the whole vertical articulation. Having said that, many of us are lovers of symmetry and balance, and as such we will want to sample them equitably, if not equally. There are trends within the selection of global contexts in MYP Mathematics. Scientific and Technical Innovation is very popular, and I often see Personal and Cultural Expression used.

A very popular activity in workshops is one where the workshop leader will project a series of images and the participants must choose a global context that would match. The popularity of this activity lies in its efficacy – it breaks through confusion or ambiguity. I love it, as it allows teachers to visually reference how they will frame their unit development.

Take a look at this image:

Can you argue that it represents:

- Personal and Cultural Expression
- Scientific and Technical Innovation
- Identities and Relationships
- Fairness and Development
- Orientation in Space and Time
- Globalization and Sustainability?

Key feature: Reflection

Consider how you might choose one of the six global contexts to best suit your unit.

You are developing a unit where students are inquiring into linear programming and inequalities.

- How many of the global contexts would be appropriate?
- Which one would inspire the most interesting investigations?
- How is this topic relevant to your students' lives?
- Does that affect your choice?
- Are there any that would not work at all?

Where did the global contexts come from?

There had been something similar to global contexts in the previous version of the MYP, called the areas of interaction. The criticisms might sound familiar: they were too vague, too disconnected, too humanities driven, too inauthentic, above students' heads, irrelevant to our subject. It was decided that these needed to be revisited in the curriculum review, but it remained a mystery how they could be improved. Malcolm Nicolson, who was head of MYP development at the time, describes another heated debate, this time resulting in a stalemate – passions were high. This long and hard day of discussion was called to a close and the team withdrew to the local Irish pub to continue the debate, regroup and play darts. This was prior to my arrival, so I cannot be blamed for this bad influence.

The next day, with a fresh start and clearer heads, they came back to the problem but still could see no breakthrough. The team knew they needed a place for why any learning was important for 11- to 16-year-olds, beyond 'you need it for Diploma'. As it happened, a PYP colleague came in to ask a question of one of the meeting participants and her recognition of this idea as the transdisciplinary themes in PYP was just the connection they needed. It was more proof, if proof were needed, that iterative development of the continuum is possible. It can indeed work well, given time and good intentions.

Once the global contexts had been chosen and defined, explorations were added as possible examples or to give more clarity on what the titles could mean. As I understand it, it was never the intention that they would become a requirement in the 'drop-down selection' way they have.

When I joined the MYP team a short time later, there were recognised concerns and complaints from teachers. Many schools make the argument that the global contexts feel too humanities driven, a criticism I heard frequently after their release. Teachers felt that the definitions of Identities and Relationships didn't fit our understanding of these in mathematics, likewise many struggled to see the application of Globalization and Sustainability in our subject. It was a fair criticism and reminded us that representation matters. If there was no mathematical or scientific voice during development then how could the examples reflect it? To this end, Robert Harrison managed to accelerate the process somehow, and I managed to get out an additional document of further guidance, which exemplified and empowered more discipline-specific explorations for use.

Since then, I still observe a lazy tendency to connect certain global contexts to certain areas of mathematics. I am guilty of using Identities and Relationships with algebra often, and I always seem to have a very valid reason to use Fairness and Development when I am developing statistical literacy. I have to stop myself from taking the path of least resistance too often. It is reported that Scientific and Technical Innovation is one of the most popular for mathematics teachers, but I do see a lot of Personal and Cultural Expression, often used for geometry, regularly with Islamic art.

There was also once an excellent question from a teacher at a workshop: why was it Scientific and Technical Innovation and not Technological Innovation, as surely it was technology and not technique that was changing our lives? I did not have a good answer for them, and the question still haunts me over a decade later.

Practically speaking, I also like the choice of global context to inspire the summative assessment, so it becomes more than a vague idea in students' minds. It can be useful in generating an authentic idea for a Criterion D assessment, where there is a great deal of mathematics to be done, within which a context can affect the validity of your results. Another great example problem, which can be mathematically interesting purely in itself, is the optimisation of the volume of a box. It can require students to extend their answers by asking them to consider sustainability, waste or circular economies. It can also be helpful to link or connect the global context to worded problems or to introduce complexity to Criterion A questions 5–6 or 7–8.

Key feature: Reflection

Pick icons to represent the six global contexts. I am often surprised by what is chosen on sites like Teachers Pay Teachers (TPT, www.teacherspayteachers.com) for their global context posters.

I really like 'context'. It feels like such a grown-up word: 'What you need to understand about the context is ...', 'understanding the broader context ...'. It is a word that invites both clarity and complexity. Context can help us to understand something in detail, and with so much more meaning and integrity. It has become a regular feature of daily life, and most recently in an era of edited media and deepfakes, when we need to know more before we make a judgement – for example, 'That remark was taken out of context!' Context reminds us that we must consider more than the basics, just as we expect the students to do with the knowledge and understanding from our classes.

For the longest time I simply accepted the term global context as a given idea, something that was a key component of adding a reason and importance for learning the specifics of a unit. I must have said over a thousand times to educators and students that it gives the why to what we are doing in class. That is how I have always used it in principle and in practice. The global commits us to embodying the international mindedness and global engagement required by the mission statement, and it is rather unique to the IB in terms of planning, that every unit of learning must bear this in mind. It brings a reason to our inquiry and deliberations.

Only very recently has it occurred to me that there is an apparent contradiction in the term: for me 'context' is specific and narrows the focus, while the 'global' opens it up. It has been possible to reconcile the two by wondering, 'How is it specifically important to me but also globally relevant?' It is a term I will continue to wonder about and refine. Perhaps a better term might have been 'global relevance'.

Key feature: Provocation question

If global contexts come from the PYP, where do they go in the DP? Are they assimilated into the theories of knowledge (TOKs)? Do they have a role or a natural home in Diploma Mathematics?

What are statements of inquiry?

The statement of inquiry (SOI) is a crucial part of any unit. It announces the purpose of the unit. Teachers construct the statement of inquiry for a unit by using an enjoyable mathematical equation:

Key concept + Related concept + Global context = SOI (starting point)

Teachers must combine a key concept, one or more related concepts and a global context for the unit into a meaningful statement that students can understand. This statement should express the connections between concepts and context for this particular unit of mathematics. It also important that the content of the unit can be identified too, as factual knowledge.

The SOI should be a transferable idea, which can be recognised as lifeworthy knowledge by a mathematics teacher as well as teachers of other subjects. These SOIs should be age-appropriate and increase in complexity as students progress through the MYP. They must describe something worth knowing and a suitable line of inquiry into a complex relationship that is worthy of inquiry, i.e. both what they are learning and why it is important. They often vary in sophistication and specificity.

I mentioned that the formula above gives an SOI starting point. The reason I made this distinction is that I have scores of examples where the different terms have been stuck together and yet they are meaningless. These vague statements give no indication of what a student will engage with, and end up as white noise to students and teachers alike.

How do we create SOIs to ensure their efficacy? As mathematicians we naturally crave an algorithm here, at least I do. I like to start with the formula above and then read it several times over. Then I insert indicators and specific details of the mathematics within the unit. There will be several drafts and rewording at this point. The key question I ask myself is, 'Why is this unit interesting for their future?' I read and reread the SOI until it sounds like something concrete and reasonable. These statements must be constructed, then crafted and, finally, stress-tested by the classroom. The best SOIs are creative, i.e. resourceful and resilient to criticism and changes over time.

'We are resourceful and resilient ...'

Teachers are the main creators and consumers of statements of inquiry. Parents are usually somewhat perplexed by them. The students see so many of these I was often worried that they became little more than background music to their educational experience. To counteract this, we experimented with assessment cover sheets, which made the key concepts, related concepts and global contexts explicit, and highlighted the statement of inquiry too. It added to the page count and paper consumption but gave a uniform approach to all assessment, and students had a visible reminder of the importance.

Can we use a powerful or inspiring quotation as a statement of inquiry? Yes, absolutely. Nowhere does it say you *have* to use the words exactly. Neither does it say you cannot use the words exactly.

Statements of inquiry should not be so specific that they cannot be transferable beyond the content of the unit. It is ideal if another teacher happens to see your unit, in a classroom or an assessment. It is important that you feel comfortable evaluating them and having them evaluated by others. It should make them go, 'Oh, I didn't know you did this then' or 'Ooh, this could be a cool unit for ...'.

Key feature: Reflection

Consider some of the following good and bad examples of statements of inquiry, and see whether they are too short, too vague, too long or meaningless. I've included one that I really like, one that is too specific, one too vague and one that has potential.

- The process of mathematical simplification in two-step equation solving is a process of inversing not balancing.
- Accurate measurement and representation are essential to fairer societies.
- Humans access logic to help us understand mathematical relationships.
- Geometrical richness requires an understanding of the history and culture of geometry.

It can be a good idea to use AI prompts to road-test your SOIs. This can be an interesting experiment. It might reveal some improvements and ideas, but beware: it is important to be discerning, as they can be very repetitive and a little dry. Sometimes they will give you absolute rubbish too! Here is one I generated as an example for 'Mathematics can be a tool for simplifying relationships in identities'.

Key feature: Anecdotal counterexample

Some teachers have tried to have students craft SOIs. This is allowed, if not encouraged. Of course, I have found myself arguing or suggesting this in workshops – 'there's no reason why you couldn't co-develop these with students' – until I tried to do it with students myself, on re-entering the classroom. I have never made this work as an exercise. The time invested, and occasionally authority ceded, simply wasn't worth it for me. If you have a sufficiently motivated and eloquent group you can of course give it a try.

How do we ensure excellent unit plan completion?

Accepted wisdom online with regard to clickbait-style headlines seems to be that a non-conventional number of tips is more likely to generate interest. To test this theory, here are the top 13 tips for completing the unit planner and producing excellent unit plans.

1. Remember the importance of reflection. Always complete the reflection before unit planning – this is an important step in setting the aspiration as well as expectation. Set a reminder in your phone or calendar for a mid-unit reflection, maybe around the time of a substantial learning check or a formative assessment.
2. Use the strategies of pairing, i.e. always complete two tasks together so you don't forget one or the other. Make sure to complete the reflection section of the planner straight after the assessment, when putting the grades and feedback in. This way the immediate feedback is fresh and it will help you formulate the lessons learned. Another great time to do this is when standardisation is happening in the department. Build it into the routine before closing a standardisation meeting by completing the reflection. Make sure it feels like part of the process.
3. Remember you have to choose your global contexts, but you don't have to explicitly choose one of the explorations provided if it doesn't fit. Remember to check the further guidance suggestions too.
4. Make sure you include two or three lines on the unit's content so everyone is clear on the rigour and content required in this unit. Distil the content to three to four lines to define the floor as well as the ceiling for all students, where there is a spread of abilities within the groups.
5. The statement of understanding might include a conceptual understanding statement and a statement of inquiry – only the SOI is compulsory as a part of the unit planning.
6. Always state three to five inquiry questions that relate to the unit. The factual questions can and should be drawn from the content; the conceptual questions link explicitly to the concepts chosen. I also like to vary my debateable questions between issues arising from the global context as well as interesting TOK-style questions pertaining to that unit or branch of mathematics.
7. 'Meet a mathematician or meet a mathematical symbol!' The learner profile attributes block is a great opportunity for students to reflect on or discuss the selected IB learner profile attribute. It can offer a useful way to integrate Nature of Mathematics into normal discussions. Identifying a person or a mathematical process to feature in a unit builds up students' confidence and familiarity in communication, and is handy for unit cover pages too.

8. Two or three ATLs have to be selected for the unit, which support the content and identify how they will be used. Every ATL skill should have a connection to various learning experiences, and ideally will be linked to the summative assessment in some way.
9. MYP objectives block: identify the objectives. You can choose all four (as there are very few units that don't deal with patterns, communicating, understanding or the real world in some way), but it is more effective to concentrate on addressing the same criteria as those being assessed.
10. Content block: can be arranged under bullet points – e.g. a few points that students will 'know', 'understand' and 'be able to' by the end of the unit. I find it a great opportunity to link 'know and understand' to Criteria A and C, whereas I like to link 'be able to' to Criteria B and D.
11. Always give detail on the summative assessment, with task-specific clarifications and clear command terms. Make sure to upload or capture a copy of these. If possible, scan some examples for future use, usually one high, one middle and one low level of achievement, to ensure the standard and quality expected does not drift year on year.
12. It is always useful to review all materials and resources used in the unit, to conform with some kind of sensitivity check. There is a huge focus on DEIBJ (diversity, equity, inclusion, belonging and justice) appropriate resources, and this can have a positive, inclusive effect on your choices. We will discuss these ideas and more in the application of ethnomathematics in chapter 9.12.
13. The unit flow is where the sequence of teaching is outlined. Check the unit has a flow. I call this 'the pointillism moment' – do all the dots come together to form a cohesive picture? I always take a moment and we do a common-sense check together, savour the green ticks and see if the unit comes together.

Key feature: Resources signpost

Do you need sample units or subject group overviews?

- Save: check out the teacher support materials on My IB in the Programme Resource Centre.
- Spend: AI models can help sequence units, but it is limited in terms of formatting and detail.
- Splurge: try some pre-populated units from Hodder, Toddle or InThinking, which have been authored and evaluated by MYP teachers.

'I've written an SOI and a unit overview, which I think is good. How can I check it?'

Initially the best place to get feedback from is your MYP coordinator and other members of the department. The MYP coordinator acts a conduit to, or the official voice of, the IB. It is assumed that the IB can rely on coordinators' independent understanding of its processes. Any registered teachers can access readily available material through My IB, but coordinators have a direct connection to the IB through a school representative or manager. They can seek clarification in the case of disagreement or misunderstanding.

Remember that the IB is not in a position to give feedback on units, SOIs or anything else that has been created in these channels. It might welcome you sharing them in the IB exchange but will not quality-assure them for you now that BQC is a thing of the past. (BQC was a service called Building Quality Curriculum, which would review units for more than a hundred dollars per unit, but the service is no more.) I see many people reaching out for help or feedback on various platforms, predominantly Facebook and WhatsApp. These can be a great source of ideas, but be sure to fact-check anything you are told. Many people have internalised their own interpretations over the years and present their opinions as fact, with the very best of intentions. When in coubt, check the IB publications and ask IB Answers if you are still unclear.

What is the purpose of the subject group overview?

'... we work cooperatively and independently ...'

It is with very good reason that the IB insists on detailed overviews of curriculum before it will authorise a school. Without an idea of what will be learned and taught throughout, captured in writing and with detail, it is game over! Schools may not even get past the consultant or application stage withcut a decent understanding of how to set out a **horizontal** and **vertical** curriculum overview. This act of sequencing has so many functions: the detangling of requirements, the actual delivery and content of classes, the vast amount of learning and upskilling that will be required. It is a sober reckoning for many, of the sheer amount of work involved in designing and then sequencing units in the IB manner.

Each unit must 'speak' to the others. They all have to work independently to a certain extent, as a standalone piece of important learning and knowledge acquisition, but no unit is an island. Now that we have discussed the various parts of the unit planner, we must tie these together and minimise dangerous risks to our curriculum spectrum.

One of these risks is that we make assumptions about **prior learning**. If we get this wrong it can manifest as delays or frustration, when we discover gaps in competencies. Before long, it will become apparent if students are not where you think they should be. This fact is essentially a black box in planning until we are in the delivered curriculum – we can make reasonable assumptions, but we are surprised over and over again by the levels of knowledge walking into our classrooms from elsewhere.

Key feature: Anecdotal evidence

Don't fall into the trap of bad-mouthing the primary or previous teacher with statements such as 'What on earth did they learn in primary?', 'What do you mean you haven't learned this yet???' Another trap is to try to re-teach everything from first principles. There will be no time for this and even less motivation on the part of the students. If you have the chance, it is an enlightening experience to visit a PYP classroom. You will be mind-blown by the detail and thought that is put into the painful process of acquiring the reasoning and skills we take for granted. These primary teachers have to be wizards of inquiry to make these simple skills relevant and exciting. It's humbling to remember that we get our students already partially formed.

We fall into a trap of thinking of ourselves as the constant and the students as the new phenomena when in fact the reverse is true. Their learning has been a continuous experience for them and we are the intruder – the new phenomenon that imposes on their lives. A phenomenon who may be trying to introduce them to a very new, different or complex way of doing things. Empathy and realism can work wonders in situations of massive knowledge gaps.

There are various ways to try to address this in advance, such as SWOT and sequencing analyses to check these, or in a practical way using diagnostic assessments and mapping by each branch of reasoning. The appeal here is that these are logical, and aim for both coherence and completeness. We tick off each part of the framework once it has a home and, better still, once it has been revisited later, retrieved and consolidated. We know then for sure that the DNA is structurally sound, the ingredients are ready for the cake, the outline of the painting is taking shape.

But does this mechanical approach fully address what we need in a complete articulation of the curriculum?

My friend and queen of publishers at Hachette Learning, So-Shan, has an inspiring way of moving through the world. She is both a keen gardener and a talented campanologist, which means she spends a great deal of time looking up as well as down. Her Instagram account documents her commitment to finding the beauty overlooked by others, and I have been inspired by her posts with the hashtags #lookup and #lookdown. Any mathematics lover looking through her feed is rewarded with complex geometric patterns of manhole covers, views of spiral staircases or the organic sequencing of nature in bloom, and much more. She reminds me to take stock and appreciate the beauty in mathematics everywhere, often overlooked.

If we approach subject group overviews in the same way, we will move to a more complex and multidimensional planning model. In our analysis we must identify areas for attention. Naturally, the continuum is our first concern, which we facilitate or make possible by looking forwards and backwards. Looking backwards and forwards comes naturally in planning, but looking 'up' and 'down' less so. It is crucial that we remind ourselves to look up, finding inspiration and novelty to test. We must take the time to look down into the foundations and misconceptions of students' understanding.

In the words of the great Oscar Wilde, 'We are all in the gutter, but some of us are looking at the stars!'

Key feature: Reflection

Does mathematics in primary or secondary always have to follow a comprehensive, sequential approach? Can the inquiry lines determine what needs to be addressed mathematically? This is probably a bridge too far for many. It certainly is for me! Thinking of the definition of Risk-takers – is it safer to develop independently or collaboratively?

Mapping can be a tedious job, but software can facilitate it, filtering by almost any parameter you need, so that you can instantly see where ATLs are, how different criteria are over- or under-assessed, etc. It cannot be overstated how crucial this is to the processes of authorisation and evaluation in the IB world. Be careful not to do this before you are happy with the logical sequence and development of concepts across the years or grade levels.

Case studies

I have had a few opportunities to carry out this work on a large scale outside my work in the IB. Each had different contexts, different outcomes and varying levels of risk, and each taught me unique and valuable lessons.

Case study 1: Private international school with MYP only

In this case, the sciences curriculum had suffered from teacher turnover and sudden departure and was in dire straits. There were units in place, but the scope and sequence did not match up or meet IB expectations. I worked closely with the inspiring MYP coordinator, Rheanne, over several evenings and we soon had a curriculum to be proud of. This was then set in stone, and future science teachers could pick it up and deliver without worrying if they came from a lower knowledge base. The risk level here was low as there was huge parent support, flexibility in what was taught and when, and no Diploma Programme requirements.

Case study 2: Private international school with a long-established DP and MYP

The curriculum was already in position but needed augmentation. Most teachers were doing their own thing, and there was a very clear inverse relationship between how long they had been in position and how closely they adhered to the plans. We (I) decided to do a complete curriculum overhaul, to increase buy-in from the department and to bring our subject out of the silo we felt we were in. It was not a unanimous or shared mission, with several established team members unhappy with frequent change, as they perceived it. At the time this sort of exercise was referred to in management speak as 'open kimono', which felt wrong at the time and now feels utterly abhorrent as a concept. I hope there are better terms for a warts-and-all analysis these days.

We took time off-timetable to encourage deeper thinking and proper alignment. I incited colleagues from sciences, geography and business to come and review our epic Post-it display and feed back where we could make changes to better align the mathematics needed by our students at different phases. It generated some good feedback, such as 'Now that you ask, we in science would find it much better if you taught scattergraphs before grade 7 as we are already drawing them with them in grade 6.' We also had some fruitful discussions as to why we were doing percentages in grade 6 but waiting to introduce algebra in grade 7.

Two things I learned from this curriculum sequencing experiment were, first, that several staff felt affronted by the process itself. These staff members were outwardly hostile to the idea that I was presenting the opportunity to other departments to dictate to us what our sequence, or spiralling, of learning should be. They felt strongly that we were making mathematics lesser than or subservient to other subjects. In this situation, a reserve of grace and flexibility was required, along with a dash of humility and humour, to get results. I risked a great deal of my interpersonal capital with these colleagues, but we got a much better understanding of where students would encounter mathematics outside our classroom, and it allowed us to feel interconnected.

Second, I had not appreciated that some preferred splendid isolation, or to the extent to which some people feel ownership over units they have created and taught in the past. It was a heady clash of ideas, and one I am not sure I was victorious in. One positive was that in subsequent meetings we had fruitful discussions about the changes, why something did or didn't work well, and fostered some green shoots of growth. The risk expended may have been worth it in the long run.

Case study 3: Start-up school

In Dublin, as a start-up school with a tabula rasa, we established a STEM department from the outset. Here the risk budget focused on the time pressures and the desire to create a world-class curriculum in almost no time. Each team member held a dual responsibility in educating the other departments as to their curriculum, while identifying opportunities to blend and converge their disciplines with one another. There was a fluidity to this collaboration that I think was born of the optimism of a start-up, and from giving extremely competent practitioners freedom and flexibility. These colleagues – Leif, Shannon, Andy and Raemie – were an inspiration and it happened by design, not organically. These meetings were energetic, co-determined and good for the soul. As with all good things in life, though, nothing lasts for ever. The outcome was a highly collaborative and exciting curriculum, which is still in place and hopefully still resilient and resourceful.

Case study 4: State school

In a state school in the UK, the curriculum was mandated by government, with zero input needed, which left me feeling uncreative and unfulfilled. Although it was certainly easier for planning, I had to find other creative outlets for my professional ambitions. Recalling our Risk-takers learner profile attribute, here there was no risk and therefore very little reward, creatively speaking.

Of course, none of this tells us what is happening or going to happen in the classroom. It can only tell us the framing, the underlying and often unspoken ideas and motivation for the unit. We do not often communicate this to students, and they interact with a unit as if it has always been there and that it knows exactly what it is doing. Our hard work should be invisible, like good design.

Here endeth the planned/designed curriculum guidance. Now you have the essentials to map out the year, let us put further detail on the planned curriculum, and add flourish and depth to it. How do we bring inquiry to life, given the risks we have taken?

Self-assessment

Complete the reflection:

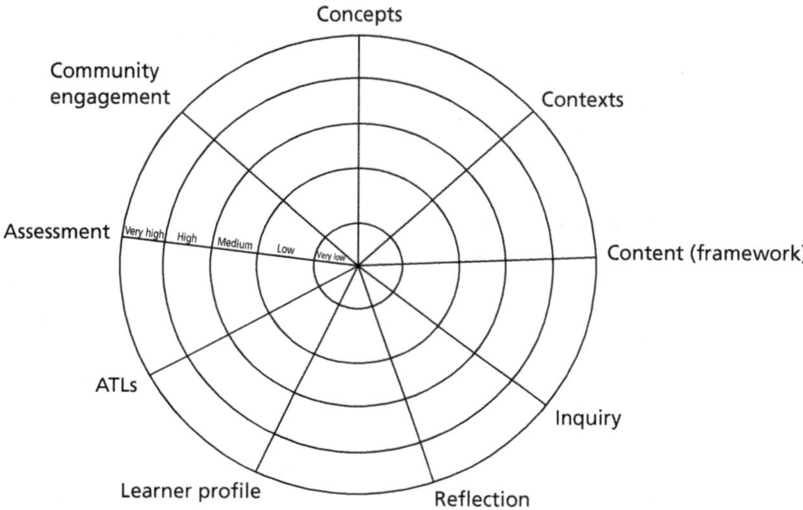

Shade in your knowledge level from low to high as you feel your comfort level lies.

Action item

Consider trying one non-conventional approach in your vertical and horizontal articulation. Not ready to take major risks with the curriculum? Don't worry, there will be more opportunities in the delivered curriculum in the Inquirers chapter (chapter 5) as well as the Communicators chapter (chapter 7).

Glossary

Global context A common language for powerful contextual learning, identifying specific settings, events or circumstances that provide more concrete perspectives for learning and teaching.

Horizontal planning/articulation Planning horizontally involves a team of teachers of the same grade level working together to plan for learning.

Prior learning The MYP mathematics framework is based on the expectation that students in MYP Year 1 have at least five years of prior mathematics experience and are familiar with the topics and skills, as outlined in the MYP Mathematics Guide.

Statement of inquiry This statement expresses the relationship between concepts and context; it represents a transferable idea supported by factual content.

Unit In the context of the MYP curriculum, a unit can be defined as a period of study that concludes with a summative assessment. Also can be defined as a series of lessons, focused through a statement of inquiry and inquiry questions, designed to enable students to achieve some of the objectives of an MYP subject group summative assessment.

Vertical planning/articulation The goal of vertical planning is to sequence learning (in terms of subject-group objectives and ATLs) to ensure continuity and progression from Year 1 to Year 5.

CHAPTER 5
INQUIRERS

> We nurture our curiosity, developing skills for inquiry and research. We know how to learn independently and with others. We learn with enthusiasm and sustain our love of learning throughout life.

Key thinking points

In this chapter, there are explanations/discussions of:

- the reasons for choosing Inquirers as the learner profile attribute for this chapter
- who this chapter is useful for
- what is meant by inquiry-based learning
- how the IB cultivates inquiry
- the various opinions and experiences with inquiry
- how mathematical inquiry can be introduced in a mathematics classroom (with exemplification)
- designing inquiry questions to fit within a unit of inquiry.

Why choose Inquirers as the learner profile attribute for this chapter?

Now, why on earth would I choose Inquirers as the best fit for our chapter on inquiry? It is clear to see the IB's commitment to the process of learning by inquiry, by placing it within the learner profile attributes and by connecting it to the approaches to learning (ATL) skills. We also see traces of it in Criterion B: Investigating Patterns. During the extensive review of the learner profile attributes, which ultimately resulted in showing that the current ones were fit for purpose, the learner profile attribute 'Curious' was considered. This would also have been a good fit, I think. The best way to define what the IB expects from an inquiry-based approach is to interrogate its interpretation of what that should look like, by examining its own definition of what makes a great Inquirer. An Inquirer is independent and curious, they enjoy learning, and our role is to nurture this as far as we can.

Who is this chapter useful for?

This chapter is designed for inquiry newbies, sceptics or the exhausted! If you have been in IB circles for a few years, you may have heard a lot about inquiry, but simply not had the time or inclination to go too in depth with it. Alternatively, you may be a Diploma teacher who is interested in how it might apply to the MYP. This chapter should help realign your opinions on inquiry-based learning, having a balanced approach between direct instruction and student-centred approaches. There is a place for all styles in the IB, and a curious attitude is all that is required to continue to improve the teaching and learning in your mathematics classroom and curriculum.

What is inquiry in the MYP?

Inquiry (pronounced either as *ink*werey or ink-*wire*-ee, depending on where you are in the world) is a core tenet of MYP philosophy and features in the approaches to teaching. If students have joined you from a PYP setting, they will be very familiar with these ideas from units of inquiry throughout. We build on these ideas, with lines of inquiry, statements of inquiry and inquiry questions forming such a big role in our planned curriculum. In this chapter we will consider these various aspects of inquiry-based learning and how it relates to MYP Mathematics.

When writing about primary teaching, the author Sean Delaney suggests that, 'Teachers should introduce students to ideas and insights that are enduring' (Delaney, 2016). This should be our motivation when deciding how and where to introduce more inquiry in our teaching and learning. Notice how I say when '*deciding* to introduce' – there is a definite misconception in the wider MYP community that inquiry is the 'be all and end all' of the MYP. That is certainly not the case. Nor is it true that every unit and every assessment you have written before needs to be started over. It is possible to introduce inquiry incrementally in units, building up to as many inquiry-driven opportunities as you feel appropriate to each sequence of learning.

Now that we know that demonstrations, memorisation and explicit instruction are not forbidden, let's talk about content. Another mistaken idea abroad is that the IB expects your school to develop inquiry-based units in isolation. Some people in the community feel strongly that textbooks are bad and should be eschewed. This is not the case either. There certainly were those in the early phases of MYP development who felt it should closely resemble the PYP in this regard. The IB itself certainly does not reinforce this. We can see this by the variety of units and sample subject group overviews provided in the online curriculum resources in the Programme Resource Centre (PRC).

These artefacts, including assessments and achievement levels, are called Teacher Support Material (TSM). The IB even authorised textbooks through Hachette Learning, on the condition that the books were authentically concept driven. It insisted on the provision of rich, meaningful activities, and that the practice questions usually found in other, traditional, books were to be kept to a minimum. Its feeling was that most of these traditional textbooks, while not bad, are not appropriate in most cases for an inquiry-led, concept-driven curriculum.

With this in mind, I wrote the *MYP by Concept: Mathematics 4 & 5* (Bateson, 2017) textbook for Hachette Learning and, with Irene Amlin, other textbooks in the same series for MYP 1 to 3. It is true the books don't have tons and tons of questions, but they do include many inquiry ideas, looking at how to introduce it in topics, activities and assessments. As one experienced educator, Gurpreet, explained so articulately to a teacher querying the absence of questions in bulk, 'What do you need that for? You have shelves and shelves of books with questions? What you need is how to use them for inquiry and deeper learning!' She expressed it so succinctly that I was jealous but also inspired by her words.

The textbooks and workbooks on the shelf are useful still. They are a healthy source of skills and drills, and often have hidden gems of questions that will help extend your students' and your own repertoire. Inquire into what is within and what can be repurposed as a springboard, or trampoline, into inquiry. There are very few bad textbooks – they were simply created for a different type of curriculum, either content driven or standards based. As we saw previously, when the IB created an exclusively concept-driven curriculum, it featured a non-linear approach to each concept in isolation. Practically, we need the questions and rigour of a traditional textbook but approached from an inquiry-based perspective, with all the MYP requirements to make it holistic.

Why choose inquiry?

As teachers, we aim to model our own curiosity and lifelong learning to our students. We want the same inquiring nature in our students, keeping them enthusiastic about learning in a way that can be sustained. We are actively embedding in them an immutable desire to 'stay curious' about learning. Beyond modelling enthusiasm – which is not always infectious – how do we inspire this attitude towards inquiry?

Inquiry takes the pressure off you – you do the work out of the classroom, the students do the work in it. But what does this actually look like?

Inquiry should spark curiosity by presenting a phenomenon or artefact that invites exploration. It makes sense to ground this in the chosen concepts for the unit (see chapters 3 and 4) and context, too, where possible. This inquiry-based learning can be highly collaborative or intensely personal in development. It can take many forms, some of which we will discuss later, but it is generally agreed that authenticity and agency are the most important considerations. If inquiry does not allow for reflection or action, then it is not meeting expectations. Inquiry-based learning can lead to assessment, or could be inspired by assessment goals, and it should be age-appropriate in length and depth. See later in this chapter for ideas on how to use inquiry in assessment design.

'Not all approaches to teaching in the MYP will take place in an inquiry setting' (IBO, 2014). I wish more people understood this. In this statement, we are given the indication that inquiry-based learning is not a 100% commitment. This is one of the issues that is often misunderstood or misquoted, as mentioned previously. Some days, and some topics, are better than others for inquiry. Some days the most I can manage is to deploy the 'inquiry box'. This is a resource-collection of mathematically fascinating objects, which I pass out to groups and ask them to investigate. Even these stand-alone activities foster the curious Inquirer in students.

For more ideas on suitable contents for an inquiry box, see the resources list in chapter 13 – you want students to think 'inside the box' to explore their power to think outside it. A few items I include as 'must haves' are games such as mancala, as well as an old-fashioned calculator (students adore this one – no instructions as to what it is or how it works), which was one of my most appreciated gifts from Andrew and Howard at the IS Hamburg. I have some 'magic tricks', too, such as a monkey puzzle, great for starting important debates, and a book of 'mathematics for men', which is another great conversation starter.

There are also a few aesthetically beautiful objects in my inquiry box, such as a Klein vase, several kaleidocycles, self-closing nets and spirographs. I start simply with a 'What is this and how is it mathematical?' I will give groups five or ten minutes to discuss (having first ensured that it is an object that is new to the group). They feed back at the end, but I never give any answer to their observations. They particularly love to figure out the calculating machine, with its satisfying clicky buttons and levers. The inquiry box is a very useful activity to have close to hand, especially if you need a quick breather to recover from a parent meeting or a crazy-busy morning. It can also form part of a routine if you have a class period longer than an hour, rather than letting students out of the classroom for a break.

By the intentional design of meaningful, and occasional, inquiry learning moments, students grow in their capacity for making connections through experimentation. Direct instruction, demonstrations, memorisation, and skills and drills are still an important component of the delivered curriculum.

What is the nature of inquiry?

Structured inquiry	Controlled inquiry	Guided inquiry	Free inquiry
Students follow the lead of the teacher as the entire class engages in one inquiry together.	Teacher chooses topics and identifies the resources students will use to answer questions.	Teacher chooses topics/questions and students design product or solution.	Students choose their topics without reference to any prescribed outcome.

Types of student inquiry

There are different levels you might aspire to or that suit your context and abilities better. Consider where your comfort zone is. I am a big fan of comfort zones when we consider them as zones of competence. I prefer structured inquiry, controlled inquiry and guided inquiry, where I feel a measure of control and comfort.

'... nurture our curiosity ...'

I have worked only once with a teacher who truly believed in free inquiry at all times. He often proposed out-there ideas, such an entire year dedicated to slime. When I tried to understand how it could form the basis for an entire year of inquiring into slime (the history of slime, the mathematics of slime and the science of slime, as he suggested), there were some nice ideas. He suggested a unit on invertebrates, and plenty of experiments. I could see a valid unit on non-Newtonian fluids leading to mechanics but nothing beyond that. It certainly didn't lend itself to a year full of essential numerical and abstract reasoning or geometric reasoning, for example. The suggestion was dead in the water, but at least it gave us all food for thought. More importantly still, it forced me to consider where I swam in the inquiry pool and maybe, just maybe, to take a few more risks in letting go of control. And, to give him his due, he returned to the next meeting with the suggestion of a year in the study of bubbles! His resilience and creativity were quite impressive, and this led to an exciting interdisciplinary unit on the geometry and topology of bubbles in mathematics, and the science of medicinal bubble use in biology.

It is helpful to visualise the types of inquiry in relation to the states of matter shown in the illustration here. In a formal, directed level of inquiry, students move within a crystalline solid where the teacher has set very clear limits and paths to the inquiry. In the liquid state of inquiry, the students have a greater degree of freedom, but the teacher still keeps control of the topic and resources where the students inquire. In the gas state, student inquiry can take them in a variety of directions to create their own solutions and outcomes. In the unique plasma state, students can be in a variety of conditions, from highly effective to ineffective, depending on their choices and the direction of the inquiry.

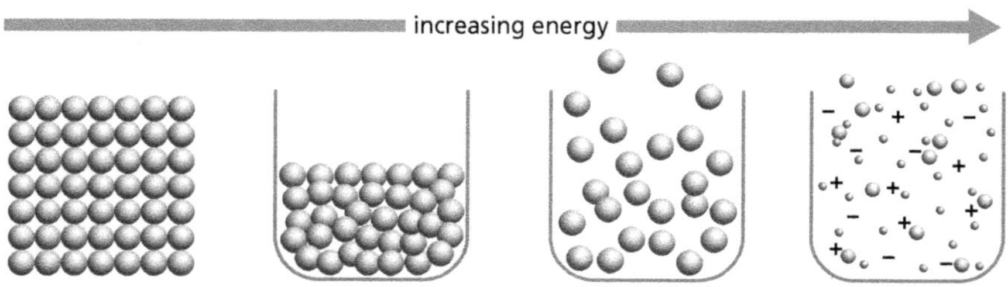

Solid
The molecules that make up a solid are arranged in regular, repeating patterns. They are held firmly in place but can vibrate within a limited area.

Liquid
The molecules that make up a liquid flow easily around one another. They are kept from flying apart by attractive forces between them. Liquids assume the shape of their containers.

Gas
The molecules that make up a gas fly in all directions at great speeds. They are so far apart that the attractive forces between them are insignificant.

Plasma
At the very high temperatures of stars, atoms lose their electrons. The mixture of electrons and nuclei that results is the plasma state of matter.

Source: Encyclopedia Britannica

Ultimately, the end goal of any inquiry should be to lead the students to knowledge and/or action. This makes sense if we think of it in terms of police lines of inquiry (a mystery has been solved and justice is served). For teachers and students, concepts, global contexts and even ATL skills can provide a means to inquire into subject content by questioning, explaining, discovering and doing.

Is there any downside to inquiry in the planned or delivered curriculum?

There has certainly been a lot of pushback to inquiry-based learning in past years, particularly in the UK where there has been a resurgence in what is described as 'direct instruction'. For a considered approach to this debate, I recommend reviewing some of the back catalogue of the *Mr Barton Maths Podcast* from the incomparable Craig Barton. He has several interesting podcasts from both perspectives, with Greg Ashman on the direct instruction side and Andrew Blair defending the use of inquiry. In the IB world, the commitment to this style of teaching and learning shows no signs of abating at all. In fact, if anything, the Diploma Programme has shown evidence of movement towards more conceptual understanding and inquiry in learning.

Some of the common critiques are that this style, with particularly reference to the ideas of free inquiry, is a 'hippy dippy' waste of time. What if students go wildly off base? What if their selections of inquiry and resources are what we might consider trivial or irrelevant? How can we control to ensure they don't travel off in random directions or off at a tangent to the general learning curve? To those critics I would acknowledge that this is a recognised tension and suggest they consider less free versions of inquiry. I would also ask them if they truly believe there is such a thing as irrelevant learning?

They may well counter with, 'No, there is no irrelevant learning, but I have so much content to get through that I don't have time to spare for those messing about with inquiry.' For these risk-averse colleagues I like to encourage them to consider what are they already doing to make their subject interesting and relevant. Usually, they can speak passionately on this, unless they are complete walnut trees! (Take a look at chapter 7 to find out more about these walnut tree types.) With the evidence they usually offer of the ways they make learning engaging, we discuss how to make tiny adjustments in the style of introducing students to new material. Instead of introducing SOHCAHTOA to students as established relationships, could they begin it as a Criterion B investigation into pattern spotting. Can they consider what they see developing in the table of ratios? It works very well in extensions into asking them to plot and reveal the value of $\sin^2$ and $\cos^2$ too. This method of modelling is also seen in the DP Mathematics book, see especially the official Oxford University Press versions (for example, Forrest et al., 2019).

Key feature: Reflection

If inquiry can be seen as a journey to discovery, what are you already doing in your classroom towards this? How can you reflect it in the written or planned curriculum? Are you doing it already?

Ask yourself:

- Am I facilitating the journey to a good thinker or a good knower through this activity?
- For each of the assessment criteria, can I think of ways I am building inquiry implicitly?
    - In Criterion A assessments, am I giving students the opportunity to transfer ideas in a new way?
    - In Criterion B assessments, are they having enough chances to inquire into different patterns?
    - In Criterion C, can they communicate clearly what they've uncovered?
    - In Criterion D, are they inquiring into accuracy and truth in a non-trivial way?

It is helpful to consider the best times for inquiry learning in your classroom, to avoid the pitfalls of wasting time or inefficiency.

Ask yourself:

- What are the times or topics where inquiry is less appropriate or is inefficient?
- Will I spend more time and effort setting up the inquiry when it might better to let students inquire into the application of the concept later?

Inquiry should, in principle, take the work off you and put it onto the student. You are the coach in the learning process – you give them enough information to complete the task and improve, but no more than is necessary. As coach, you know what they need to do and you want to get them started, so you open a curiosity gap for them. Reflect on how much you speak in class compared to them – what percentage of class 'airtime' is filled by you versus their work? Can you shift the percentage more and more in their direction? In the world of movies and TV there is a measure of equity called the Bechdel test. This test considers the role of female characters and their representation in the media. Are there more than two named female characters in a work of fiction and do these females have a conversation about something other than a man? Are they given names?

Consider an analogous approach in your classroom practice. Have your students had sufficient representation in the inquiry? Do they have conversations about the mathematics with one another rather than you? Are they protagonists in their own learning?

Is home learning antithetical to inquiry? Personally, I have gone back and forth on homework. Often, I have set it because it was school policy or because parents expected it. I never felt strongly about it, as I felt we had sufficient time in school to master concepts, skills and knowledge. More recently, I have heard the opinion expressed that it is now completely redundant, as students head straight for AI models such as ChatGPT, or similar, making it a fruitless endeavour. My old boss and mentor, Robert Harrison, believes the horse has now bolted from that particular stable and that teachers will need to shift their mindset completely in this regard. I sense that he is, as usual, right on this. To what end should we set home learning unless it is personalised and meaningful? I'm interested to see how we address this in coming years.

Key feature: Reflection

- What is your personal stance on homework and home learning? Is it a valuable precursor to good study habits, or a waste of time? What is your school policy?
- Do you have particular views on noise levels during learning engagements?
- Is the role of the teacher to calm chaos? To instigate a curiosity gap? Or to impose order on confusion?

Key feature: Anecdotal evidence

During one curriculum review meeting for the last guide, we tried to completely rethink the MYP curriculum into an inquiry-only sequence, to see if it would be possible. The closest we came to this goal was when we mirrored an approach taken by a colleague, Jenny Gillett, in the development of a 'Big History' course. We wondered if it would be possible to make a similar 'Big Mathematics' course ...

Our first aim was to **scaffold** inquiry into Mathematics in the order that humans discovered and understood mathematical ideas, instead of spiralling different branches in terms of complexity.

It is my greatest professional regret that we could not make this work. It was exciting but unworkable.

What are inquiry questions?

We encountered statements of inquiry in chapter 4, while looking at the process of selecting key and related concepts, and combining them with a global context to give a unit relevance. To support the choice of content, concept and context, we create inquiry questions. These inquiry questions are crafted from the statement of inquiry, and their purpose is to add detail and scope for the unit. I like to connect them in the following ways.

Factual questions:

- Link these to procedural knowledge from the unit. What processes or algorithms will students use? What facts will they be expected to recall?
- Use questions that have a factual basis, where the answers are generally accepted or non-controversial. These can be related to skills or content from the unit.
- Concentrate on recall or comprehension by choosing the most important or key understanding from this unit, when considering what will be most useful or important to carry forward from the unit.

Conceptual questions:

- I regularly phrase a question that explicitly uses the concepts by name. If the statement of inquiry includes approximation or relationships, then I will formulate a question that includes those words, which connects them to the content of the unit.
- This should spell out the *big ideas* from the unit, again connecting them to the facts and topics.
- Try to build connections for students where they might see transfer within mathematics or between other subjects, to promote their ability to apply big ideas to new situations.
- I have tried using these questions as exit tickets, with limited success. The time required to do justice to the big ideas is not conducive to assessing students' understanding while they are rushing out the door. I switched

the exit tickets to factual questions and moved the conceptual questions to the unit cover page to add detail, which was much more successful.

Debateable questions:

- These can sometimes be the harder questions to craft. As a starting point, consider why you chose the global context. Why is this learning important or relevant to students?
- Decide what level of **provocation** you would like to create.
- I like to use these questions as a soft launch for students to start thinking about thinking and knowing, as an introduction to TOK (Theory of Knowledge in the Diploma Programme).
- Find a place to consider these multiple perspectives – perhaps include a debateable question during a summative assessment, or ensure time in class to have a robust discussion. This becomes easier as students get older and are more confident in presenting or advocating for their own ideas in class.

Speaking of which, students can also play a role in developing these questions. I have not tried this very often as I found they just stared back at me in response, with an expression on their faces that I can only describe as benign confusion: 'I thought you were supposed to be the teacher, not me.' Feel free to add questions as the unit develops, as the students will have important questions that might make a strong contribution to next year's planning.

Let's look at some sample questions that might arise from each of the four branches of reasoning in the MYP Mathematics framework. These are simply samples and there are many more available in the guide and the TSM (Teacher Support Material) on the IB website.

Numerical and abstract reasoning

Type of question	Examples
Factual	1. What properties do the commutative and associative laws describe? 2. How do ratios help in understanding proportional relationships? 3. What is the purpose of using variables in algebra?

Type of question	Examples
Conceptual	1. Why is algebra considered an abstraction of basic *numerical* concepts? 2. How does understanding *equivalent* expressions aid in solving algebraic equations? 3. In what ways do the associative and commutative properties impact the *simplification* of expressions?
Debatable	1. Is the traditional way of understanding algebra through symbols and variables the most effective method for abstracting mathematical concepts? 2. Should financial literacy be a compulsory component of any mathematical education? 3. Are real-world applications necessary to fully understand algebraic concepts, or can these concepts be taught effectively in a purely theoretical context?

These questions are designed to provoke thought at varying levels, from straightforward recall of facts to deeper analysis and evaluation of mathematical concepts and their applications in different contexts.

Reasoning with data

Type of question	Examples
Factual	1. What statistical methods are used to determine the measure of spread in a dataset? 2. How do we calculate the interquartile range for a set of data? 3. How can we use a scattergraph to determine correlation?
Conceptual	1. Why is it important to understand both theoretical and experimental probabilities when analysing data? 2. How does identifying outliers enhance the interpretation of datasets? 3. What is the significance of the law of large numbers in predicting outcomes?
Debatable	1. Is the reliance on large datasets potentially misleading when making individual predictions? 2. Should statistical literacy be considered just as important as algebraic literacy in the mathematics curriculum? 3. To what extent should ethical considerations impact the collection and use of statistical data in research?

These questions encourage a range of responses, from straightforward factual answers to more complex discussions about the implications and methodologies of statistical analysis, enhancing both the understanding and critical evaluation of data handling in mathematics. Notice how the conceptual questions did not explicitly call out a concept but implicitly connects to them, giving a variety of strategies for development.

Spatial reasoning

Type of question	Examples
Factual	1. What is a formula for calculating the area of a triangle? 2. How do you use coordinate geometry to find the distance between two points? 3. Describe the steps involved in performing a rotation on a figure on a Cartesian grid.
Conceptual	1. Why is it important to understand both two-dimensional and three-dimensional geometries in spatial reasoning? 2. How does understanding symmetry contribute to solving problems? 3. What role does the concept of congruence play in spatial transformations?
Debatable	1. Should spatial reasoning be prioritised over algebraic skills in early mathematical education? 2. Is the use of technology, like graphic calculators and software, diminishing students' ability to understand spatial reasoning independently? 3. Can mastery of spatial reasoning enhance cognitive abilities more significantly than other areas of mathematics?

These questions are crafted to stimulate different levels of thinking, from simple factual recall to more profound conceptual understanding and critical debate on the relevance and application of spatial reasoning in the mathematical curriculum and beyond.

Thinking with models

Type of question	Examples
Factual	1. What is the standard form for a quadratic function? 2. Describe how to transform a quadratic function graphically. 3. What is the purpose of using function notation in algebra?
Conceptual	1. Why is *modelling* with functions useful in representing relationships between variables? 2. How do *transformations* of functions help us in understanding different mathematical concepts? 3. What is the significance of using different types of function models, such as linear and quadratic, in solving real-world problems?

Type of question	Examples
Debatable	1. Is algebraic modelling more effective than numerical modelling for predicting real-world phenomena? 2. Should mathematical modelling be integrated more extensively into other subjects within the MYP curriculum to enhance interdisciplinary learning? 3. How essential is it for students to learn manual graph plotting in an era where computer software can perform these tasks instantly and accurately?

These questions are designed to address different aspects of thinking with models, encouraging students to engage with factual knowledge, deeper conceptual understanding, and broader debates about the role and methods of mathematical modelling in education and its practical applications. Sometimes questions from the abstract reasoning branches can work well with models too, given the overlap between these branches.

Is an inquiry-based approach the best preparation for the DP?

It is fair to say that, despite the emphasis over past review cycles on concepts and conceptual development, much of the DP course content in all subjects is still very content driven. How does inquiry-based learning at MYP support DP, then, if there is an apparent mismatch? Quite simply, I would argue that the mismatch is not as great as some would lead us to believe.

Fortunately, many more teachers are now including inquiry in their teaching practice at Diploma, thanks to the approaches to teaching. This gives MYP students a solid throughline and familiarity when they reach DP. Their metacognition and thinking skills development throughout MYP (both creative and critical thinking) will stand them in good stead as preparation for theory of knowledge (TOK) in the DP. This subject in the Diploma Programme has a structured focus on ways of knowing and will help students formulate different areas of knowledge, as constructed in human societies and through history.

If a student is already familiar with inquiry and questioning strategies, they will be familiar with conceptual and debateable questioning, having had a variety of experiences and learning engagements in the MYP. Global contexts will also provide a springboard for inquiry into the nature of knowing and understanding the limits of what we know. When students see inquiry-based approaches in mathematics classes, they are comfortable with questioning and evaluating other people's ideas and thoughts. Ensure you make time to find inquiry-based opportunities, and even assessments, to strengthen students' metacognitive muscles. This will make for satisfying learning experiences now and will foster ease of practice for TOK.

How can we use AI – nquiry?

One use of AI models is as a way to generate ideas that we can improve and refine, to level them up to match our requirements and standards. This section looks at some ways we can use AI to augment our curriculum development in inquiry-based learning. I try to be responsible in my use of AI because of the energy requirements brought about by overuse, so the following suggestions should be used wisely, to reduce teacher overload.

Eight ways to use AI when considering inquiry questions and activities

1. As a tutor and guide: AI models can assist by explaining different types of inquiry questions and how they differ in purpose and depth.
2. As a content generator: AI can generate bespoke inquiry questions for you, but make sure to vet them before use.
3. Feedback: AI can analyse the appropriateness of given inquiry questions and suggest improvements.
4. Integration: If you ask for help in integrating inquiry questions into units, AI can suggest how to weave questions into lesson planning for authentic and continued inquiry.
5. Treat ChatGPT or other AI as a waiter in a restaurant. Allow it to present you with a variety of ideas, from which you will select and digest the most delicious-looking option.
6. Ask ChatGPT to give examples of bad answers or poor articulation of ideas. This helps to set the standard of what you will accept and what you will support in your students' answers.
7. Use AI models to help weave inquiry questions into assessments to encourage critical thinking or explicit problem-solving.
8. My favourite activity with ChatGPT, and the one that gives me the richest ideas – is when I upload a photograph as a stimulus. Before AI, I would often find myself looking around and taking photos, thinking, 'Oooooh, look at that railway bridge/tiling pattern/parking fine sign/company logo ... That would make a great question.' I would get formative or summative assessment 'vibes', but rarely would I dedicate the time to sitting down and developing an assessment that matched the SOI completely from my picture.

Recently, I have begun to experiment with advancing these ideas using generative AI. In updated models of ChatGPT it is possible to upload a picture and ask it for ideas. It can then regenerate with different models almost instantly. I often play with it in the following way, with a series of requests. Sometimes the answers are intriguing and show me something I would not have considered. Other times they are mediocre, predictable, or make me regret wasting the time and energy on input.

Case study: The wonderful barn

The following is a summary of the types of questions I used to develop a variety of resources from this one image.

Look at the photograph of this building. Using Criterion D in MYP Mathematics suggest a possible investigation suitable for grade 9 extended class and using ideas of area and volume.

Initially, the response was extremely impressive, as it located, and named, the building correctly. Bear in mind, this is effectively an abandoned, relatively unknown barn in a quiet suburb outside of Dublin in Ireland. Here is what ChatGPT suggested as a starting point:

Title: 'The Geometry of Historical Architecture: The Case of The Wonderful Barn'

Overview

This investigation will require students to explore geometric shapes and structures by examining the photograph of an unusual historical building, such as The Wonderful Barn. The task will involve calculating the surface area and volume of the building, including its conical shape and adjoining structures.

I was less impressed with the task description, which was effectively just making a cardboard model of the building with annotations as to area and volume calculations. It was an interesting jumping-off point though.

Next, I decided to test the parameters and see how adaptive it could be. Here are the prompts I used, with mixed results:

Create a task-specific clarification for this assessment. In one column provide the official rubric by level, and expectations specific to the task in the other column.

Here is what ChatGPT provided:

MYP Criteria Rubric (Level)	Task-Specific Expectations
Level 1–2	Identify geometric shapes present in the building
Demonstrates limited understanding of area and volume.	Students identify basic shapes but make significant errors in estimating dimensions.
Level 3–4	Estimate dimensions and apply formulas
Demonstrates an adequate understanding of area and volume with some correct application of formulas.	Students accurately estimate dimensions of simpler shapes and correctly apply area and volume formulas in some cases.
Level 5–6	Calculate the surface area and volume of the building
Demonstrates a good understanding of area and volume with mostly correct application of formulas.	Students perform accurate calculations for both the surface area and volume of most parts of the building, showing good use of formulas for composite shapes.
Level 7–8	Create a mathematical model and detailed report
Demonstrates a thorough understanding of area and volume with correct and creative application of formulas.	Students create a detailed and accurate mathematical model, including annotations of calculated areas and volumes. The written report is comprehensive and reflects a deep understanding of geometric properties.

Expectations Specific to 'The Geometry of Historical Architecture' Task:

- For **Level 1–2**, students might struggle with the complexity of the shapes and provide only basic calculations with limited accuracy.
- At **Level 3–4**, expectations include more precise estimations and some evidence of understanding the formulas for area and volume, though errors may be present.
- Students at **Level 5–6** are expected to demonstrate good competency in applying the formulas to calculate the surface area and volume, with minor errors likely due to the complexity of the composite shapes.
- At **Level 7–8**, students are expected to not only calculate areas and volumes accurately but also to interpret the historical and architectural significance of the building through their mathematical model and report.

This felt like an inauthentic task with not enough **inquiry** or **alignment** with the actual strands. And so, I decided to train or 'feed it' the required text. My next question was:

Here are the specific threads of Criterion D. Generate the table again with these in the left-hand column and the task-specific clarifications in the right-hand column:

Criterion D: Applying mathematics in real-life contexts Maximum: 8

At the end of Year 5, students should be able to:

i. identify relevant elements of authentic real-life situations
ii. select appropriate mathematical strategies when solving authentic real-life situations
iii. apply the selected mathematical strategies successfully to reach a solution
iv. justify the degree of accuracy of a solution
v. justify whether a solution makes sense in the context of the authentic real-life situation.

Giving it the correct context and wording created a much better clarification rubric:

Criterion D Threads	Task-Specific Clarifications
i. Identify relevant elements of authentic real-life situations	Students will examine the provided photograph to dentify and document the various geometric elements that comprise the building, such as the conical shape, cylindrical sections, and prismatic bases.
ii. Select appropriate mathematical strategies when solving authentic real-life situations	Students will choose and explain the mathematical processes and formulas needed to calculate the area and volume of the identified shapes within the context of the building's architecture.
iii. Apply the selected mathematical strategies successfully to reach a solution	Students will demonstrate the accurate application of geometric formulas to calculate the area and volume of the building's components, showing how these calculations contribute to understanding the structure's design.
iv. Justify the degree of accuracy of a solution	Students will discuss the limitations and assumptions in their measurements and calculations, such as estimating dimensions from a photograph, and how these might affect the accuracy of their findings.
v. Justify whether a solution makes sense in the context of the authentic real-life situation.	Students will reflect on their final calculations and model to evaluate whether their solutions are realistic and make sense architecturally, considering the historical context and purpose of the building.

And a mark scheme:

Criterion D threads	0	1-2	3-4	5-6	7-8
i. Identify relevant elements	The student does not identify relevant elements of the situation.	Identifies very few relevant elements with significant inaccuracies.	Identifies some relevant elements with minor inaccuracies.	Correctly identifies most relevant elements of the real life situation.	Accurately and comprehensively identifies all relevant elements of the real life situation.
ii. Select appropriate strategies	No appropriate strategies are selected.	Selects strategies that are inappropriate or applies them incorrectly.	Selects mostly appropriate strategies with some errors in application.	Selects appropriate strategies and applies them correctly with minor lapses.	Selects highly appropriate strategies and applies them correctly and effectively.
iii. Apply strategies to reach a solution	The strategies are not applied, or the application is wholly inappropriate.	Applies strategies with limited success, many solutions are incorrect.	Applies strategies with some success; some correct solutions are reached.	Applies strategies successfully with mostly correct solutions.	Applies strategies with high success; solutions are correct and well-reasoned.
iv. Justify the accuracy of the solution	Does not justify the degree of accuracy at all.	Provides weak justifications for the degree of accuracy of the solution.	Justifies the degree of accuracy of the solution with some logical reasoning.	Provides a good justification for the degree of accuracy with clear logical reasoning.	Provides thorough and convincing justifications for the degree of accuracy of the solution.
v. Justify if the solution makes sense	Does not justify or the justification is not related to the context.	Justifies with limited reasoning that does not fully connect to the real life context.	Provides a reasonable justification that the solution makes sense in the real life context.	Justifies well that the solution makes sense in the context with good reasoning.	Provides an excellent justification that the solution is sensible and fully contextual.

Marking scheme for 'Geometry of Historical Architecture'

We don't have enough space here to go through all the iterations and changes I experimented with but here is a summary of some of the experimental prompts I used:

List the relevant elements of this real-life situation. What mathematical calculations should they produce?

Add a GRASPS framework to this assessment.

Create inquiry questions to frame this unit.

Suggest three different MYP subjects that would be suitable for combining with this assessment for an Interdisciplinary Unit and state reasons why it is suitable for each subject pairing.

How could this assessment, and supporting unit, give rise to Service Learning?

Now write three inquiry questions to support this investigation

Scaffold this assessment for a non-native speaker

Create some sample problems that use the 'low floor high ceiling model' that students can do in advance of this assessment to get them ready

Create a three-part problem in the style of Dan Meyer

Naturally the output was variable, with some questions answered extremely well and other responses vague and mediocre. The important thing my experiments with AI have taught me is that I must use my professionalism and discernment to follow any novel ideas, and discard the rest.

Often the most terrible or vague ones actually help me to identify what I *don't* want, which in turn crystallises what I do. And – voila! – the assessment is nearly ready.

To learn more about these assessment details, turn to chapter 11.

Self-assessment

Complete the reflection:

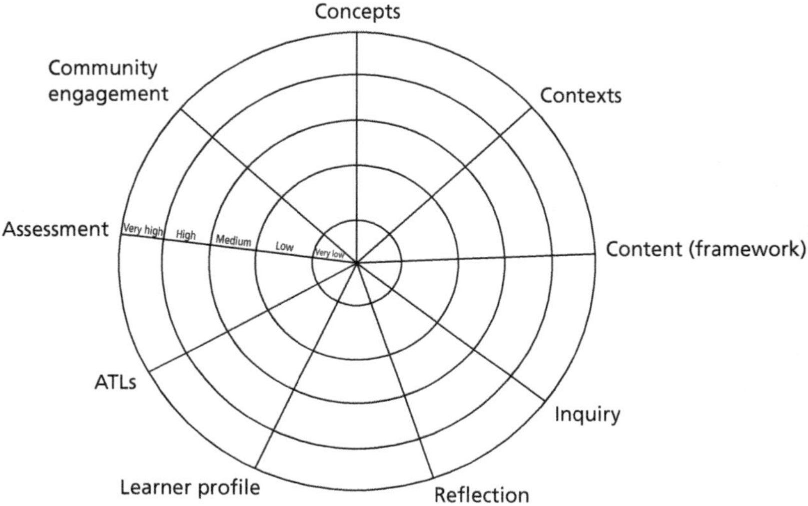

Shade in your knowledge level from low to high as you feel your comfort level lies.

Glossary

Alignment Agreement in principle and practice between shared values and aspirations for learning (designed/ planned curriculum), how teachers actually work (delivered curriculum) and what students actually learn (assessed curriculum).

Inquiry A perspective on learning, emphasising that meaning is actively constructed.

Provocation An open-ended stimulus to engage student thinking.

Scaffolding The use of a variety of teaching strategies and tools to support a student's progression in their learning. Scaffolding is temporary, appropriate and responsive.

CHAPTER 6
OPEN-MINDED

We critically appreciate our own cultures and personal histories, as well as the values and traditions of others. We seek and evaluate a range of points of view, and we are willing to grow from the experience.

Key thinking points

In this chapter, there are explanations/discussions of:

- why Open-minded is an appropriate choice of learner profile attribute for a chapter on the MYP content framework
- who this chapter may be useful for
- the importance of content in an inquiry-driven curriculum
- an introduction to the MYP Mathematics framework
- what is meant by numerical and abstract reasoning
- What is meant by thinking (reasoning) with models
- how we support spatial reasoning
- how we develop reasoning with data, both past and future
- comparing and determining.

'We critically appreciate ...'

Why choose Open-minded as the learner profile attribute for this chapter?

Open-minded struck me as a most considered learner profile attribute for a chapter on the framework and content of MYP Mathematics, thanks to the emphasis on evaluation, and appreciation of value, tradition and growth. What a wonderful starting point for looking at the content that will bind our concepts to skills and bridge the DNA (see image). As curriculum developers, we have to remain open-minded about so many things, from tradition to innovation. We must make critical choices, as time is not infinite and the curriculum can already be overloaded with so many demands.

Current mathematics skill framework	Focus on reasoning
Number	Numerical and abstract reasoning
Algebra	Thinking with models
Geometry and trigonometry	Spatial reasoning
Statistics and probability	Reasoning with data

In this chapter, we will explore, in detail, the MYP Mathematics framework, the **branches** of reasoning, how this current curriculum configuration was developed and how it will influence future MYP frameworks. I will outline the thought processes and research that went into the compilation of knowledge and skills, and how it was determined what would be in and what must unfortunately be out. All of this required a great deal of open-mindedness, both on my part but also on the part of the many teachers and educators who contributed to curriculum reviews.

As mentioned previously, curriculum development is a process of refining value judgements. To ensure I made informed, reasoned and evidence-based decisions before imposing it on schools, it was imperative to seek a range of points of view, from the reported needs of schools to the opinions of experts. The Assessment division had a great deal of input, as they are always responsible for implementing the limits of this content in the **on-screen examinations**. I read hundreds of books, and spoke to as many schools and teachers.

Curriculum development is itself an act of appreciation. All knowledge is worthy. To lose anything mathematical can feel like a betrayal to the subject and a disservice to the students. We must determine what is most essential. What is realistic to expect of students and teachers alike? And are we showing a willingness to grow over time?

Who is this chapter useful for?

This chapter is designed to be used by, and useful for, teachers who have the freedom to determine what will be in their units, adding detail to the exact content included. Teachers who have not had a focus on reasoning until now, as they have been busy teaching the content, should find the reasons for change interesting and it will inform their teaching practice. The mapping will help DP teachers to understand how the curriculum of each programme dovetails, and where there might be overlaps or underlaps in your school's sequencing or spiralling of curriculum.

The breakdown of the required and enriched curriculum content will assist MYP coordinators mapping and overseeing coverage of content. It is a good chapter for those new to teaching in a concept-based manner, or those who are developing a deeper understanding of the distinction between content and reasoning skills. The information in this chapter will help with populating and completing the subject group overviews, and finishing the scope and sequence documentation and unit plans.

Curriculum planning is an infinite loop of decision-making, trapped in a finite time. This chapter is designed to offer an insight into how the MYP Mathematics framework was last redesigned to feature reasoning rather than facts. Moreover, it should refresh familiarity with the branches themselves, and engage with the differences between *standard*, *extended* and *enrichment* in the framework.

In summary, this chapter is for those who have no time to read, digest or memorise the extensive pages in *From Principles into Practice* (IBO, 2014) or the *MYP Mathematics Guide* (IBO, 2020) in its entirety. When I first joined the IB global centre, I was so overawed by the sheer quantity of everything that had to be considered that (as I noted in chapter 1) I literally slept with the guide under my pillow. Reading it every night helped me to memorise the content, so I could speak confidently and competently in the face of any question at all. Embarrassingly, I also stuck individual pages of FPIP all over my apartment (including the bathroom, as also noted earlier), for the same reason. To prevent this fate befalling anyone else, this chapter is design to meet the needs of anyone who is overwhelmed, intimidated or confused.

Why do we need content?

'We critically appreciate … the values and traditions of others …'

If mathematics really is a manifestation of the urge to understand, and the urge to create, as we discussed in chapter 2, then why do we even need **content**? What are the 'values and traditions' of mathematics, and why should we adhere to them? These are the questions that a curriculum developer asks themselves to get to the heart of what matters in the designed and planned curriculum. It is precisely the same process in the IB as would be practised by a school or a teacher seeking to develop the knowledge, skills and facts needed.

Is there a robust argument or evidence base to suggest that there should be a content-free curriculum? If there is, I've never seen it. More importantly, I'm not sure I would be convinced by it. I did complete the thought experiment process with colleagues and trusted educators as part of the curriculum review, with mixed results. What would a world without prescribed (or suggested) mathematical content look like? Give it a try. Imagine handing a blank sheet of paper to mathematics teachers. What would they do? What would they say?

My experience was that teachers would not thank you for this, especially not in a subject as interwoven and dependent on prior knowledge, as spiralled a knowledge base, as mathematics is. In fact, they often report being frustrated with even the current level of detail (ref. 'The Vague' nickname for The Hague discussed in chapter 3).

Clearly this is the thinking that led to the unusual exception within the MYP of a framework, when no other subject had the same. It is one of the causes of the 'mathematics is just different' attitude. We have a fairly secure consensus as to what constitutes valuable knowledge in mathematics – if not strictly at which age, then certainly agreeable at certain phases of learning. This learning is comparable, if not identical, and seems to transcend teaching styles and pedagogical differences. As a community, we seem to broadly agree, globally, on what is most important in the wide world of mathematics, for students at primary school, at 16, and again at the graduation age of 18 or 19. The sequencing may vary, but the finish line is approximately the same for all.

What is the MYP Mathematics framework?

'... our own cultures and personal histories ...'

The goal of the last curriculum review was to completely interrogate the framework for MYP Mathematics at all levels, and test to see if it was fit for purpose. I was tasked with checking the content, the structure and articulation of every part of it, which was both terribly exciting and terrifying in equal measure. To read more about the findings and changes due to that interrogation, see the 'Mathematics curriculum development report' (IBO, 2019) available in the Programme Resource Centre (PRC). In this, the outcomes of the curriculum review meetings showed that the framework scope was still relevant, but there were desirable changes to be made, some motivated by Assessment, others by our changing world, and this led to the publishing of the new framework, in a new structure. We had the opportunity to remove duplicate entries, realign certain topics or skills, which felt misallocated, and to provide more clarity.

The change that I was most excited by, and proud of, was the shift towards reasoning in the way we think about the mathematical branches. I was highly impressed early in my research by a book called *Key Ideas in Teaching Mathematics* (Watson et al., 2013).

Key feature: Who to follow

I continue to be impressed by Anne Watson (one of the co-authors of Key Ideas in Teaching Mathematics) in all she creates, and she is definitely worth a follow online: www.pmtheta.com/anne-watson.html. I also highly recommend this book for anyone interested in the granular detail of reasoning in all areas of mathematics, with examples of misconceptions that I had simply never encountered before.

In this book, I found research-based guidance for reshaping mathematical education by reasoning required through best practices from ages 9 to 19. I was intrigued to see if rethinking our branches would make it possible to bring reasoning to the fore.

Whereas the authors suggested the following branches of reasoning, I did not see a need to adopt their thinking fully:

1. Relations between quantities and algebraic expressions
2. Ratio and proportional reasoning
3. Connecting measurements and decimals
4. Spatial and geometrical reasoning
5. Reasoning about data
6. Reasoning about uncertainty
7. Relations between variables.

To remain true to the scope of the review, I wanted to stay as close as possible to the existing branches in the framework. I found that our branches already had cohesion of thought, but that I could bring out the reasoning emphasis by reconsidering what belonged where, according to thematic reasonings. We would use the reasoning as a fixed point in the curriculum review, and move the content according to the experience and opinion of my experienced contributors. I was excited about the possibilities.

Over a series of meetings, we determined that the four branches would be better served if we could remove duplication or overly advanced topics, and if we could emphasise mathematics in modern life (e.g. algorithmic thinking and probabilistic literacy). See the below extract reproduced from the 'Mathematics curriculum development report' (IBO, 2019):

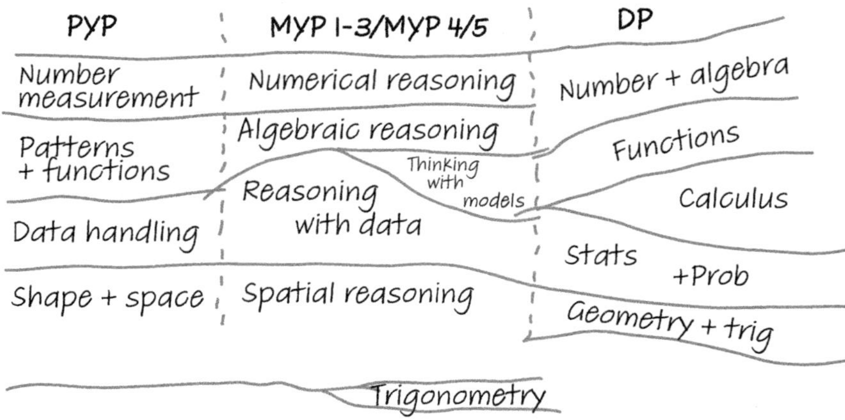

Mathematics is unique in the MYP, and has been for the longest time. It has always had a framework. When I first encountered the MYP in Bermuda, I wasn't fully appreciative of this. My husband, the design teacher, was spending weeks deciding what to teach when I finally asked him why he wasn't just using the syllabus. When he told me there wasn't one, I was horrified. 'How do you know where to start!' I shrieked. Then I felt a rush of relief for my own subject. It was only after a few years that I found the detail restrictive, which I now see as a natural development in terms of experience and expertise.

But why should reasoning be a priority? We all know the well-trodden argument that students have facts at their fingertips thanks to Google. Now that they have apps such as Photomath too, and ChatGPT is getting better at calculations, this is sadly becoming ever more true. So, our winning argument should be that we are teaching ways of thinking and engaging with the world, to banish ignorance of invisible factors. The work of Carol Dweck and Jo Boaler was gaining prominence at this time; now they are deservedly well known in education. Also highly influential was the work of Cathy O'Neil, with her fascinating book, *Weapons of Math Destruction*. So, I kept coming back to reasoning ...

We have a framework, then, that comprises four branches broken into expected content for MYP 1–3 and differentiated content for MYP 4–5. As per MYP philosophy, the expectation is that classes are mixed ability until MYP 4 and only then should you offer different levels of mathematics to the students, in the form of the standard or extended courses. Again, this is exceptional to mathematics in the MYP. Any mathematical topics that were deemed to be outside the expected, assessable curriculum for MYP standard or extended (and that I couldn't bear to cut completely) I placed in a new section called 'enrichment'. This way schools could add this to their curriculum if desired, but those doing **eAssessments** would have a more limited curriculum from which to be examined.

Schools are expected to define their own distinctions between standard and extended, and you can go beyond the indicated framework if it better suits your students. Be careful not to design less than the curriculum indicates though, as this will prove a disadvantage for them as they progress through the MYP and into the DP. If you feel a topic in extended or enrichment would be suitable for your students, go ahead! It is a great source of extension, and will keep them challenged and focused in the long run. There is no real danger here of robbing Peter to pay Paul, as will be evidenced when your students make their DP course debuts.

It is not a requirement that schools address all branches in every year. Indeed this would be difficult in certain situations – for example, in the US where modules are clearly defined by year. That being said, you must ensure that all branches are addressed in your curriculum over the various years. If you have a degree of flexibility, I would highly recommend that you do try to have at least one unit per branch per year. This shows the students how the individual branches develop over time and how they support the concepts between their various domains.

For each branch, we will discuss what has been placed and where, and how can you approach this in an open-minded way to suit your school context. The importance of using real-world examples to build reasoning in students will be a key focus.

So how was it determined which content would be mapped to which level, given the global difference in expectations and outcomes? In the initial stages, I completed curriculum comparisons from international curriculums and cross-checked with Pisa to ensure that I had the full spectrum of what was considered 'important to know' from 11 to 16.

Later, in subsequent meetings, I intended to have the educators determine with me where each item should go, attempting to be as open-minded and flexible as possible. For example, I know many schools avoid algebra with grade 6 and wait until grade 7, but my preference has always been the reverse. To map these out, I had imagined we would vote, discuss and debate, which to a certain extent we did. When I outlined the plans, and described how we vote on paper, one of the participants (Zach Wissner-Gross, a particularly impressive contributor who I had invited from MIT/Amplify) offered to write quick code that would aggregate our individual preferences and colour-code them in real time, and place each item along a spectrum of complexity. Our minds were blown by this magician.

Each time I proposed a topic, everyone would vote on where they expected students to encounter it, and we could see where there was or wasn't a consensus. It was such an elegant solution and resolved so many disputes much more quickly than at any of the other curriculum review meetings I had run up until then. Wherever there was disagreement, say between the teacher from the private boarding school in Switzerland and the teacher from the inner-city London school, then we would focus on those controversial topics. There were some clear outliers and some grudges (I particularly wanted to get transformations of trigonometric functions *off* the standard list), but we took an open-minded and balanced approach to each decision. Hence the 'extension' section was born.

What should students know when they come to you?

'... we are willing to grow ...'

Prior learning

The MYP **Mathematics framework** is based on the expectation that students in MYP Year 1 have at least five years of prior mathematics experience and are familiar with the topics and skills listed below. Teachers must therefore ensure that any skills listed here that are unknown to their students at the start of the course are included at an early stage.

MYP prior learning expectations

To ensure students are ready for MYP Mathematics, they should be able to:

Numerical reasoning (PYP: Number)

- use the base 10 place value system to represent the magnitude of very large and very small quantities
- use the associative and commutative properties to express quantities and expressions in multiple equivalent forms
- use the relationships between the operations of addition, subtraction, multiplication and division in order to process information to solve problems
- use fractions and decimals to represent whole–part relationships
- model complex operations in a variety of ways, such as algorithms or flow charts

Abstract reasoning (PYP: Pattern and Function)

- analyse and identify rules for patterns
- use functions or rules to extend patterns and describe patterns
- apply a range of procedures to measure different attributes of objects and events

Spatial reasoning (PYP: Shape and Space)

- describe the accuracy of measurements with reference to the situation and the precision of the tool
- convert units and measurements to describe the world we live in in terms that make sense
- transform shapes using rotation, reflection and translation
- use geometric vocabulary to show that changing the position of a shape does not alter its properties
- use geometric shapes and vocabulary useful to represent and describe objects and events in real-world situations

Reasoning with data (data handling)

- collect, organise, display and interpret data in different ways
- use different graph forms to highlight different aspects of data
- express probability in numerical notations
- use data to describe the probability of events in daily life.

Without these skills or procedural knowledge in evidence, students will struggle to meet the MYP objectives. This should be the basis of your transition discussions for mathematics, whether students are coming from PYP or otherwise. It can be helpful to use the above prior learning expectations as a diagnostic assessment, with questions geared to each checklist item, giving multiple opportunities to demonstrate each one. This would give a very reliable baseline of skills, rather than cognitive ability as indicated by other diagnostics.

It is crucial to understand the learning needs of incoming students, identifying those who may require support or intervention. You may find the checklists' wider use with any newcomers beneficial too. It always surprises me how many joiners in different years or grades have vastly different knowledge bases, especially now as many cohorts are experiencing different educational lags following the pandemic. Prior knowledge is no longer assumed knowledge.

What is meant by numerical and abstract reasoning?

Numbers do not exist in real life – they are an abstraction, a representation. I think our students forget this and think of them as absolute truths. Numbers systems are models that describe real-world operations and needs. They are so deeply ingrained that students' minds are blown by different number representations (see Arabic clock story in chapter 8, or their acceptance but mistrust of Roman numerals).

Algebraic reasoning involves generalisation of both number in spatial situations and the relationships between them. Students must also be able to use symbolic models to understand or explain or predict in many situations. Algebraic manipulation should not be the 'be all and end all' of understanding. Algebraic reasoning must be given time in the curriculum to advance beyond manipulation into deep engagement through, wherever possible, practical examples or real-life applications. This can add to the depth of this understanding.

In our branch of numerical and abstract reasoning, it can be argued that number and algebra dominates the earlier years of the MYP to the disadvantage of statistics, probability and other exciting fields of mathematics. That's not to say we cannot make number and algebra exciting, just that it seems to take a disproportionate focus in curriculums globally.

Ratio and proportional reasoning can also often be underserved in our curriculum, and the idea of covariance or sharing and scaling of those rates is incredibly important for students, although we are often guilty of presenting proportional analysis as algorithms, routines and procedures.

The ability to work with numbers and symbols is an essential skill in mathematics. Students are expected to have an understanding of number concepts, and to develop the skills of calculation and approximation. Algebra uses letters and symbols to represent numbers, quantities and operations, and employs variables to solve mathematical problems. Algebra is an abstraction of the concepts first used when dealing with numbers and is essential for further learning in mathematics. Students should understand that the use of numbers and symbols to express patterns and to describe real-life situations goes back to humankind's earliest beginnings, and that mathematics has multicultural roots. Other branches will require strong numerical and abstract reasoning skills – with graphs, gradients, similarity, measure of spread. They will appear simply everywhere.

In Criterion D assessments especially, students will need to distinguish between things that have inherent properties associated with their number and numbers themselves, which are property free.

What is the reason for algebra in our curriculum? Are we teaching students about the relationship between quantities and variables? Or is it a technique to uncover solutions? Or must they transform between these two ideas. How do we make them do that fluently in our curriculum design?

In abstract reasoning, students can find the ideas of equivalence versus identity really hard to express. They are less intuitive about which is a sum to be solved and which is a transformation or version of the other. For example:

$$2(x+3) = 2x+6 \quad \text{versus} \quad 2(x+3) = 11$$

where one is always true and the other is true only for a certain value of x.

Abstract reasoning includes modelling realistic situations and the construction of algorithms, which helps students when presented with a problem. We don't want them to simply learn a rote method, but process is important.

When designing your planned curriculum, decide where and when the algebraic and abstract reasoning will happen and map it considerately across the years. If you introduce linear sequences to plotting to understanding functions or if you approach from an equation perspective to solutions to representations, then remain consistent in your approach, but make sure to move in both directions in multiple units.

Topics and skills

The topics and skills in numerical and abstract reasoning will help students develop an understanding of:

- number sense and operations
- commutativity, associativity and distribution of operations
- estimation and approximation
- measurement and units
- decimal places and significant figures
- equivalence in number and representation
- proportional reasoning using ratios and percentages
- how proportional relationships lead to linear equations and modelling
- how ratios associate quantities that vary together
- solving versus satisfying an equation

- equivalent expressions
- application and limitations of accuracy
- money and financial literacy
- appreciation of errors.

Change these into essentials of proportional reasoning, and consider what else we want students to be able to do instinctively, naturally, useably in ten years' time.

Framework content for numerical and abstract reasoning

MYP 1–3	MYP 4–5 (standard)	MYP 4–5 (extended)
Number		
Number operations		
Forms of numbers (integers, fractions, decimals and percentages) and transforming between them	Number systems and notation (set of positive integers and zero (N), integers (Z), rational (Q), irrational (Q'), and real (R))	
Estimation, including using appropriate forms of rounding to estimate results, decimal approximations and significant figures		Lower and upper bounds
Recurring decimals	Absolute values	
Time zones, clocks and timetables		
Number lines and simple inequalities	Representing inequalities, including compound and double inequalities	
Factors of numbers	Number sequences (prediction, description)	
Prime numbers and factors, including greatest common factor and least common multiple		
Squares and square roots	Surds, roots and radicals including simplifying	Logarithms, including laws of logarithms and use of technology to find values

MYP 1–3	MYP 4–5 (standard)	MYP 4–5 (extended)
Exponents	Laws of exponents including integer and negative exponents Standard form (scientific notation)	Laws of exponents, including fractional/ rational exponents
Ratios	Direct and inverse proportion	
Algebra		
Find and verify rules for sequences	Find, justify and prove general rules/formulae for sequences	
Forming equations	Solving simultaneous equations, including algebraically and graphically. (See also 'Thinking with models')	
Operating with algebraic expressions	Solving inequalities, including compound and double inequalities	
Substitution into expressions		
Expanding brackets		
Factorizing algebraic expressions	Factorizing quadratic expressions	
Rearranging and solving simple equation	Solving quadratic equations using factorization, the quadratic formula and graphically	
Using formulae	Rearranging formulae	Using notation and formulae for arithmetic and geometric sequences to continue a sequence, find specific terms and the progression
Flowcharts and simple algorithms		

MYP 1–3	MYP 4–5 (standard)	MYP 4–5 (extended)
Enrichment		
Number Rationalizing the denominator Number bases **Algebra** Exponential equations Use notation and formulae to find the summation of an arithmetic sequence and a geometric sequence Sigma notation Convergence and divergence		

Source: IBO (2020)

Questions to consider from this branch of reasoning

- If your class is familiarised to a graphical display calculator (GDC), then it is likely they will be using the nSolve function, or similar. This incredible menu option quickly becomes their 'new favourite thing' as they simply input the equation and identify the variable to be solved. The danger of nSolve is that it inevitably hides the problem-solving. It diminishes the experience of step-by-step solving and the associated steps or structure. Is this important? Is it a time-saver?
- How are algebra and coding related, and are we making enough of this connection? Consider this with your more techie-focused students.
- Diagrams are often underused in algebra, with the exception of multiplication or the box method. They can often be used to explain collecting like terms, squaring of terms and why x cannot be combined with x^2, or why conjoining terms (like $2a + 5b = 7ab$) does not make spatial sense. Why not experiment more with these ideas to expand students' visualisation of algebraic operations?
- In numerical reasoning when we discuss forms of representation such as measurement with decimals or changing between forms, we often concentrate on communication as a key aspect (Criterion C) without considering uncertainty in measurement of mathematics, which is of course Criterion D. Lead students to an appreciation of the loss of information when we lose precision. Can that impact our judgements, leading to valid solutions over correct ones?
- The phrase 'for every' or 'for each' can help with proportional reasoning and support the idea of 'per' when talking about gradients and rates later.

How can we connect this to real-life contextual learning?

To overcome students' reticence to move to abstraction, it can help to build up a bank of real-world examples, citing the importance of fractions, decimals, measurement and negative numbers in real life. Similarly with algebra, even with its contrived examples. Wherever possible, have a real-life example up your sleeve, such as the taking away of a debt, or a double negative in speech making something a positive.

In your department or personal resources, attempt to build a repertoire of real-world authentic (or semi-authentic, simplified) examples. It is time to retire the mobile/cell phone plan investigation? Cell phone plans are rarely available any more, with unlimited data and pay as you go. Still relevant and valid examples of real-life algebraic relationships include: health insurance and copay charges, comparison of tradespeople such as plumbers or electricians, booking fees, credit cards, Airbnb deposits and cleaning charges, holiday planning and budgeting, fundraising, and many more.

Numerical and abstract reasoning – link to MYP-related concepts

Approximation	Change	Equivalence
Generalisation	Models	Patterns
Quantity	Representation	Simplification
Space	Systems	Validity

As any of these concepts are considered appropriate for use with numerical and abstract reasoning, you can match the most appropriate to the focus of your unit. Are you concentrating on simultaneous equations/systems of equations? Choose systems or equivalence. Maybe you want to investigate Sigma notation in algebra? If so, then I would suggest quantity or approximation. Either way, choose one of the concepts when creating your statements of inquiry for this branch.

Key feature: Reflection

Consider the development of reasoning in this branch. One useful exercise is to map certain approaches to learning (ATL) skills to different curriculum focuses. How could reasoning be supported by the ATLs?

- Choose the most immediate or suitable ATLs for this branch.
- Now choose a different one for content from both standard and extended.
- How can you link the ATL authentically to reasoning we want students to develop in this numerical and abstract reasoning?

What is meant by thinking with models?

Function ↔ Models

First, we must clarify the different uses of models and functions across the continuum of IB Mathematics. From the PYP scope and sequence, which has a strand of learning called Pattern and Function: 'repetitive features of patterns can be identified and described as generalized rules called functions. This builds a foundation for the later study of algebra.'

In MYP Mathematics, we refer to models as depictions of real-life events using expressions, equations or graphs, while a function is defined as a relation or expression involving one or more variables. This is similar to the Diploma Programme courses, where the definition states: 'Modelling refers to the way in which mathematics can be used to represent the real world.' Thinking with models is heavily dependent on students' algebraic skills and knowledge, so make sure to take this into consideration when planning the progression of learning.

'All models are wrong but some are useful' is a quotation from the mathematician George Box (Box, 1976). This insight can rock students' worlds! It leads to rich debates and deeper understanding, and I usually use it at the beginning of modelling in MYP 4 and 5 to give them a grounded approach to this branch.

Creating different representations of functions to model the relationships between variables, visually and symbolically as graphs, equations and tables, represents different ways to communicate mathematical ideas. The goal is for students to move easily and fluently between these different understandings:

- Models are an important technique to make sense of the real world. They are 'sense-making tools' only.

- Sets of points can be ordered to make a table, and the reverse process is also possible. This must be understood in order to represent the function graphically.
- Students should understand ordered pairs as examples taken from the function model.
- Models can be viewed as objects, as representations, as an algorithm or as a truth approximation.
- Functions can in turn be viewed as an input–output machine, a pattern describer or a point-to-point relationship. Some stucents find it challenging to hold these ideas simultaneously, at a conceptual level. They compartmentalise these ideas and require support to connect them and transfer knowledge between them.
- The underlying process of modelling is to reveal covariation of one variable to another.
- Assumptions are an important part of the modelling process, as is adaptation. This makes it an excellent match for Criterion D assessments as there are multiple opportunities to discuss accuracy and sense-making throughout.

Links to MYP concept

A full understanding of functions goes beyond connecting equations and graphs, and requires a variety of experiences and time to develop.

Topics and skills

The topics and skills in thinking with models will help students develop an understanding of:

- representation and shape of functions
- algorithmic thinking
- transformations of functions
- modelling with functions
- applications and limitations of models.

Framework content for thinking with models

MYP 1–3	MYP 4–5 (standard)	MYP 4–5 (extended)
Not considered age-appropriate	Mapping	Domain and range
	Function notation	
	Linear functions of the form $f(x) = mx + c$ (see also 'Spatial reasoning')	Rational functions of the form: $f(x) = ax + bcx + d$
	Parallel and perpendicular lines (see also 'Spatial reasoning')	
	Systems of equations/ simultaneous equations including solving algebraically and graphically (see also 'Numerical and abstract reasoning')	Linear programming, including inequalities
	• Quadratic functions in the various forms, including the significance of their parameters	• Transformation of quadratic functions, including translation, reflection and dilation
	• Representation and shape of exponential functions and their horizontal asymptotes	• Representation and shape of cubic, rational, trigonometric and logarithmic functions and their asymptotes
	• Algorithms (analysing and using well-defined procedures for solving complex problems)	• Networks, including edges and arcs, nodes/ vertices, paths • Calculating network pathways • Weighted networks

Enrichment

- Transforming cubic, and trigonometric functions
- Functions including *ln* and e
- Composite functions
- Inverse functions
- Logarithmic functions

Source: IBO (2020)

Things to note in this branch of reasoning

In previous frameworks there had been a 'discrete mathematics' branch, which then later disappeared in subsequent reviews. I really enjoyed teaching networks, which was done in a fun way in one of my early textbooks, so I was excited to bring it back. The more we discussed networks and algorithms as a group, the clearer it became that it was probably the most life-lasting mathematics that students might take from this branch.

It came as a surprise to me that some schools have units of inquiry involving logarithms in grade 9 standard, which seemed to me a little early. Likewise, it surprised me to see that transformation of trig functions was in standard level too, as expected content. I held the view that schools could do it if they wanted to but needn't at standard level at least. In the end it was contentious, even at extended, which gave me all the permission I needed to put it in enrichment.

The biggest change to come to this topic is the vast improvement in technology, through the general availability of online graphing sources such as Desmos, as well as the expected GDCs in use at Diploma level. The earlier you can get students used to a GDC the better, but it remains a challenge for many schools as these are expensive pieces of equipment. If you can get an emulator for your whiteboard, to show students the functionalities until they have one, then this is a good start. One caveat is that the calculator in the on-screen examination is a more basic model, so your students will have to be downskilled if they are to do well in the exam, i.e. not dependent on the ease of the GDC to do all the work for them.

The benefits of using tech-enabled models and functions are that students have a much better grasp now of axes and scales through the intuitive use of zoom, scaling and scrolling on Desmos or the GDC. There seem to be fewer now who view the graphs as a static image beyond or within which it is impossible to move. This is a vast improvement in conceptual understanding, a genuine positive benefit of technology. Likewise, the addition of sliders in Desmos has given us a way to inquire authentically into, and manipulate, the difference between parameters and variables, in an instant, animated way. Within a static image, some students misinterpreted models as 'dot to dot' relationships, more similar to a line graph. With the ability to extrapolate and interpolate this seems to be less of a problem. Technology allows us to remove their misunderstandings, too, that all models are smooth or continuous, as we can easily plot piecewise functions to describe better. Make sure to design a coherent experience of mathematical technology over time.

But what about the manual skills? That's a great question, particularly as many of our MYP students will still be faced with non-calculator papers in the future. More importantly, there are fundamental processes done by hand that give students certain skills, which are invisible when using technology, such as generating a table of points, choosing and constructing axes increments, and paying attention to precision and accuracy in representations. Will they lose these skills?

As with shape construction, I make time for the skills to ensure the students 'get their hands dirty' and to develop motor skills. So many of them now struggle with using tools that do not involve swiping, so I make sure to keep construction skills front and centre. We reinforce hand-done work to ensure that our students are not short-changed either in experiences or understanding.

How can we connect this to real-life contextual learning?

The more experience students get with the concept of modelling real-life behaviour the better. Linking real-time data to a representation that can lead to a model can be very powerful. The use of light gates, temperature sensors or noise levels can give instantaneous feedback, which students can use to model.

Wherever possible, introduce students to linear and quadratic functions rooted in the real world. When they encounter the modelling in their future lives, it will begin with a specific need or a consideration drawn from a genuine context. This will not be artificially created, so wherever possible the same should go for examples used in class.

Thinking with models – links to MYP-related concepts

Approximation	Change	Equivalence
Generalisation	Models	Patterns
Quantity	Representation	Simplification
Space	Systems	Validity

As any of these concepts are considered appropriate for use with thinking with models, you can match the most appropriate to the focus of your unit. Are you concentrating on different quadratic forms? Choose representation or equivalence. Maybe you want to investigate rates and change in models? If so, then I would suggest change or simplification. Either way, choose one of the concepts when creating your statements of inquiry for this branch.

Key feature: Reflection

Consider the development of reasoning in this branch. One useful exercise is to map certain ATL skills to different curriculum focuses. How could reasoning be supported by the ATLs?

- Choose the most immediate or suitable ATLs for this branch.
- Now choose a different one for content from both standard and extended.
- How can you link the ATL authentically to reasoning we want students to develop in thinking with models?

What is meant by spatial reasoning?

Spatial reasoning skills provide students with the tools for analysing, measuring and transforming geometric quantities in two and three dimensions. Geometry is essentially an ancient form of mathematics, which has never been more modern. Thanks to 3D modelling in games and design, many of our students are more familiar than before with 3D geometric principles, even if they can't articulate or calculate with them.

Spatial reasoning, in both geometry and trigonometry, can inform students' understanding of concepts such as equivalence and patterns. There are other important concepts that can be extracted too: invariance, similarity, transformation. These could be included in your curriculum development to deepen students' reasoning and transferability. Invariance is such an important idea, and I like to introduce it to them before they start TOK, to enrich their arguments.

The branch of spatial reasoning consists of geometry across MYP 1–5 and trigonometry introduced at MYP 4. This was a little later than I wanted, as I often begin trig in MYP 3 (grade 8). You will see this in the Hodder textbook, *MYP by Concept: Mathematics 3* (Bateson and Amlin, 2018), as an intentional choice. Nevertheless, with some trepidation, based on school feedback, I placed it in the standard course for MYP 4–5. One of the positive side effects of this was that it gave a little extra space in MYP 1–3, which I hoped teachers might use to emphasise enrichment and joy before students are effectively streamed and looking towards Diploma. One last chance to really play!

I thank my lucky stars that I get to teach spatial and deductive reasoning in an age of dynamic geometry systems. GeoGebra, Desmos and other systems have made teaching this subject so much more accessible. Students who you've lost during an explanation, can light up when you show them a slider. Suddenly they can investigate and manipulate a phenomenon that had stumped them a minute earlier. When I reflect on the series of static images of quadratics from my old textbooks, I don't think I truly grasped the transformations between them. It seemed that each function was a uniquely generated, unconnected tool.

This digital technology, and future improvements no doubt, has such potential for expanding what we can investigate with students at different ages. It makes me reflect on how far I could have gone in the field of mathematics before I met my own personal 'wall' – grad, div and curl – which essentially ended my progress. Now I see that, with the aid of technology, I could have experimented with it rather than give up. Now I ensure that I use tech, especially sliders and models, whenever it fits – I've even been known to show a motivated group of grade 7s some circle theorems to push their reasoning on.

We must also recognise the role of intuition in spatial reasoning. This is a strength for visually gifted people and area for growth for the rest of us. Pity those who prefer numerical reasoning and struggle to rotate projections or unfold nets in their mind's eye. Spatial reasoning involves creating a mental model that can be manipulated or transformed at will. You would think this would be second nature. Visual intuition should come naturally to us all, as it is reality based on the world we inhabit. It is the only branch that we live in – the others all exist on a different plane (pun intended!).

In abstract reasoning, you do not have to focus on axioms, postulates and theorems, unless you want to. There is an elegance in proof that many will enjoy. And it still remains elusive to artificial intelligence at the time of writing, in that AI can reproduce proofs but seems to struggle to create them. For how long, though? It is also a key element in supporting students' deductive reasoning.

Construction as a part of reasoning can be overlooked. Students are less and less familiar with the phrase 'measure twice, cut once'. They often find handling measurement and construction tools, such as a compass or protractor, frustrating. Is there a value in continuing these skills, given the advances of technology? I leave that decision with you, but it is noticeable with students over time that they are becoming more and more removed from their intuitive checking of valid answers. If I ask them, 'Does that answer seem right? Does it make sense? Could that angle be 0.04 degrees?' I find that they don't have an anchored feel for the right scale.

What is lovely to see is the simultaneous growth in students' understanding of spatial and geometric reasoning, where it occurs in parallel.

Topics and skills

The topics and skills in spatial reasoning will help students develop an understanding of:

- construction and manual skills
- visualisation and representation of 3D shapes
- moving between dimensions
- algorithmic thinking in trigonometry.

Framework content for spatial reasoning

MYP 1–3	MYP 4–5 (standard)	MYP 4–5 (extended)
Geometry		
Classifying shapes and angles	Metric conversions	
Calculations with angle properties		
Angles in intersecting and parallel lines	Circle geometry and theorems, including angles, radius, diameter and tangent	
Perimeter (circumference) and area of plane figures including triangles, circles, parallelograms, rhombuses, rectangles, squares, kites, trapezoids and compound shapes	Length of arc and chord, perimeter and area of sector and segment	
Volume, surface area and nets of cubes, cuboids, cylinders and prisms	Volume, surface area and nets of pyramids, cones and compound three-dimensional shapes	Capacity
Coordinates	$y = mx + c$ gradients and intercepts (see also 'Thinking with models')	
	Gradients of parallel lines	Relationship between gradients of perpendicular lines
	Coordinate geometry, including distance, midpoint and gradient formulae	

MYP 1–3	MYP 4–5 (standard)	MYP 4–5 (extended)
Symmetry and reflection	Rotation around a given point Similarity and congruence, including proving similar and congruent triangles Movement on a plane – isometric transformations, enlargements and tessellations	Enlargement around a given point Enlargement by a rational factor Identical representation of transformations
Trigonometry		
Not considered age-appropriate	Triangle properties	
	Bearings	
	Pythagoras' theorem	Converse of Pythagoras' theorem
	Trigonometric ratios in right-angled triangles	Sine rule and cosine rule, including applications (link to trigonometric functions)
Enrichment		
Geometry Fractals (informal introduction) Dilation Inscribing and circumscribing shapes Arc length and sector using radians Polar coordinates Vector notation Vector spaces **Trigonometry** Three-dimensional coordinate geometry Area of a triangle rule Unit circle Radians Equation of a circle with centre at the origin Trigonometric identities		

Source: IBO (2020)

Things to note in this branch of reasoning

- One thing that jumps out from the enrichment section is an informal introduction of fractals. These can engage students of any age and form excellent stand-alone classes. I try to introduce them in or around spatial thinking units, to allow students to connect scale and shape in an expansive way.

- My research indicated that there were some schools that were going as far as trigonometric identities in MYP, but it was a small number for whom it was important. It was kept in enrichment as a result.
- I wanted to keep the mathematics of 'inscribing and circumscribing shapes' in the minds of MYP teachers as a source of inspiration for Criterion B: investigating patterns investigations.
- It is important to remember that many cognitive tests assess spatial reasoning and use this to indicate students' ability (e.g. MAPS, CAT4). This can lead to a difference in students' predicted grades for the MYP from their in-class performance of understanding. How can we shift focus from geometric theory to spatial thinking and visualisation? Would this make a difference in these score discrepancies? Or do we know our students better?
- In terms of visual intuition, remember that presentation matters. Students will show evidence of struggle when you rotate an isosceles triangle, hide the Pythagorean question in a context or present an image in a different orientation to the one used for instruction. This should be remembered when designing our examples and explicit introductions. Don't just save it for your level 7–8 questions.
- Speaking of which, one interesting discussion in mathematics research in the past few years has been about the examples we use in teaching. Something that might be worthy of experimentation in your classroom is the idea of exemplification in a slightly different way. Can you use boundary examples? Counterexamples? 'Almost' examples? When does a triangle stop being a triangle and become a line?

How can we connect this to real-life contextual learning?

Teaching spatial reasoning involves knowing how to recognise problems around you and identifying interesting problems around us. We are surrounded by interesting geometrical patterns and uses, thanks to the modern proliferation of design everywhere we look. Perhaps we place too much emphasis on naming shapes and finding symmetry, and not on the geometric entities themselves, proofs are still important to introduce deductive reasoning.

Where can students see spatial reasoning in their lives, either now or in the future?

- In virtual worlds, moving in and between planes, such as in *Minecraft*. All manner of CGI, augmented reality, virtual reality, and more to come. These versions of reality can strengthen students' awareness of moving through three-dimensional space and lay the foundation for vectors later. *Minecraft* especially explores visual phenomena and gives students an informal language to connect to symmetry and congruence when they are constructing their imagined worlds.
- Future interdisciplinary employment, where spatial reasoning is the foundation for creativity (e.g. artistic crystallographers, synthetic biologists, astro-architects and carbon farm management). The possibilities are endless and prediction virtually impossible.
- Drone technology will continue to develop throughout students' lifetimes and we have to assume that autonomous cars will also be available for flight. How to navigate space, and how to share or regulate it, will be a theme for them to consider in a practical way.
- 3D printing is becoming more readily available and affordable for many schools. This brings the importance of structure, supports and symmetry into sharp focus. Printer fails generate rich discussions of layers, balance and projections that support this spatial thinking.

And now I must confess something. I have never mastered the art of the manipulatives. I see them, I buy them, I look at cool ideas to do with them and yet I rarely use them. In my formative teaching years, we didn't have the budget, and when I joined well-resourced schools they always seemed to sit in drawers, unused by everyone but the support classes. In the past few years, I decided to change this and began to investigate their use. To my surprise I found it a mixed bag. Some I found helpful, particularly in 3D geometry. I recommend a 3D wire cuboid for this purpose. Using 2D technology to represent 3D shapes can sometimes open the door for misconception, so I now provide nets and solid objects if students are completing a Criterion B investigation such as Euler's formula. I saw improved scores when I gave them solid, hollow representations of different polyhedra.

Visual intuition and common-sense understanding must be emphasised throughout this branch, to enforce students' reasoning. They should learn to self-check during and after every problem-solving, to see if a unit is appropriate, for example, or if an answer makes sense in context. This becomes abundantly clear in geometry and trigonometry if they are not used to checking if the answer is in the realm of reality or sense.

Spatial reasoning can have some fascinating diversions – something to research online with students is the work being done by scientists to create a geometry of smell. What at first seems ludicrous expands in a fascinating discussion of distance and differences (see Castro, 2024).

You will find lots of these very modern interpretations of spatial thinking – for example, how hard different languages are to learn relative to English, or the mathematical madness of Möbius strips. Twitter (now X) used to be a wonderful source of ideas for these connections, but many newspapers and magazines online like to feature novelties of this kind too, so keep your mathematical eyes open at all times.

Spatial reasoning – links to MYP-related concepts

Approximation	Change	Equivalence
Generalisation	Models	Patterns
Quantity	Representation	Simplification
Space	Systems	Validity

As any of these concepts are considered appropriate for use with spatial reasoning, you can match the most appropriate to the focus of your unit. Are you concentrating on angle properties? Choose patterns or equivalence. Maybe you want to investigate transformation of geometric shapes? If so, then I would suggest space or change (also invariance might be more appropriate!). Either way, choose one of the concepts when creating your statements of inquiry for this branch.

Key feature: Reflection

Consider the development of reasoning in this branch. One useful exercise is to map certain ATL skills to different curriculum focuses. How could reasoning be supported by the ATLs?

- Choose the most immediate or suitable ATLs for this branch.
- Now choose a different one for content from both standard and extended.
- How can you link the ATLs authentically to reasoning we want students to develop in spatial reasoning?

What is meant by reasoning with data?

In this branch we concern ourselves with reasoning in statistics and probability. When reasoning with data, it is important to differentiate between statistical reasoning, based on the past, and probabilistic reasoning used to predict a possible future. The difference between variability and noise in these two different modes of reasoning is often muddled in students' minds. The idea that both statistics and probability are different perspectives on data I found to be an elegant connection. These two areas of mathematical knowledge can be harmonised into 'reasoning with data' in terms of curriculum design, to make those connections between qualitative and quantitative reasoning in both. I love this idea – that statistics and probability are the same thing, depending on the direction of your view. It's almost philosophical.

Statistical literacy is so important, but so too is students' understanding of probability and how it affects their daily lives. The reasoning with data requires students to make inferences from what they collect or see, and then often to make judgements based on those inferences. They must be the keepers of their own knowledge so they can make well-informed decisions such as investments or surgery or risk-taking behaviours. They will have opportunities to make judgements of chance in their lives, and reasoning gained from data can help them in these.

Most mathematics can be undertaken in a context-free way, but reasoning with data is almost entirely contextual – you need the context to proceed. Think of a probability question without the details, or calculating measures of spread without a situation. Without a context it would be meaningless. This makes the reasoning highly valuable and useful but depends so much on the application within, and interpretation of, the situation. That is what makes this branch of reasoning different, and connects us as a subject to many more disciplines and subjects, which can be great for developing interdisciplinary units (IDUs).

Probability itself is a challenge to introduce in a very practical way as the situations where it is relevant are far too complex. We must simplify the universe, and so students could be forgiven for thinking probability is obsessed with spinners, dice, socks in a drawer or marbles in a bag. Creativity is required and we should be drawing upon real-life. It becomes easier when students move to binomial probabilities in the form of tree diagrams or dependent events in the form of Venn diagrams. And the questions get easier to write too, without the risk of sounding utterly irrelevant.

Variability in data can be explained as the effect of various factors; it can be annoying when you are looking for uniformity of relationships. We want the students to understand that the trends can be identified, despite confusing or unexpected results. In probability they are investigating randomness in a different way. Often probability has been introduced informally in primary – verbally or numerically, involving fractions. This can be a help or a hindrance.

Through the study of statistics, students should develop skills associated with the collection, organisation and analysis of data, enabling them to present information clearly and to discover patterns. Students will also develop critical thinking skills, enabling them to differentiate between what happens in theory (probability) and what is observed (statistics).

Students will often have experienced the beginnings of data handling and reasoning in primary school. They may have seen, but not inquired into, averages and simple data representations. They may even have carried out simple calculations of mean, mode or median. They will certainly only have considered monovariate (univariate) data. Our goal is to introduce students through bivariate data analysis into understanding that covariation, or how the variables interact/behave relative to one another is what we seek.

How probability distribution can be demonstrated by ChatGPT and other AI systems

Make sure that students understand that, when reasoning with probability, all the information or outcomes are visible, as though they were playing chess. When dealing with statistics, not all the data are available when making judgements, more akin to poker. In artificial intelligence models, all the probabilities are known by the AI and we see only the most likely output for our request.

As mathematics teachers we know about probability distributions and how they are useful, but ChatGPT gives an excellent visual example to students as to how probabilistic reasoning can be used for algorithms involving predictive text or probably suitable matches.

Take for example a request to complete random sentences. I started with the following, context-free, request:

Rita Bateson had a ...

It looks like your message got cut off. Could you let me know what you'd like to know or discuss about Rita Bateson?

Finish the sentence please. Rita Bateson had a

Rita Bateson had a profound impact on the way mathematics is taught in primary schools, revolutionizing methods with her innovative approaches and educational materials.

Now if we ignore for a moment that it is not fully correct (I have published more in MYP and DP than PYP, and I'm not convinced I have had a profound effect), it has chosen a probable answer, based on the information available to it. It has added a dash of hyperbole and has produced a moderately appropriate response. If I make it vaguer:

Johnathon had a …

Johnathon had a remarkable ability to solve complex problems, which made him a highly valued member of his team at the tech company.

ChatGPT assumes I am writing complimentary insights into team members. So, I try again:

Ellie had a

Ellie had a vibrant personality that lit up every room she entered, making her beloved by friends and colleagues alike.

Notice how the implicit bias fed to the large language model (LLM) has been reproduced in the most likely matches for personality and attributes. Johnathon is a complex problem-solver in a tech company, while Ellie makes a valuable contribution with her lovely personality (which happens to be true, if more than a little gendered). Let us give ChatGPT more detail, so it can make a more informed decision with a higher probability of success:

Complete Castro had a

Castro had a significant influence on 20th-century politics as the leader of the Cuban Revolution, reshaping Cuba's government and policies with his socialist and later communist ideologies.

By now, the students are beginning to understand what is happening in the 'black box' of the LLM. It is combing through the distribution of similar terms or combinations that have been fed into it and is returning best matches in what it thinks is the most suitable response. Lastly, I ask the students to predict what the AI will give us about someone called Mary. We discuss the probable matches and many stay in a similar vein, talking about how Mary might be and what she is like. Finally, to reinforce the role of data reasoning here, we try 'Mary had a':

Mary had a

Mary had a little lamb; its fleece was white as snow.

Of course those students who are familiar with this nursery rhyme immediately recognise it, and others can sense it differs from what came before. Most importantly, though, through this inquiry they have understood more about the mathematics of AI models and its applications.

Probability is meaningful and relevant, and we need to make this connection explicit by moving beyond our well-trodden, and well-meaning, examples of spinners, dice and coins.

Remember that graphical representations can hide all manner of sins, and individual cases can be lost or hidden in certain forms. Sometimes the opposite can be true, where the results are grossly exaggerated, on a box plot with an outrageous outlier changing the appearance dramatically.

Students adore the concept of 'random', often using it pejoratively: 'Ugh, that's so random', 'You're so random', etc. Life shows them bias and fairness in a variety of ways. They struggle to see how this is relevant to the mathematics curriculum. To bridge this gap, give them multiple opportunities to understand both the power and limitations of statistics. They should be aware of the legitimate use of these in hypothesis testing, but also how they feature in misinformation or persuasion.

Topics and skills

The topics and skills in reasoning with data will help students develop an understanding of:

- variability and randomness
- causation versus correlation
- inferences and informal inferential reasoning
- prediction and hypothesis testing
- sampling, resampling and aggregation
- the role of context in statistical inquiry
- the connection between purpose and utility
- outliers and how to separate the signal from the noise
- critical literacy in statistics, considering sources and evaluating techniques
- data distribution and how they can be analysed or compared
- the law of large numbers
- theoretical and experimental probabilities
- listing strategies.

Framework content for reasoning with data

MYP 1–3	MYP 4–5 (standard)	MYP 4–5 (extended)
Simple discrete data and classifications	Sampling techniques and response rates	
Data collection and generation, including surveys	Data manipulation and misinterpretation	
Limitations and context in statistical enquiry (reliability of data, bias in sampling and estimation in calculations)		
Graphical representations, including pie, bar charts, stem and leaf plots, pictograms	Graphical representations, including bivariate graphs/ scatter graphs, box-and-whisker plots, cumulative frequency graphs	Histograms for continuous fixed interval groups
Data visualizations and infographics	Lines of best fit	
Data processing, including mean, median (measure of central tendency) and mode, for discrete and grouped data	Data processing, including mean, median (measure of central tendency) and mode, for continuous data, and quartiles and percentiles for discrete and continuous data	
Measures of dispersion, including range	Measures of dispersion, including interquartile range (including application and relationship with the median)	Measure of dispersion, including standard deviation (including application and relationship with the mean)
	Describing correlation, including positive, negative, none, strong and weak	Use of technology to find the numerical value for correlation and its meaning
Qualitative handling of probability	Sets, including notation and operations up to three sets	

<table>
<tr><th>MYP 1–3</th><th>MYP 4–5 (standard)</th><th>MYP 4–5 (extended)</th></tr>
<tr><td>Probability of simple events</td><td>Probability calculations with Venn Diagrams, tree diagrams and sample space</td><td>Probability calculations for dependent and independent events (using the addition and multiplication rules) including conditional probability</td></tr>
<tr><td>Sample spaces</td><td>Mutually exclusive events</td><td rowspan="3"></td></tr>
<tr><td>Probability scale, including significance of number</td><td>Combined events</td></tr>
<tr><td>Theoretical probability and experimental probability</td><td>Relative frequency</td></tr>
<tr><td colspan="3">Enrichment</td></tr>
<tr><td colspan="3">Manual calculation of standard deviation and correlation coefficient
Histograms and frequency polygons
Covariance
Interpolation and extrapolation
Confirmation bias
Counting principles
Combinatorics
Permutations
Factorials
Geometric mean
Regression – interpretation of results
Networks and probability, Pascal's triangle</td></tr>
</table>

Source: IBO (2020)

Things to note in this branch of reasoning

This branch of reasoning links very well to debateable questions about chance and fairness in both aspects. There can be some very powerful questions that arise from discussions, such as 'Is it your lived experience that life is lived fairly?', 'How does that affect your judgements of chance and fairness?', 'What do you know of the improbable and the impossible?'

Students are making probabilistically influenced decisions all the time. We see this on a human level when they are trying to reason with simultaneous events or repeated events. Who will be cast as the lead in the school play? Who will get head prefect? What will be for lunch today? How much trouble will I get into if I don't submit this assessment? How many times can I do this before I get caught?

They are making inferential probabilistic statements and judgements all the time, using subjective estimation.

I added the law of large numbers in this branch specifically to underpin this idea that repeated sampling leads us closer and closer to the 'truth'. Teachers should design learning engagements that allow students to experiment with small samples, and then compare them to greater and greater aggregations. The eAssessment online exam did this really well one year to illustrate a recursive mean, which many students may not have seen before. It scaffolded the interactive graphing software to allow students to manipulate the input and see how the aggregate changed. Similar simulations of data and chance experiments for large numbers are available online.

How can we connect this to real-life contextual learning?

When reasoning with data in statistics-based units, the context will present itself. Use examples that have individual, local and/or global relevance, to add variety. When they are younger, students are engaged in a process of prediction and then, over time, they begin the painstaking process of hypothesis testing, leading to judgement-making. The process of making generalised statements based on the data in front of them is ideal source material for Criterion D assessments in real-world contexts and situations.

An excellent progression of learning in this branch will include many opportunities for students to address bias or other blocks to logical decision-making, such as recency bias, confirmation bias or the availability heuristic. Humans developed these intuitions to help them survive things such as poisonous plants and risky behaviour. All of these are experience-informing decision-makers that students' mathematical reasoning should minimise over time. We want to them to think less like 'I haven't rolled a 5 on this die for ages, I must be due one soon' and more like 'Each roll has an individual, identical probability of rolling a 5.'

Ultimately, I wanted students to have the foundation they need for hypothesis testing, for which they must keep an open mind. Reasoning with data, in an open-minded way, is the antidote to confirmation bias, decisions impacted by recency and misinformation or disinformation in modern life.

For older students who struggle with the idea of probability distribution it can be a useful model to choose a controllable scenario, model single instances and then aggregate them. One of the most insightful examples I have seen of students' engagement was when they had to predict where a bubble would pop or a piece of confetti would land on a certain space on the ground. They made their predictions and, with more and more trials, began to see a distribution of results and made the connection quickly.

The simple fact is that AI, algorithms and Big Data will have a profound effect on their futures. Many other examples spring to mind, helping to give more detail: game design, genetic editing, simulations, futurism, data visualisation ...

Key feature: Case study

Recently in a class, I heard a discussion of how a children's TV show had become virally popular online. This Australian show, called Bluey, had spawned memes of people crying at the wholesome, heart-warming content. I led the students in a discussion of how likely it would be for different people to cry during an episode. We discussed the probability that I would cry (they all agreed that the probability was 'certain', as I am such a softie). We then discussed the likelihood a parent might cry (fairly likely, they said) or a small child (very unlikely, as it would not resonate as emotionally), or that a teenager would well up (there was consensus as to who were the criers in the group). There was broad agreement of each person qualitatively.

As soon as I asked for numbers of likelihood, there was vast difference. This is one of my favourite aha moments with a class when reasoning with data. They give a variety of responses and then place them on a probability scale to see their differences. It gives them a great insight into how different individual perception of risk is. For some students, almost certain means 99%, while others thought it was closer to 90%. A similarly valuable experience can be to take a TikTok fail video and pause before the big finish. What is the sample space and relative probability of all the things that might happen – fall over? Probable. Hit in the face? Highly likely. Small baby will suddenly start speaking (unlikely but not impossible). It is an engaging and conceptual learning experience. Don't let them distract you though, and make sure to choose the examples carefully and sensitively.

Possible real-life contexts and connections for this reasoning branch are seemingly endless. In food design, which muffin will rise? Which will burn? How can we determine the probabilities of either?

My nine-year-old daughter, Ellie, shows us that children grasp these concepts informally at a very young age, as she demonstrated to me recently. There is a television show in which masked singers appeared and a panel of judges has to ascertain their identity. It is creatively named *The Masked Singer*. When a judge guessed that the masked singer was Taylor Swift, my daughter could already assess the probability that a superstar would appear on such a regional television show, week after week, given her status. 'As if!?!' she cried, and could give several reasons why it was almost impossible. When challenged, she would admit although not technically impossible, it was highly unlikely. We should make use of this inbuilt cynicism in our students to assess the likelihood, but then foster a sense of open-mindedness in the face of all possible possibilities.

In statistical literacy, it is a complex process to introduce them to the concept of separating the signal from the noise. I like to show them Tyler Vigen's spurious correlations (www.tylervigen.com/spurious-correlations), carefully chosen of course. The idea that margarine sales correlate to divorce rates is a humorous intro into students' ability to question data. These funny connections help them grasp the idea of correlation and causation in a meaningful way from a meaningless context! They also offer an opportunity to introduce the idea of a correlational activator (to a high-ability class), which is so important to inference and decision-making.

'... evaluate a range of points of view ...'

Cultural challenges can also crop up when engaging with games of chance. Ensure that communication is in place, for example, for a 'chance carnival'. It may be a joyful event, filled with games, but may be differently received if advertised as a casino afternoon. Some families may object to gambling, for ethical or religious reasons. Make sure information is sent home about the unit or learning engagements in advance, to allow reflection. Allow students to opt out of any biased games, but encourage the deeper learning to continue, such as comparison of fair and unfair games, as an essential part of their lifeworthy learning.

Reasoning with data – links to MYP-related concepts

Approximation	Change	Equivalence
Generalisation	Models	Patterns
Quantity	Representation	Simplification
Space	Systems	Validity

As any of these concepts are considered appropriate for use with reasoning with data, you can match the most appropriate to the focus of your unit. Are you concentrating on bivariate graphing? Choose generalisation or validity. Maybe you want to investigate relative frequency and expectation in probability? If so, then I would suggest approximation or change. Either way, choose one of the concepts when creating your statements of inquiry for this branch.

Key feature: Reflection

Consider the development of reasoning in this branch. One useful exercise is to map certain ATL skills to different curriculum focuses. How could reasoning be supported by the ATLs?

- Choose the most immediate or suitable ATLs for this branch.
- Now choose a different one for content from both standard and extended.
- How can you link the ATL authentically to reasoning we want students to develop in reasoning with data?

Lastly, it always happens that statistics and probability units are timed for later in the academic year. It happens so regularly I feel there should be a name for this phenomenon. It means that if this learning is placed at the end of a busy period, with trips and exams, it may be rushed, reduced or skipped over entirely. For this reason, I recommend never leaving the reasoning with data units until the end. I have committed this exact mistake twice – in the framework and now again in this chapter! I am disappointed in myself. I must do better next time.

Whether we sample from each of the branches equally, or match the reasoning with external expectations, we are ensuring that our students have a broad and balanced experience with mathematics. Remember that there is no 'best way' to teach or learn any of these branches. Choices of curriculum content need to be informed by the following factors:

- external requirements
- external assessments
- imposed standards (state, national, international)
- resources available
- best preparations for DP choices
- student needs
- student, teacher or community interests
- choice of textbook
- scope and sequence defined by the school/network/district.

The whole framework is a recommendation, from which you can design the most appropriate mathematics curriculum for your schools and students. If you are in a school that takes part in the eAssessment you must ensure that all the framework content outlines are addressed fully. Students will complete

Criterion A and D style questions and a Criterion B investigation, with Criterion C marks awarded throughout. This is done on-screen under timed conditions. For each examination session, the IB releases particular guidance to that session which will give a contextual grounding. The number of schools that register for these is very much a minority in the community.

For all other schools, they can take, leave, move up or move down the content and skills as they wish. This can be done by consensus or individually, and the creative permutations are unlimited.

Self-assessment

Complete the reflection:

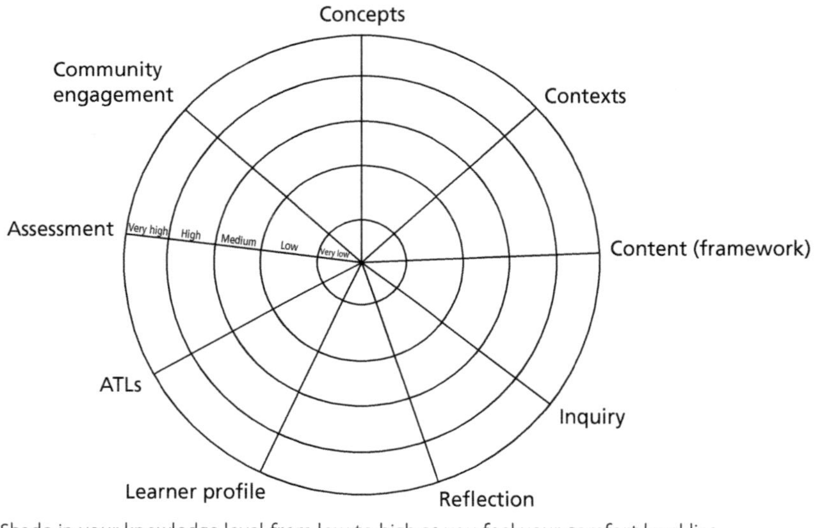

Shade in your knowledge level from low to high as you feel your comfort level lies.

Glossary

Branches A division of the mathematical domain of knowledge, organised by types of reasoning featured within.*

Content An IB education encompasses disciplinary knowledge and understanding that meets international university standards for rigour in terms of depth and breadth, which content articulates.

eAssessment Assessment carried out on a computer or similar device.

** Not an official IB definition.*

Mathematics framework A detailed document showing the mathematical content suggested to schools and required by schools engaging with eAssessments.*

On-screen examination A formal, timed, externally produced, media-rich examination comprising a series of tasks related to the subject designed to be answered in a secure exam environment.

CHAPTER 7
COMMUNICATORS

We express ourselves confidently and creatively in more than one language and in many ways. We collaborate effectively, listening carefully to the perspectives of other individuals and groups.

Key thinking points

In this chapter, there are explanations/discussions of:

- why the learner profile attribute Communicators fits for a chapter on communication in the delivered curriculum
- how this chapter can support and improve our communication in MYP Mathematics
- what an MYP classroom should look, sound and feel like
- differing teacher profiles, including the optimal traits for an MYP teacher
- differing student profiles
- classroom culture and counteracting mathematical anxiety
- how we can use verbal communication to reduce anxiety, including advice on specific language switches
- the power of non-verbal communication, for example through environment and routine.

Why choose Communicators as the learner profile attribute for this chapter?

Communicating is the single most important skill in teaching. One cannot excel in the field of education without it. We have all seen teachers who know their subject matter so well, and feel passionately about their chosen field, but simply can't connect this with students. The communication I discuss in this chapter will cover many aspects that we may take for granted in how we communicate to our students, beyond the verbal and visual. This communication is multimodal and all-encompassing, and as such offers us many opportunities to fine-tune our craft. Within the scope of this chapter will be hundreds of minor decisions we make every day in communicating with and about mathematics, both consciously and unconsciously.

The IB loves communicating! Granted, that's not a universal opinion, but bear with me ... I have evidence of how much it values communication. There is no other logical explanation for how it appears in so many places. We see from this chapter title how it begins as a learner profile attribute as well as an approaches to learning (ATL) skill. Communication is a key concept but also addresses and assesses a full criterion, Criterion C: Communicating. It's everywhere! We can infer from this that communication is so important that it compels us to consider it in curriculum development in as many ways as possible.

Communication is not always verbal, but it is always improved by collaboration and creativity. In this chapter I try to codify whatever magic can be possessed in the classroom, and how to fake it until we make it. This chapter will further focus on the delivered curriculum in the form of classroom culture and ethos through the focus of Communicators.

I adore teaching mathematics, and my students appreciate the thought and kindness I communicate to them, which can be felt in the collective effervescence in the room. It is quite probably my only gift and almost entirely the reason why I wrote this book.

Who is this chapter useful for?

This chapter is designed to challenge and support everyone! It is especially useful for those teachers preparing to enter an IB classroom for the first time or who might be worried about imposter syndrome. What follows is a quick guide so you can make the magic happen. It is helpful for those going to interview for their next MYP position and who know they will be asked about their classes. Whether you are a teacher new to international schools, whether established, start-up or growing, you will find practical advice and fresh perspectives on your practice to consider.

How can we ensure that all students are being heard and seen? Or that we are communicating as effectively as possible? What are students perceiving, and therefore believing, about themselves? In this chapter we will review all aspects of communication, from verbal to visual and everything in between. One fellow teacher once remarked upon this throwaway comment I made to him: 'Please don't encourage them by saying "come on, this is easy". It may not be easy for them. By showing them that you think it is easy and yet they cannot do it, that is negative reinforcement.' He said it changed completely how he thought about motivation. It even affected how he spoke to his own daughter whenever she struggled with comprehension of anything new.

Most importantly, this chapter is enriching for teachers who want to elevate their practice to discover, or rediscover, the joy of delivering the MYP curriculum in the classroom. None of us are perfect in every class. Even more importantly, we cannot know what we don't know. This chapter should help those who want to improve their classroom dynamics or engagement. I have been looking forward to writing this chapter so much, so eager am I to share what I have seen and learned, that I postponed writing some of the other chapters to get here!

How do we best deliver the curriculum in an MYP classroom?

'... listening carefully ...'

What should an MYP classroom feel like?

Putting aside the fact that this is a classic interview question, it is an excellent time to consider genuinely how an MYP classroom differs from any other. An MYP classroom should be filled with enthusiasm, inquiry, activity, action and discussion. Consider if this describes your classroom, being as honest and authentic as possible. It is impossible that this utopian learning environment would exist in every single class on every single day, so let us take a pragmatic approach to what the IB expects to happen within the walls of your classroom.

An MYP classroom should be dynamic but not chaotic. Students should move between individual and group work, with a sense of purpose and responding to their needs, all the while guided by their teacher and/or the inquiry underway. It is a balanced classroom, balanced between the active pursuit of understanding but also developing skills and attitudes. To achieve this, teachers are expected to use a range of teaching and assessment strategies and resources, but this varies massively between schools, considering the content, context and resources available. We are expected to make the most of what we've got.

Learning in an MYP classroom must build on prior learning and skills, be engaging and age-appropriate. The delivered curriculum should be flexible enough to accommodate the different learning needs and styles of students while maintaining rigour and high standards. Not a lot to ask for. Teachers need to be skilled in supportive, open-ended questioning, to encourage students and allow them to develop their learner profiles too. Students must also be given lots of opportunities to assess themselves, reflect on their development and seek out their own pursuit of excellence. If students are experiencing this in the majority of classes, what an enriching MYP experience they will have! How do we make this seemingly perfect, unattainable, classroom situation a reality?

In summary, an MYP classroom is a place for thinking and where the expectations are high. It is an environment that is focused on learning.

IBO (2014)

What should an MYP Mathematics classroom sound like?

You might think that a class filled with inquiry, discovery and activity is a wall of noise. In contrast, it may indeed sound active, or quiet learning may be taking place. There is no hard-and-fast rule. I am not a big fan of noisy classrooms, as I find that it's harder to target who needs an intervention or a motivation. I truly hate chaos in class as it plays havoc with my control issues! Reluctantly, to meet the needs of an authentic MYP classroom, I have learned to embrace discussion and collaboration, and reduce my need to take the majority of the speaking time for myself. It required me to tune my ear to differentiate between chatting, messing and productive work.

The key is to be clear with yourself and your students about what can be tolerated and what cannot. Is there a certain volume level or active behaviour that makes you regret starting the activity? In *From Principles into Practice*, it is clear that 'an MYP classroom is itself a model of a community – it is a lively place, characterised by collaborative and purposeful activity' (IBO, 2014). You are free to develop your thresholds for duration and intensity of active learning. Again, it depends on the day, but the goal should be a collaborative place, where students feel comfortable contributing to discussions, support others and reflect honestly to communicate this.

Something to note for all teachers is to protect your voice at all times. The single best course we were given in teacher training was projection and voice protection. I am shocked that this is not standard practice for all teachers. Be sure to experiment with your voice, both volume and variety, all the while using your diaphragm and staying hydrated. It is the single most important tool of your profession, so protect it. Assume that at least one student in your class will have auditory challenges or processing issues, and that in meeting their needs you will actually be supportive for all.

Be mindful of your voice and use silence as an effective tool too. I experimented with this once with a student who came to class looking a little shifty. He was a good kid, quite naughty though, so I decided to bluff and ask him, 'Well, is there anything you want to tell me about from your way to school here today Jordan?' His automatic response was, as always, 'I haven't done anything.' Cue my disbelieving face ... Bear in mind I had no idea if he had done anything at all, I was just curious, and a little suspicious from his entry into the classroom. Thanks to the power of silence, he started to spill the beans. He simply had to fill the space I was patiently holding. (I found it really hard, by the way, not to fill it myself!) He started off by confessing he had taken a shortcut through the field to school. More silence ... 'OK, I stopped at the butchers for a bacon sandwich.' More silence ... 'Oh, is this about me smacking Ben in the head in the corridor outside your class or is it because you know I haven't done the homework?' I had to laugh – and as a result I have learned the painful process of knowing when to speak and when to let students lead the conversation, sometimes to surprising results!

What should an MYP Mathematics classroom look like?

As we have seen before, this can depend on the day as, naturally, different activities lend themselves to different points of the learning process. While I have very strong views on noise and sound in a classroom, I feel less concerned about how a classroom looks during active learning. Some might accuse me of being clutter-blind. The buzz and the words I hear from groups working give me a solid indication of the efficacy of activities and engagements. Having said that, I am always on the lookout for physical manifestations that students are off-task or unengaged. I often prolong an activity if they are very engaged and clean it up myself afterwards, rather than cut the learning short. I realise that others may hate this approach, and that completion of the task should include an ordered conclusion and tidy-up. Know yourself, your limits and boundaries, and police them carefully.

When I recently had the opportunity to revisit a more traditional, non-MYP, teaching environment, I could immediately feel the lack of commitment to experiential learning. There were markedly fewer visuals and resources. There was even less colour in the rooms, and I felt the lack of creativity instinctively by the visual environment and what that communicated to me. It did not make me think, 'I can ... we can ... it's possible ...', as a good MYP classroom should.

What about the teacher?

'We express ourselves ... in many ways ...'

What does an MYP teacher look like in the classroom? What kind of person can make all this perfection happen?

I have met so many different types of MYP teacher over the years, in hundreds of schools. We are nothing like our reputation and also exactly like our reputation! So, who are these MYP teachers? Are there certain types or tropes that we encounter in IB schools? There's:

- the one who loves photocopying and then hugging the warm pages (this one is me!)
- the one who comes up with great ideas but never does anything about them, talks a great game in meetings but there's no follow-through
- the one who lets the kids do the work in class and they drive from the back of the room
- the one who is also balancing coordinator, and has one foot in and one out of the department
- the one who has taught 'more lessons than you've had hot dinners'; you can't tell these teachers a thing! They may avoid initiatives or change, but they have great life advice and do actually know a thing or three ...
- the one who is actually a sciences teacher but prefers mathematics because there is (almost) no set-up or clean-up
- the one who lives for mathematics – presents mathematical ideas simply or directly, assuming that students will see the magic for themselves; great teacher for the best students and HL classes, but struggles to connect with younger students or strugglers; they've never struggled in this subject and can't understand why everyone doesn't breathe it like they do
- the well-meaning introvert, who knows their stuff and is very sweet or kind but veers into passive or dull without quite knowing why; they take a little longer to figure out their style
- the 'hot mess' head of department, always racing to check in with people while fielding a thousand parent emails
- the one who lives their principles – they bring their whole personality to class, and imbue teaching and learning with their personalities; this may present as their objections to animal cruelty, a coffee obsession, their political beliefs or their predilection for cute kitten memes! They are honest and warm, and give freely of their teaching spirit; they can feel hurt when others don't appreciate this or share their interests

- the warm boffin – has the aura of a well-meaning professor, often loses their glasses but never their sharp sense of humour; they can tip over into being acerbic sometimes but always makes time for younger colleagues, to help them through the rougher spots
- the one who wants to be liked – they can't admit it, but they love to be the students' favourite; they can blur the lines of friendship and may end up paying for it. This is a very valuable learning experience so teachers learn about respectful boundaries; it's usually a red flag for me, as a manager, when the students are practically giddy going into their class or they refer to this teacher as 'such a legend' – makes me worry what is happening in the classroom
- the one who wants to be left alone to get on with the job – their classroom is often undecorated and they have no time for the latest research or even the IB philosophy sometimes, but it has to be said that students respect them and seem to learn the mechanics and processes of mathematics very well
- the magic maker – the one that students try to transfer to, who communicates ideas with ease and humour but can't quite explain how or why; their classes demonstrate an effervescence that is difficult to describe; they tend to value full participation and understanding and, in that drive, cater well to the strugglers; occasionally their caring nature means they may fail to stretch the most capable students while focused on those who are experiencing challenge.

There are a few more profiles of teachers that I have seen on occasion and hope never to see again in an IB school. In this group, there's:

- the one who considers themselves an entertainer as much as an educator – in Ireland we call them a 'waffler' or a 'spoofer'. This teacher type convinces themselves they are making the curriculum engaging through their stories and anecdotes; they are often unaware that the students understand all too well that they are easily derailed and work avoided as a result. I have heard tell of students planning questions to ask to distract them, such as 'Have you ever needed this in real life, sir?' or 'Did you see the election results?'
- the one who barks at the kids – they often scoff at any proposed changes or ideas; their favourite phrase is usually 'we've tried that before'; they decry the dumbing-down of students or the curriculum. The students often display genuine fear or anxiety with this teacher type, and sometimes incorrectly correlate their strictness with high standards or their harshness with experience

- the 'walnut tree' – on her *Cult of Pedagogy* web page (www.cultofpedagogy.com), Jennifer Gonzalez wrote a blog post (Gonzalez, 2013) that so perfectly encapsulated the effect of negative teachers that I have to reference it here; it is called 'Find your marigold: the one essential rule for new teachers' (see the Key feature box). These walnut tree teachers will often comment on the behaviour of students, lack of consequences, poor leadership, the parents or the dumbing down of education, among other complaints. There is never ownership from them in improving matters, and they always seem to have more time to drink coffee and complain than the rest of us. Quite simply they enjoy the negative drama.

Key feature: Who to follow

Put down this book now and go and read Jennifer Gonzalez's blog entry immediately! You'll find it here: https://www.cultofpedagogy.com/marigolds/

And, while you're on her page, it's well worth giving her a follow too.

Key feature: Reflection

- Are you currently a walnut tree or a marigold?
- Which of these would you like to be thought of as?

If you work with one of the profiles here, then your best strategy is protection and resilience. When I had difficult colleagues or department members, I always tried to see things from their perspective, but I could never correctly anticipate what their next complaint or obstruction might be. Once, I got a tongue-lashing from a colleague as I had said she was 'out' instead of 'absent', as she claimed this made her sound as if she was on holiday rather than ill. Another time she lambasted me for telling people she was 'absent due to illness' as it was no one's business where she was!

Why would people end up as any of these negative profiles? My father was the first type (a complete waffler) and my great-aunt was the second (a classroom dragon), so I have seen these types close up. I had hoped they were simply remnants of a past era and were destined for extinction. As I join the older teaching community, I understand that this is not an inevitability. It is shocking how some teachers become one of these types somewhere along their career path, while others of us manage to keep our enthusiasm intact.

Key feature: AI prompts

One excellent use of AI is to get it to adopt one of these unique personalities, to help you strategise for future challenges. I designed an inquiry-based assessment and asked ChatGPT to 'Take on the persona of a teacher who is cynical and critical of the MYP and inquiry-based methods. Review this MYP assessment and give me your feedback/concerns.' The results were fascinating. It truly did take on the tone of a grumpy, change-resistant, work-sensitive colleague. Almost instantly, it gave me a stinging critique of all I was doing wrong.

I asked it for suggestions for improvement. It gave several, some of which could be accommodated easily and added a little without denuding the inquiry or conceptual understanding. Further feedback from the AI confirmed that, with these changes in place, concerns had been allayed and the 'persona' could think of no more excuses. I then asked it if, now pleased with the changes, would it finally collaborate with me on this project and assessment. Reality intruded as ChatGPT reminded me that it was simply an AI interface and could not work with me in the real world, but it wished me luck and enjoyment with it!

For more on these types of interactions, and how to use them to your advantage, see chapter 10.

Working with one of the tropes listed above always challenges my belief that 'we never give up on our students, so we shouldn't give up on our staff'. I've had a lot of people laugh at that belief. It is a safe bet that if you are reading this you are not likely to be any of the last three profiles listed – those teachers are always convinced that their way is the only way. They believe they have little to learn and just need to 'be left alone to get on with it'! You must be the judge as to how and when you engage with their negativity.

Why is the motivation for this negativity? A close friend was complaining about her child's teacher to our friendship group and I was asked to weigh in, as the educator of the group. She explained that the teacher is particularly grumpy and takes the hardest possible line and the most negative interpretation in every interaction. My friend asked why she would be like this as it must take so much more effort to be so 'nitpicky' and angry all the time. It might have been expected that I would defend this teacher but instead it made me rethink my assumptions about these confrontational types. It finally helped me clarify something I had been unconsciously feeling my whole career – that being this way is actually much easier for the teacher involved.

It takes effort to listen and be patient. If I choose to reprimand a student reactively, it will shut down any conversation or dialogue. This will in turn ensure the student shuts down, which will require no follow-up or support. If I don't offer empathy or understanding, I absolve myself of further support. Thus, there is no time required to dedicate to restorative practices or consequences. I have ensured that they won't bother me with questions or feedback, out of fear. So they don't speak, ask or challenge.

Sadly, the impact on the child is long-lasting. My friend acknowledges that her daughter is now a little tougher, a lot more resilient, but also less excited about mathematics. This 10-year-old is now less joyful in her work for fear of making a mistake and getting in trouble. It feels like a case study – watching the acquisition of mathematical anxiety in slow motion.

What would make the ideal MYP teacher?

An MYP class can feel magical when all is going well; it is presumably the reason why we became teachers. We can see, when observing a class, who has the 'teacher magic'.

Laura Vanderkam, an online guru for productivity, states that 'Magic is just labor, hidden well' (Vanderkam, 2024). She talks about how the magic of an event often depends on an incredible amount of work behind the scenes to make sure everything goes well and is enjoyable without feeling the stress. She considers the role of 'magic maker', and how we can choose to embrace this or not. This seems to perfectly encapsulate what we are doing as teachers – making the magic look easy when in fact it is a product of exceptional thought and planning.

What does that work look like? For me, magic is 'I don't hate mathematics like I used to' or 'it just seems to make more sense' or 'thanks, I feel like you are on our side', although the last one makes me almost scared to ask who we are against in this battle? Do they mean mathematics itself? The magic of MYP teaching may look or sound different for you.

Researchers in university- and college-level education find that the most important questions on professorial efficacy seem to be:

- Does the professor seem like a nice person?
- Is the class well organised?

These two work brilliantly together, and a successful class cannot happen without both in place. An effective teacher will communicate care and competence, connecting with students and bringing them to the learning with ease and interest.

When a child walks in the room, your child or anybody else's child, do your eyes light up? That's what they're looking for.

Toni Morrison (2000)

As a parent we are told to radiate acceptance and availability. In medicine, doctors are told that patients desire kindness and competence more than anything. I combine both of these when I communicate to my students in any interaction. Students do comment on how I always seem to be pleased to see them. Children need to experience the feeling of 'Ah great! It's you! You are precisely the person I was hoping to see today! Come and join me on this learning journey.'

What are the typical student profiles that we see in class?

'... perspectives of other individuals ...'

Broadly speaking, and ignoring individuality, students tend to demonstrate their capacity and attitude towards mathematics very quickly in class, such that I can place many of them along a spectrum of mathematical enthusiasm. This ranges from positive to negative and has several external factors too, including, but not limited to, student competence and ability, home support, parental experience with mathematics, and societal or contextual pressures.

This can lead to a cohort of the mathematically ...

- Anxious: this is a continuous spectrum from 'a little nervous, not doing well recently' to a deeply concerning inverter learner. One student manifested so badly she would immediately start pulling at her sleeves and scratching her arms as soon as we started talking about anything mathematics related. Everything is a battle with these types of students, not in an oppositional way – they feel as if they are fighting against their own brain. You can see it physically, making them shy and small, and often their confidence needs to be completely rebuilt. This can be heavily influenced by past shame, and they can almost always recall when they stated to struggle in class and how that made them feel humiliated. It is vital to build trust with this student, so they can let you in to repair previous damage in their relationship with the subject. For some students the anxiety itself is not ability related but results oriented – they are aspirational, ambitious students with a fear of failure.
- Hesitant: this is the stage before a student becomes anxious. For students like this it appears that recently the work seems to have been slipping out

of their grasp, but they have not internalised this to a negative degree yet. You notice that they seem less confident contributing in class than they have been before, and they need encouragement and support to get back on track. When I see this manifesting in the ages 12 to 14, I pay extra attention as, if it develops into full-blown mathematical anxiety, then it can be hard to get them back. This applies particularly to teenage girls, which is such a pity given that they are already receiving implicit bias from society that mathematics is not for them, so it can be conflated with this.

- Curious: this student tries hard and has some successes, some losses. This helps to maintain their curiosity and enjoyment of mathematics, but they may also be overly fixed on grades and achievement level. This student will put in the work when needed. Their work is usually presented well, sometimes even prettily, and you may need to remind them that presentation is not graded. You may need to refocus their emphasis on understanding and transfer, and have them save the intricate note-taking and representation for other areas of their life.
- Capable: this profile of student loves answering the questions and very much enjoys being correct. They often hate writing any work down, either as it slows them up or they feel it should be obvious that the answers just 'appear' to them. They may even exude the attitude that it is beneath them to communicate their thinking. What we know, and what they fail to accept, is that these mental techniques will evaporate at a certain point and they need the discipline of communication. Criterion C is an excellent training device in this regard, as they don't like dropping levels or grades here either. These students often require extension and challenge, but they may perceive extra work as a punishment for ability.
- Hungry (sometimes Precocious): this type of student has been known for their mathematical ability since early primary and their identity often rests in their successes in this subject. Other students tend to defer to them or let them lead in collaborative groups. Their family, sensing a mathematical gift or family enthusiasm, will often request additional work for them, but their appetite is hard to satisfy – and you may get lots of emails about extension or differentiation for their child! See chapter 8, Balanced, for more advice on dealing with expectation management.
- Oblivious: good-natured and not in the slightest bit bothered that they don't get it. This student is not challenging in class nor is it immediately obvious whether you are reaching them or not. They require close scrutiny and it can be very rewarding when they re-engage with the subject, sometimes to their own surprise most of all.

- Cillian Murphy: this type of student is completely disengaged. In this profile the body language is similar to that of the actor Cillian Murphy doing press interviews. If you don't get this reference, go and search online for some examples. He perfectly embodies the student that is beyond anxiety and in full-on mathematics shutdown. They are past the point where achievement in the subject matters to them, and see no need to engage or make any effort at all. This is a red flag for both MYP and beyond into the Diploma. I would attempt to act on this quickly, but it requires the pastoral support of a full team around the student, including support from home.

What are the current best practices for communicating a planned curriculum in the face of these different profile needs?

So much has been written on growth mindset and mathematics anxiety that I won't labour the points here, but it is important to be aware of the work in these areas by Carol Dweck and Jo Boaler (see the Key feature box). Both of these influential academics have changed the discourse in mathematics teaching impressively in the past decades and continue to inspire teachers globally towards rethinking their practice. Another key influencer in this field is Peter Liljegard, particularly his book, *Building Thinking Classrooms in Mathematics* (again, see the Key feature box for full details).

Key feature: Resource signpost

For anyone less familiar with the work of these educational researchers I can recommend the following starter pack of books to help you become more familiar with these complementary studies and findings.

Mathematical Mindsets: Unleashing Students' Potential through Creative Math, Inspiring Messages and Innovative Teaching, by Jo Boaler (2015a). In this book, Boaler discusses how traditional teaching methods can inadvertently create anxiety and hinder learning, and she offers approaches to transform math classrooms into environments of exploration and creativity.

What's Math Got to Do with It? How Teachers and Parents Can Transform Mathematics Learning and Inspire Success, by Jo Boaler (2015b). This book presents research and case studies that demonstrate the importance of innovative teaching methods in mathematics. This book is targeted not only at educators but also at parents who want to support their children's mathematical learning.

Carol Dweck's most famous book is Mindset: The New Psychology of Success (first published 2013), where she introduces the concepts of fixed and growth mindsets, and discusses how these can affect all areas of a person's life, including education, business and relationships.

Peter Liljedahl's book, Building Thinking Classrooms in Mathematics, Grades K-12: 14 Teaching Practices for Enhancing Learning, outlines practical and transformative teaching strategies that focus on developing a classroom environment conducive to active learning and critical thinking. Liljedahl presents pedagogical, research-based practices to help teachers create an engaging mathematical learning experience.

How can we use the twinned nature of 'growth mindset' to conquer 'mathematics anxiety' in a 'thinking classroom'?

'... collaborate effectively ...'

If we combine the important aspects of a mathematical mindset in a thinking classroom, as outlined in the books listed in the Key feature box, then we must consider their effective use in the planned and delivered curriculum. You will probably have heard the term **neuroplasticity**; it is the brain's ability to form new connections. Neuroplasticity often happens when we learn or experience something new. Students can benefit from understanding quite how incredible this phenomenon is and how much we have learned from recent advances in neurobiology. For example, we now know that mathematical anxiety appears to 'light up' the same parts of the brain as physical pain. This fact alone can be revelatory for parents and also provides an insight to students currently suffering from mathematical anxiety. Indeed, for many parents who are mathematically avoidant themselves, they will remember their own personal moments of shame or incompetence well into adulthood. I always find their own stories of mathematics trauma to be moving, and a little upsetting.

Jo Boaler has lots of good recommendations for parents and teachers, some you might think would be obvious to good teachers, but I have seen them needed more times than I would like. She mentions one statistic that I have been fascinated with since I read it: that researchers found that, as soon as mothers shared the idea that they were bad at mathematics or struggled at school, their daughters' achievement went down. Therefore, we share our stories of struggle and success but never of inability or statements like we are 'not built for mathematics'.

We need time to change these mindsets and the current generation deserves those efforts, as their parents often have fixed mindsets. But not all of them. When I taught evening adult education in the UK, a heart-warming number of those present were parents. They were there to improve their mathematical literacy simply so they could help their children with homework. The best role models of all.

So how to proceed with growth mindset ideas in the MYP Mathematics classroom?

For all the advice that follows, consider it carefully, reflect upon it and then implement it with intention. One consideration I like to use in communication is to 'beware unintended consequences' that might be inspired by your changes. The law of unintended consequences is the idea that the actions of people, and especially of governments, always have effects that are unanticipated or 'unintended'. One such example is the phenomenon that placing a scarecrow can actually attract birds as they have learned that there must be something present that is worth protecting.

I like to apply this to the classroom, as part of my intentional planning for communication and change. For example, when we introduce technology in the classroom, we intend to enhance learning and give students immediate access to information, which can be successful as an intended consequence. An unintended consequence might be an overreliance on technology, leading to diminished arithmetic skills or critical thinking. When we implement group work, it can foster teamwork and collaborative problem-solving skills, but it might lead to social friction or anxiety for some students.

When we implement growth mindset strategies we see various benefits for students. We perceive an enhanced student resilience, increased intrinsic motivation, improved performance and better coping strategies. If we encourage, and recognise, effort not ability, we give our brain's natural capacity for neuroplasticity a boost. When students are making mistakes, their neurons are firing and new neural pathways are being formed or strengthened. This is all to the benefit of our inquiry-based learning model in the MYP. Some possible unintended consequences might be that students may believe that effort alone is sufficient for success. This may result in frustration at the slow nature of incremental improvement. Moreover, attributing all struggles to a lack of effort might overlook other potential issues such as learning disabilities, external stressors or the need for differentiated instruction, which might do a disservice to students' needs.

When we implement the suggestions from Boaler's work on mathematics anxiety we see a level of deeper understanding as students engage with concepts and problem-solving in a more meaningful way. This again is perfectly aligned with our philosophy in the MYP. A reduction or removal of mathematics anxiety could mean greater equity, confidence and enjoyment in MYP Mathematics for learners. Be cautious when giving too much of your delivered curriculum time to developing this mathematical mindset though, as some students might become overly stressed or anxious if they are constantly pushed to embrace struggle and challenge.

Teachers might inadvertently create an environment where the focus on struggle overshadows the need for clear instruction and support, leading to confusion and frustration among students who require more guidance. This has been an active concern of mine, particularly around the idea of 'my favourite mistake'. I am hesitant about inviting them to share and discuss their mistakes, as I always worry about it increasing students' exposure to incorrect methods or ideas. In all other ways, I find Boaler's research and suggestions to be extremely useful in bolstering confidence and rigour.

For all of the strategies above, you will find there are certain requirements to implement them fully in your MYP Mathematics curriculum. You will experience time constraints, and will require patience, openness and an ability to communicate, by both listening to and sharing with students. Expect some initial resistance from parents and/or students too.

These examples highlight the importance of balancing innovative teaching philosophies with careful consideration of different communication styles, way more relevant to an international school with transient populations. Many schools have international student populations, some are private or independent, with high ambitions and expectations, and some are a combination of both. You can use a newsletter or content culture (Facebook, WhatsApp broadcasts, email blasts, etc.) to promote these ideas and push them out to families. This may not be taken up by all, but it might just reach the parent or carer who struggles with supporting their child in learning MYP Mathematics.

How can this impact our verbal communication?

'... express ... confidently ...'

Watch your words! The use of language in and around mathematics can be a massive factor in how students perceive themselves and the subject. I've learned so much about the power of language through observation of other teachers. When you interact with a student and have answered their query or given feedback, by necessity you move on to the next need. When observing, you get to see how that interaction lands with the student, how they look when the teacher has moved on to the next thing. You can see them inflate or deflate physically, when they ponder and when they despair. Most critically, the teacher had no time to see the impact of their communication.

Each time I saw a student react, either positively or negatively, I reflected on the communication between teacher and student and what language had been used. I also looked at other things that might have been communicated in the interaction, and saw how often implicit bias and misconceptions can mislead students. Communicators may be oblivious of their impact, by which I mean that there can be an observer effect, with the natural pride of teenagers or fear of authority meaning that the teacher will not be privy to their reaction. And so, I have modified my language and intent based on thousands of these micro-interactions I have observed and the anecdotal evidence I could glean from them.

In this section we will focus on the effect of subtle changes in language, with a view to reducing mathematical anxiety. Given the importance of what we have seen from Boaler and Dweck, what change can we effect in our communication to iteratively change students' perceptions and ultimately success? We will look at five possible switches we can make in our daily language, some of which may feel unnatural at first, but as I have seen such positive results with my own students and others, I feel no hesitation in inviting you to experiment with them.

The single most important shift I would like to make, in all cases, is to consider how you deal with student confusion. Picture a classic situation, where a student has asked for clarification of an example on the board or a test solution. It is very natural to ask them where the problem might be, using questions such as 'What don't you get?' or 'Where are you stuck?' This subtly reinforces, again and again, that the problem lies with them and their lack of ability. Instead of questions that indicate the loss of understanding is their personal fault, I always use a combination of the following questions:

- Where did I lose you?
- Are you with me to here?
- Are you with me on this line?
- Is it the move from this to this where I've lost you?
- Let's track back to where you were with me last. Did I lose you getting started or later on?

It may seem a trivial thing, but it costs nothing, in terms of my pride or competence, to take ownership of the lack of understanding, and it frees the student from self-blame. I use this language in every single interaction of confusion. It has been the most effective change in combating anxiety and deprogramming students' negative associations. It places the responsibility of accessing my explanation back on me. If they are lost, it is I that have lost them, not the other way around. They start to mimic this language back to me too – 'You've lost me there, could you go back over that bit?' – and their confidence grows. It also has the impact that they willingly accept responsibility for where the loss has happened, so they can indicate the place where I lost them. Their self-confidence grows and it empowers more students to ask questions. Another positive benefit is that I don't get the responses I did previously, such as 'I don't get any of it', as they know they are free to track back as far they need until we are together on their learning journey again.

Communication shift #1: Taking the 'blame'

This shift is an extension of the ideas above. If you are confident enough to communicate to students that you are responsible for their learning, the most powerful change you can make regarding anxiety is in this acceptance of blame on you when they are not comprehending, which allows them the mental bandwidth to focus on the important part, shame-free.

The message I communicate to them, both implicitly and explicitly, is 'how fascinating, let's see what your brain is doing here, let's learn how it works best'. It takes an extra beat in the conversation but makes a huge difference in confidence and willingness to grow. Take the time for students to explain their frustrations. Use clarifying questions such as 'Let me make sure I am understanding you properly, could you see this? Did you try this?' or simply 'Say more about that', to encourage their metacognitive skills and ATLs.

Communication shift #2: Encouraging mathematical talk and metacommunication

In all schools, but in international schools that favour the IB in particular, there are additional language needs beyond those of native speakers. A mathematics teacher will experience this a little uniquely, due to the misconception that mathematics is a universal language. You will find instead that there are multiple representations and communication styles, from the interchangeability of commas and decimal points for different uses, a variety of multiplication symbols and radically different approaches in algebraic manipulation, as just a few examples.

The IB has a commitment to international-mindedness, so you may notice a variety of methods and accepted communications in mark schemes. Aspiring for a degree of consistency however, there are certain preferences for forms of communication – certain symbols and units given in the accepted symbols list. This list is included in the guide to eAssessment. Other differences include the IB's preference for $y = mx + c$ over $y = mx + b$ or decimal point instead of comma, which teachers and students tend to simply adopt. Variation within and between systems is allowed, and you should accept this variety as long as student work is valid, correct and consistent.

When it comes to challenges in the language of instruction, the best advice is to often say less. As a naturally loquacious person, I always gave more explanation, with even more confusing vocabulary. With non-native speakers I learned to stop, slow down and give fewer synonyms. Recently, I read a blog post called 'Stop using these four words in math class' by Dan Ilaria (Ilaria, 2024). At risk of giving a spoiler, he makes an argument that the words 'cancel', 'reduce', 'plug in' and 'cross-multiply' should be eliminated, to reduce confusion, stress and anxiety. I have not yet had the opportunity to try this out, to establish my feeling as to efficacy, but I find these kinds of discussions about pedagogy to be invigorating, even if I disagree.

Communication shift #3: Collective responsibility

In the first communication shift, we looked at effective questioning and language to empower students. Another useful extension of this idea, to ensure that this 'tracking back to find them' technique is effective, is to make it a collective responsibility.

Include other students in this explanation process by making the endeavour more group-relevant; it is bound to have a positive effect on any other student who struggles, and it builds the communication of any students who were successful on this. Using revoicing and repeating as a strategy, can engage them.

Use questions and statements such as:

- Am I right in thinking ...?
- I think she just told me ... . Did I get that right?
- Why would I have lost them here? How could I make that step clearer?
- What did they just explain, but give it to me in simpler words? Different words?
- Keep talking, I'm listening ...
- I'm always learning. Tell me what your/his/her/their brain did there ...?
- Why would they have tried this?

Given the variety in techniques and methodology you will experience in your students, it can be effective to show a variety of methods and allow them to choose. I will often outline different ways and ask them to go with the 'one that makes the most sense' to them, giving them **autonomy**. I used to ask them to vote on their favourite method, or indicate which made most sense, but now I leave it open-ended, removing the pressure of decision.

I use generic sentences to give students a basis of choice, but these are essentially meaningless and more of a general indicator that different learning styles exist so they can determine their own best learning styles. Students are so much more open to this type of thinking since the increase in online language such as 'so satisfying', 'my **neurodivergent** reaction to ...' or 'that pleases my AuDHD brain'. They have a much better baseline understanding of the divergence of preferences and I use this to engage their choices.

Sentences could include:

- My visual learners will probably like ...
- People who like rules/processes will enjoy ...
- Look how satisfying it is when these cancel
- Your brain probably wants you to do this now ...

The sole purpose of these sentence structures is to give students licence to create their own style of comprehension and recall.

Communication shift #4: The language of introduction, recapping and development

There is nothing in the designed, planned or written curriculum in MYP Mathematics that does not rely on prior learning in some way. We are not the students' first teachers, and we simply cannot know much about the ability, competence or agency of previous classes. We can piece together some of their experience by talking to them, but often we may not have the capacity or wherewithal to do this, and it may not be helpful. They are where they are, and a position of radical acceptance saves time and stress.

When introducing new concepts or content, make sure to avoid questions such as 'Did you not do this in primary?' or 'Didn't you do this in geometry last year?' And remember that 'Haven't you seen this before?' can be internalised as 'You must be lying to me' or 'You are stupid for not remembering' or 'What did you even do all year, you absolute slackers.' Now you may mean some of these, but it does not benefit the students' progress or your classroom climate to engage in them. We are all guilty of these micro-aggressions when faced with the frustrations of a gap in students' knowledge or skills. So, there will be no more dumping on the last teacher, even if they deserve it.

A helpful strategy can be 'You might remember this from primary/last year/previously.' If we act like they have seen it but possibly, understandably, forgotten some of it, this gives us a useful starting point and saves time. 'Start me off ... what do we know already?', 'What might we have seen before in this topic?', 'I try to treat everything as if it is a "black box" of information – maybe you've seen it before, maybe not, but I will give you a whistle-stop tour anyway.' In IB schools this can be particularly useful for students joining from a diversity of past experiences. Prompt them with questions such as 'Which looks more familiar?' If they are drawing a complete blank, then I reassure them that this is ideal as I can teach them in my preferred way, and so we move on quickly.

Communication shift #5: Implicit bias

My most hated phrase in school, or life in general, is 'Don't worry, it's not a test.' Every time I hear some kind of version of 'Don't worry, it's not a test' I want to scream 'STOP!' We are teaching students that they are right to be afraid of tests, that they should always worry about them. Language like this might serve to ease anxiety in the short term, but it reinforces that tests are bad, scary things, just not happening right now.

Some alternatives include:

- Don't worry, it's only a test.
- You can do this, even though it's hard.

And for those with a certain sense of humour:

- You mightn't like it but it's happening, so let's get on with it.

Try not to use the word 'normal' when talking about responses. This may be internalised as 'abnormal' for those not understanding or completing something. I tend to use 'typical' as an alternative, as students seem to feel less of a stigma about finding their responses or reaction 'atypical'. For similar reasons, I always recommend using 'incorrect' rather than 'wrong' when giving feedback to class contributions or on written work.

We want to minimise their exposure to this kind of stereotypical thinking, to make their experience with mathematics shame- and stigma-free. We cannot control for the perpetuation of fixed mindsets in others, but we can in our classroom. Where it is possible, gently correct any visiting teacher, cover teacher, leader or classroom assistant when they exclaim 'I was never any good at this subject!' A gentle 'We don't really subscribe to that idea here' or 'You never got a proper chance to be good at it' or 'Everyone can be good at mathematics' can help to correct. Aside, you can explain to them that you are trying to always have good mathematical role models for students, and they will almost always be receptive to this aspiration. They often reveal their own vulnerabilities with mathematics at this point in the conversation and, again, will often express regret or frustration that they are not more mathematical.

There will always be certain frequent phrases or exclamations that we hear from students. Here are some of the usual ones and how I choose to respond to them, with intention! Naturally, different students need different responses, but these are a few to consider ...

- I hate math! I hate maths! – *That's a shame because it likes you!*
- I'm no good at this – *Yet!*
- I don't get it, I'm so stupid – *Don't you dare say that about one of my favourite students [angry face]*
- It's looks easy when you do it! – *I know, that's so frustrating, but it will get better*
- I never see the pattern in Criterion B – *Meet my best friend – the 'table'*
- Why do we need to know this? – *Because I won't let you leave my classroom ignorant of anything*
- Miss, were you a nerd when you were young too? – *Oh yes, even worse!*
- Are we doing something fun today? – *Ha ha ha, nice try or It's all fun, how dare you!*

The power of non-verbal communication

'... in more than one language ...'

Let's think about the different ways we communicate within an MYP classroom. What we communicate to students is a complex mix. So far, we have concentrated on the power of words, but we must also strive to ensure that everything that happens in the class happens with intent and acceptance – verbally, visually and culturally. It is important to consider what the surroundings are communicating to the students. What is being conveyed by the environment, the routines and the competencies on display?

During any paper-based assessment or activity under test conditions I will always place myself at the back of the classroom. This facilitates invigilation, as students are completely unaware of where you are and might be looking. I find they experience fewer opportunities, and therefore less temptation, to cheat. It also gives me the opportunity to observe and reflect on a different perspective of the room, allowing me to see what the students in those seats see. What haven't I noticed before? Is there a glare, a draughty, chilly spot? Do the displays look worn from here? Is there a visual impediment? A blind that keeps banging against the window frame, or insufficient space for a bag and jacket. This process has alerted me to many learning impediments and distractors for students of which I would be unaware from my usual vantage points. For this reason, I usually choose to have my desk placed away from the front of the room, whenever possible.

Consider a non-IB classroom. What do we often notice? There is usually a use of colour on the displays and an attempt to showcase student work. We cannot know how old this is, but I suspect the students might have an idea. The teacher desk is often always at the front of the classroom, in a traditional way, as are the student desks. In one classroom that springs to mind, there is usually an impressive display of textbooks on the teacher desk, but curiously they always point outwards. I wonder why why the teacher placed them in this way.

When observing this teacher in action, they stayed firmly rooted to the desk or the front of the class, rarely moving in the classroom. I noticed before long how the books acted as a barrier to students, that they rarely physically or intellectually approached the teacher. I felt it was a very effective way of communicating – sadly, though, it communicated 'don't bother me'. There are many aspects like this to consider that will affect the learning in your classroom. To approach each is to subscribe to the idea of incremental gain. If we limit everything that could have a negative effect on learning we will surely see an improvement!

What does your room look like, as a starter? Other sources of visual communication include the environment and equipment. I see so many different styles of classroom – from the idealised perfection of Instagram classrooms to classes that emulate cosy sitting rooms or rooms that are chaotic but functional. Some styles I have given affectionate names to are 'the cell' (complete with blank walls and minimal colour), 'the explosion', 'the messy handbag', 'the kaleidoscope', 'the boffin cove'. I have always vacillated between a classroom that is highly visually engaging, like a kaleidoscope, with a serving of messy handbag (organised chaos) on the side.

Whatever your style, there are things that everyone can check to ensure optimal learning conditions and outcomes. Is your room well ventilated? Is it well lit? Is it too bright? Clean, if not tidy? Are you a permanent fixture or are you moving from class to class? Is your writing on the board clear and large enough for everyone to read? When you display on an interactive whiteboard or beamer, is your zoom sufficient? Remember that there are students for whom the wrong date or an unwiped corner of a board is a distraction. While we cannot accommodate everyone's idiosyncrasies, it is a good reminder that the visual interruptions that the students see, I might not, but they are still valid concerns.

Habituation can also happen to teachers, by which I mean you may be used to a sensory stimulus and no longer notice or respond to it, but students will – for example, banner blindness or overwhelming air fresheners.

I've been fortunate to see hundreds, possibly thousands, of lessons as head of school, during authorisation and when supporting schools. Observing the lessons of other teachers gives you such a different perspective on what is effective and what is definitely not. I always look for a variety of communication modes in an observation, ranging from their physical communication and command, presence and gravitas, noticing how the teacher uses their hands, eyes, body placement and voice control. Observing how they respond to criticism or irrelevant contributions helps me to assess if the expectations of the classroom are well established. Is there evidence of a routine? Better still, a thoughtful routine, with purpose?

Mathematics teaching and learning is a complex interaction of power and identity, success and failure for students. They will quickly sense what a teacher will tolerate by a process of casual stress-testing.

In my years observing and supporting, I would say that almost all excellent teachers could fall into one of two categories. There are those teachers whose style says 'wow, look at this, let me meet you in the learning journey, check this out' and then there are those who hold back, creating a learning gap and invite the students to come to them. I find they are both highly effective and deeply personal. It might be too simplistic to suggest that this difference in styles, 'come to me' vs 'I'll come to you', may correlate with introverts and extroverts respectively. My husband is the introvert profile and students really respond to his calm delivery, with high expectations of them coupled with high subject matter expertise. Another teaching couple I mentored exhibited the exact same characteristics: Tanis has a similar 'wow look at this' style to mine, which David has 'I have so much knowledge that would be useful. Why not come here and check it out?' Seeing it so perfectly encapsulated in this other couple crystallised this understanding of, and appreciation for, both styles – one as an enthusiastic guide and the other a knowledge coach.

Key feature: Resource signpost

Make sure to be creative in how and where you allow students an opportunity to communicate with space. They get a high degree of excitement and disproportional enjoyment from writing on walls, windows, desks, boards or in breakout groups. I always build in an opportunity for corridor work or breakout groups on a Friday (or Thursday!) afternoon, when patience and decision-making reserves are low. Chalk, window and wipeable markers for a variety of surfaces are a good investment, and butcher paper or rolls of wallpaper are invaluable. For more resource suggestions, see the appendix.

How do I communicate through my typical classroom routine?

'... express ... confidently ...'

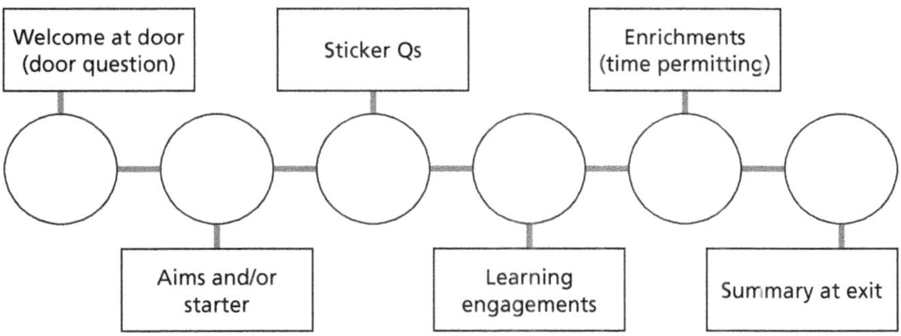

Although not every class follows this pattern exactly, I have found that versions of this routine fit well into different lengths of classes and different age groups.

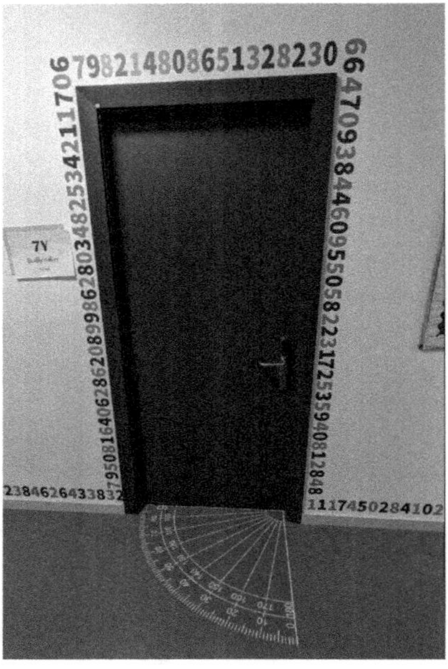

Door question

The students will enter through a door similar to the one shown here. They are acutely aware that they are entering a mathematical space (pun intended!). I stand at the door and each student gets a smile and a 'door question'. These questions will often be based on previous learning. I vary this between factual knowledge, recall and lateral thinking. At the start of the year, it might be as simple as 'How many pets do you have?' and then, before long, I know them better and they feel like a valued community participant. The purpose of the door question is beyond formative feedback for student understanding – it ensures that each student is seen by me, in the unlikely event we don't interact in the lesson at all. It helps me to check in with my introverts too, which is particularly important in larger classes.

Never let them reuse answers:

- Give me a polyhedron.

A sphere?

- Already gone, sorry.

A dodecahedron?

- Nice! Come on in and get ready.

Regular questions include factors, fractions, prime numbers, factorials, means of spread and centre, anything I think might be forgotten prior learning. The questions are chosen either as open-ended, 'Give me a ...', or I will vary them to differentiate for the various skills of the students and to reflect what would be an appropriate challenge for each. Competitive and able students will strive to find the most complex, impressive answer for you; others will try to put in the least effort and you can use this as an opportunity to motivate.

The negative version of this is as a gatekeeping exercise, where a teacher stands at the door and polices the entire line-up, possibly for uniform infractions or misbehaviour. The teacher may feel this is setting the standard for the class, but I have seen so often that it starts off the lesson with a negative climate and ensures that there will be some level of conflict or hostility throughout. It hurt for me to observe the sighs, slumped shoulders and eye rolls, the walk of shame to the back of the queue, the audible relief of those who were 'allowed in'. Far more enjoyable for all involved if the lesson begins with a greeting and a grilling!

Aims and/or starter on board

I always write the aims on the board, with a starter activity on the interactive whiteboard/projector, which is a real remainder of pedagogy from the early 2000s. I have kept it as it still has a function. Writing the aims in their books occupies the students when they enter the room and focuses their mind as to the lesson expectations. The starter, such as 'Which one doesn't belong?' or 'dot counting', gives them material for contemplation and discussion. For certain classes I will also have inquiry objects on their desk groups when they arrive (see the appendix and the Inquirers chapter, chapter 5, for more on the contents of an inquiry box).

Sticker questions

I regularly begin the lesson proper, following a brief discussion of the starter question or inquiry, with 10 refresher questions on the last lesson, or something that is relevant to today's work. I still use scratch-and-sniff stickers as mini rewards for good answers, either correct or very interesting. I use this in every class, no matter the age: the stickers are awarded with enthusiasm to younger students, delivered with irony to the older ones (who secretly love it!). I employ a variety of stickers, with a range of smells, from cola to stinky socks. You may not be a sticker person – the same is true for some students too – but it works for me, so I keep doing it!

Learning engagements

In the main section of the class there will be a variety of activities and engagements with different focuses, content, skills and drills, conceptual understanding, ATLs or inquiry.

Time permitting

On the aims list I will always give an idea for some extension or differentiation that could be done in class, time dependent. Sometimes it might be a visible thinking routine like choosing an icon or image to represent the lesson experience.

Summary at exit

When summing up the lesson, make time to tick off what was accomplished during the class, to give a sense of progress and completion. This can also be done on OneNote; it is not a paper-centric idea. You can also build in homework or home learning depending on school ethos or policies. For next-level communication, you could try 'breadcrumbing', by which I mean use the opportunity of exit questions to challenge or raise intrigue around future concepts or ideas, or to lay some assessment hints.

There are many ways for you to communicate the classroom ethos and culture, your expectations and standards. While this is certainly not a book which addresses behaviour management, I have found the following tips incredibly helpful in communicating and maintaining high standards.

Teach yourself to write on the board without having to look at it. I learned early in my career how to write on the board for the length of an equation or a sentence. This means now I often write on a board with my body still facing the class, which they find impressive and also a little disconcerting, but it allows me a greater visibility on the class while explaining or introducing.

Once you have mastered this skill, learn to type without looking at either the keyboard or the screen. This again helps you to monitor the class while replying to the inevitable interrupting email. It encourages accountability in students. If you have to track back and correct a few words, what's the harm? It communicates confidence and a degree of control to the students and keeps them on task. It serves as an attitudinal adjuster.

Our goal is not to create the next generation of mathematicians, although that would be nice. Our true aim should be to develop members of society who confidently move in and out of a relationship with mathematics over time and through their lives. If they are not anxious or reluctant with mathematics, if they can move through life seamlessly, sometimes seeing mathematics in action, other times using it invisibly, we will have done our jobs well. When a challenge or unfamiliar context comes before them, we hope that they will pause, reflect, transfer and/or self-regulate. They will communicate mathematics, creatively and critically. I often tell them that my only aim for them is success – whatever that looks like for them personally – that my only wish for them is to become lifelong consumers of mathematics, rather than being consumed by it.

Key feature: Reflection

A final reflection on communication

What can I use from this chapter immediately? What do I want to mull over or consider? How do I want students to feel when they come to my class? How do I want them to feel about mathematics in 10 years?

- Consider the following questions to reveal your own personal philosophy as a teacher:
- Are you an introvert or an extrovert?
- How can you use this to model best thinking around success for introverts or extroverts?
- What is your least favourite compliment as a teacher?
- What is your most dreaded complaint?
- What are your passions? Do you use them?
- How do you bring your enthusiasm to bear in the classroom?
- Why did you choose mathematics?
- Where and when did you reach your limit? How can that help you communicate with your students?

Self-assessment

Complete the reflection:

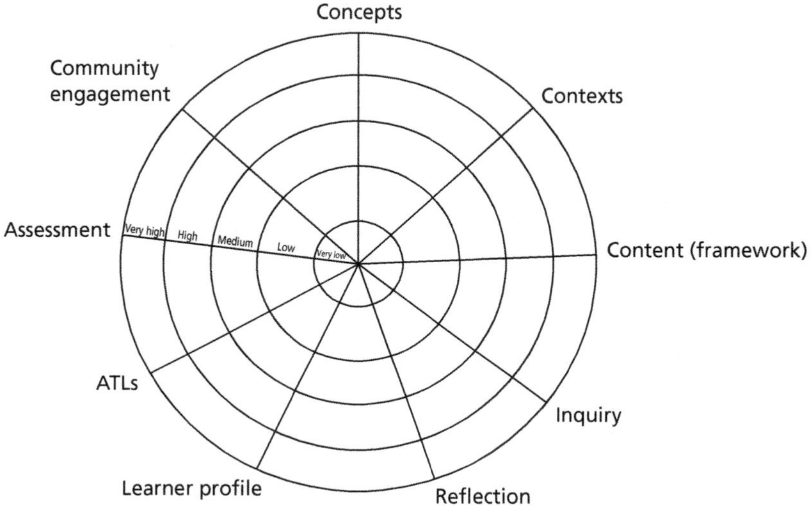

Shade in your knowledge level from low to high as you feel your comfort level lies.

Glossary

Anxiety A feeling of worry, nervousness or unease about something with an uncertain outcome.*

Autonomy The freedom to decide for oneself and pursue a chosen course of action.

Neurodivergence Variations in the human brain regarding sociability, learning, attention, mood and other mental functions. A term often used to describe individuals whose brain functions differ from what is considered typical or neurotypical.*

Neuroplasticity The brain's ability to reorganise itself by forming new neural connections.*

* *Not an official IB definition.*

CHAPTER 8
BALANCED

> We understand the importance of balancing different aspects of our lives – intellectual, physical, and emotional – to achieve well-being for ourselves and others. We recognize our interdependence with other people and with the world in which we live.

Key thinking points

In this chapter, there are explanations/discussions of:

- the reasons for choosing Balanced as the learner profile attribute for this chapter
- the IB's commitment to a broad and balanced curriculum
- how we can achieve balance in the curriculum and in our work–life contexts
- potential indicators of an imbalance in the planned, delivered or assessed curriculum
- ideas to lessen cognitive burdens on teachers while maintaining rigour
- the need to balance routine and variation in the delivered curriculum
- balancing needs through differentiation
- reasonable strategies and limits to supports.

Why choose Balanced as the learner profile attribute for this chapter?

This chapter will focus on developing the planned/designed curriculum, through the learner profile attribute Balanced. A key feature of teaching is achieving, then maintaining balance inside and outside the classroom. We strive for balance in all aspects of the planned, delivered and assessed curriculum, and have to recognise that this is a very tall order indeed.

Many teachers speak of spinning plates or juggling many balls in the air, and I wonder why we unwittingly cast ourselves in the role of clown-entertainer? Personally, it can feel more inert or stationary – more like the old-school game Buckaroo! or indeed whack-a-mole. In both of these games, pieces have to be carefully placed, one after another, each causing a measure of strain until eventually it all has to give. Such anticipation is fun in a game but causes heartache in the classroom. We hear regularly about teacher **burnout**, disenchantment with the profession and teachers 'leaving in their droves'.

The IB can be a labour-intensive commitment and the international school network competitive. By necessity or design, this adds to the emotional, as well as cognitive, load of educators. Requirements are usually increased and it is rare to feel that something has been taken away to compensate. Expectations from schools and families are high, the curriculum is rigorous and the planning seemingly unending. I hope that this chapter, and the whole book, helps to lessen that burden through advice, reframing and contextualising what can feel like a very solo experience.

In previous chapters, we have analysed the key elements of an IB curriculum, so this is a good time to address the effects or consequences of those previous chapters. If you are reading the text in a non-sequential way, feel free to jump back to any chapters on the framework or conceptual development earlier in the book before proceeding.

If you are reading this, then I take it that you are a conscientious and curious teacher. I can imagine that you're putting a great deal of effort into planning. You've been doing your best to 'live' the IB philosophy and bringing your whole authentic self to class each day. It's not hard to guess that you're probably exhausted. Now you have to do this, and a few more things, until you retire. Or maybe you've considered taking on a responsibility post just to get 'out of the classroom' and a break from the treadmill? If you used to love teaching and now you like it less, let us consider how to get back a sense of balance in all things curricular and school relevant. It should mean the difference between burning bright and burning out.

The IB commits to balance in the learner profile. It also intuits and references it in the frequently used phrase 'broad and balanced curriculum'. There is an implicit commitment to a balance in everything, especially in what we learn. In mathematics we endeavour to find the perfect balance between rigour and joy, while recognising their interdependence. Our students will not experience joy without skills, and the mastery itself can also be joyful. For ourselves, we must balance home and work, workload and desires, expectations versus sustainability. The goal must be a broad and balanced life, from curriculum to needs and relationships, and beyond.

Who is this chapter useful for?

'... balancing different aspects of our lives ...'

Very few of us who have it all figured out. Over the last 20 years I certainly haven't. I have worked far too hard and dedicated myself disproportionately to projects I should have had clearer boundaries with. With this in mind, the ideas in this chapter are hard won and would have been really helpful to tell myself at any point along that journey. They are particularly relevant for teachers who are feeling under pressure, either external or self-imposed. I have seen far too many excellent mathematics teachers, particularly since the pandemic, suffer from this, and they have left the classroom as a result. Many have internalised perfectionism; others simply could not find a balance in these areas

As a newly qualified teacher, these would have been helpful rules to live by, to set up for a successful and sustainable career. It is rare to work in a school that doesn't have some sort of imbalance. This chapter is also useful for those who have now left the classroom and are at a distance from the factors that cause imbalance in a curriculum or teachers' lives more generally. The pressures of leadership can, over time, lead to a diminishing of empathy and memory for the classroom challenges, and this chapter may clarify or refresh this for school leaders. It may also be useful for coordinators and heads of departments, as they should support and advocate on behalf of their teachers and hold them accountable for their performance, in equal measure.

What about those of us who love the classroom? How do we achieve a balance, sometimes despite ourselves?

Ideally, to achieve this gargantuan task of balance we would need several things in place. Our knowledge of curriculum needs to be thorough. We would be highly confident and competent in the classroom, and part of a strong team enriched with trusting relationships. The students would be engaged and engaging, and we would all feel that we are part of something special, making a positive difference in the world. Throw in a massive salary and it is the perfect job! As one of my best colleagues and the person who was the most vocal advocate of me writing this book, Marnie, often says, 'Is that really too much to ask?'

How can we manage a work–life balance?

Can wellbeing ever truly be achieved in mathematics teaching? I used to think it was inescapable that teachers always had more to do and had to give 1000%, and the few who were quite relaxed were the miserable ones who said no to everything and everyone. I definitely didn't want to be one of those walnut trees in the staffroom (see chapter 7), so I resigned myself to the fact that most of us would wait until the holidays to have any balance at all.

Warning signs – if you are worried that you are out of balance, consider if you have experienced any of the following:

- dreaded going to school on more than one day a week
- lack of empathy for students
- found yourself saying 'because I said so', 'I don't even care any more' or 'do what you want, I don't care'
- bad-mouthed another colleague or senior leadership in front of the students (that includes eye-rolling when the person in question leaves the room)
- leaving marking more than a week
- never ever going to the staffroom, as you are 'too busy'
- not getting any exercise, fresh air or leisure time on a school night
- missing a social occasion because you 'need to mark'
- crying at work. Ever. For any reason.

If you recognise a change in your behaviour, or you are feeling an imbalance, it is important to remember that burnout can be addressed. Be on the alert for decision fatigue: 'I'm too tired, I don't care, you choose.' This can manifest in your home life when you have spent all of your attention and decision-making energy at school. My husband can also recognise when my empathy reserves are running low, as I make snippy comments and am less charitable in my interpretations of events. Thankfully he balances this out with his reasoned perspectives, so seek out a colleague or friend who can provide you with this counterbalance. If that proves to be insufficient, talk to your line manager about strategies and plans to stop the tide or make adjustments.

There can be so many root causes of feeling any or all of the sentiments above. The most common causes in IB schools are due to workload, expectations, relationships, working environments, needs and resourcing. We will try to tackle each of these in turn with some suggestions and minor tweaks, in the hope that this may release the pressure valve a little. Incremental changes are good here because so many of the school factors are out of the control of the teacher. We can only modify our own behaviours, expectations and outputs, and we need to find efficiencies wherever possible.

Consider the following reflection questions about factors in your work–life balance.

	Always	**Regularly**	**Rarely**	**Never**
How often do you bring your laptop home?				
Do you check emails on your phone?				
Have you ever read emails on your phone while walking down the stairs?				
Are you properly hydrated during the school day?				
Do you get enough sleep on school nights?				
Do you get outside at some point most days?				
Is there more than one set of marking to do at any given time?				
Do you eat at the appropriate times during the school day?				
Can you go through a whole day without having a non-work-related conversation with someone else?				
Are your shoes comfortable?				
Do you have an appropriate level of extracurricular school commitments?				
Does your classroom have good ventilation?				
Do you find yourself printing resources or assessments right before you need them, adding pressure to the day?				
Are you completely aware of who to go to for what in your school?				
Do you know what to do with an aggressive parent or an inappropriate request?				
Are you clear on where your time goes?				
Do you actively care for your voice?				

Consider your answers to these questions, and where you might make adjustments or improvements? You need to balance the needs of now, but there will also be needs tomorrow.

Having seen thousands of teachers over the years, the single most important question above is the last one. We overlook the importance of voice protection. If you are a younger or early career mathematics teacher, then you have not yet fully grasped the essential importance of protecting your voice. It is the single best thing I learned in teacher training. I speak to so many teachers and student teachers whose teacher qualification was a blur of paperwork and evidence, but never once discussed the need to project and protect.

It could be argued that this becomes even more important in an MYP school, where the students are so often the guides and the noise level can rise in proportion to the excitement of genuine inquiry. MYP students often need independent working time and vast spaces in which to measure, explore, expand and create. All of these physical spaces will put pressure on the human vocal cords. Your best investment would be to start your teaching or MYP journey from a position of strength. Being able to make yourself heard is crucial and cannot be underestimated as a relevant component of classroom management.

Key feature: Reflection

Given the answers you gave above, and considering what a balance would look like for you, answer the following questions as honestly as you can. Aim for clarity and conciseness:

- What are my goals for this school year (or what remains of it)?
- What has the most negative impact on my work–life balance?
- Is that within my power to change?
- What aspect of my curriculum (planned, delivered or assessed) do I find the most fulfilling?
- Can I increase the time I dedicate to this without neglecting others?
- If I change all that I can and the work–life balance is still unachievable, what will that mean for me longer term?

Early in my career, I had an inspirational head, Peter Harding, who helped me handle a parent who kept demanding more and more differentiation for their child. I was at my wits' end when he intervened: 'Rita, stop now. You will never be able to do enough for them. They want a tutor or an accelerated programme written for him. They think he is exceptionally gifted. Maybe he is, I can't say.

What I do know, they will either accept what we offer them within reason or they will leave.' The principal was correct – they left in high dudgeon not long after, and the cycle repeated in their next school.

This principal was also the source of invaluable insight about a parent who was trying to whip up a frenzy of complaints about certain teachers in the department. This had been stressing me out as I tried to defend those colleagues against these slanders. This head calmly explained that a potential reason may be that the family can no longer afford the school or resented the cost of the fees. He explained that this can sometimes happen as a precursor to a family withdrawing from the school so they can have reason to make a tactical withdrawal. And this proved to be the case, although my inexperience meant I could not have perceived this. Both these pieces of advice taught me to not take all claims at face value or let them imbalance my perception of the planned or delivered curriculum without evidence.

Another trap for super-keen teachers, and a fast track to imbalance, is taking work away with you on a holiday or break. If you leave things to catch up with over the break, you will not properly recharge. I made this mistake and learned the lesson the hard way when I left papers on an airplane. Later, when I saw a colleague, Shannon, almost fall into the same trap, another very sensible colleague, Huw, and I stole the papers from her and locked them in a cabinet. So that she wouldn't worry about the work and not relax, we promised to mark them with her on her return. I think she was touched and frustrated in equal measure. She still tells the story, though, so the lesson must have been a successful one.

A useful trick to avoid 'end-of-term-itis' it is to schedule your assessments earlier than most colleagues. Look for the sweet spot in the third- or second-last week before a break (see the example below). Most units are timed naturally to span a half term or six- to eight-week time frame. This means that all assessments land around the same time and students become grumpy. Teachers too.

Example: Sample probability unit with staggered assessments

Unit	Probabilities – quantitative and qualitative
Week 1	How to describe probabilities and then quantify them. Sample spaces and outcomes.
Week 2	Binary probabilities Prob. trees. Dependent and independent events.
Week 3	Mid-unit assessment. Criteria B & C. Patterns in Pascal's triangle.
Week 4	Using Venn diagrams to represent probabilities. Calculate conditional prob.
Week 5	Summative assessment. Criteria A & C: Probability calculations.
Week 6	Assessment feedback. Understanding the use of probabilities in modern technology, e.g. weather, simulations and mineral exploration.
Week 7	Enrichment activities that are valid while accommodating early departures: Criterion D formative on using probability to analyse games of chance.
School break	

Following a similar model, this short unit of inquiry would generate two formative assessment judgements, but – more importantly – give an assessment opportunity for four criteria assessments (A, C, B, C) with an optional possible Criterion D in the enrichment 'buffer zone'.

If you have your assessments done by the pre-penultimate week, it gives you time to chase those who inevitably missed them, have them levelled, possibly even moderate them with colleagues and the levels entered in the system before you go on holiday. By simply avoiding the assessment logjam your stress levels will not be as elevated as you go into your well-earned break.

I also hold firm to the view that the second-last week of any term is the worst. People are more frantic and argumentative. More accidents happen and this is the time when you are most likely to be fraught, make mistakes, and harbour grudges or disagreements. The week afterwards, students have started to leave early, so assessment is virtually unworkable, and everyone gets a lift thinking of the holidays.

One last note regarding work–life balance: as imbalanced as it might feel now, this will someday be the dim and distant past. So many of the memories of this time will fade away. Make notes for yourself about your daily experiences. I keep a 'funny book' and most of the entries I had completely forgotten until I reread it in research for this book. From the time a student locked himself and the heads of year into their office and swallowed the key to the time we had to have a bird funeral, or the German trip where we accidentally took the students to the most graphic art gallery ever, these all remind me that even imbalanced to the point of exhaustion there are good memories to be made and savoured.

How can we have balance in our relationships with colleagues?

'We recognize our interdependence with other people ...'

Sean Delaney cites several different types of teacher–teacher relationship his book, *Become the Primary Teacher Everyone Wants to Have* (2016), categorising them in the following ways: parallel play, **adversarial**, **congenial** and **collegial**. When I read this, I spent a long time reflecting on all the teachers I knew and whether I had an imbalance in those relationships too. Delaney is missing a few categories, presumably because he was speaking in a national system context. In international schools it would be reasonable to add that some teacher relationships can be toxic, cliquey, overly intense and/or community-driven.

A long time ago, a well-meaning teaching assistant took me aside at the annual Christmas party to warn me I was getting overfamiliar with the student teacher who was training at our school. She said it had been noted I was flirting with him, and that people were talking. She was very sweet, so I was a bit embarrassed to have to tell her that he was my husband – I just hadn't changed my maiden name when we married. What I learned from this incident was that there are colleagues who are principled enough to tell you an uncomfortable truth. These people are to be cherished and, occasionally, listened to.

To maintain the balance, notice these relationships early and decide how you wish to navigate them. In many contexts, the local community can be difficult to break into, or there may be a language barrier. In Bermuda, when we shared that we were leaving, one of our Bermudian friends threw her hands in the air and exclaimed, 'I don't know why I bother with you expats, you break my heart every school year!' Mentioning this to a colleague in Germany, Tim, he advised that the key was to meet people from the local communities where they were. He said to leap at the chance or mention of any offer at all. If they give a little, meet them at 80% to their 20%! This was good advice indeed. And some I wished I'd had earlier in my international school career.

If you do have adversarial, toxic or cliquey colleagues, don't lose heart. It's never too late to build trust. There may be some conflict or trust issues to overcome. And both parties must be interested in growth, or any mediation will be for nothing. As the author Gretchen Rubin advises, 'The best time to plant a tree was twenty years ago. The second-best time is now.'

It may be that you are in an intense work–life local environment. For many of us in international schools our home life is intermingled with a unique location. Many teachers live on a base, a small island, in a gated expat community or high up in the mountains. If you live in close proximity with students' families, you know them and feel connected. I have often given free tutoring, after-school sessions or done families a favour, as I felt I should. It is nice to feel part of a community. But remember that in many countries there is now a legal obligation to switch off and be unavailable. There is certainly a moral right to do so, if you can. Make sure the wrong kind of concessions are not getting through the door of good intentions.

One of my most embarrassing examples of this took place when I was working in Leeds and driving to school in a panic because I was late, it was raining and the traffic was awful. There was a student I vaguely recognised getting soaked through at the bus stop and my heart went out to him. 'He is going to be even later than me,' I thought, 'I'd better off him a lift.' In my defence, this was long before the much improved safeguarding understanding we have now. As I indicated to pull in to the bus stop, I racked my brains for what his name could be so I didn't freak him out. And I wondered why he was wearing a different school tie. 'Probably rushing and made a mistake,' I reasoned. The only name I could summon was Nigel or Neville, and that was when I realised, to my horror, that he wasn't a student at my school at all, but the actor who played Neville Longbottom in the *Harry Potter* films, who attended a nearby school. In my pure mortification, I could not get out of there quickly enough, and I can only hope I didn't drench him completely as I fled.

'... balancing different aspects of our lives – intellectual ...'

'What does this have to do with MYP curriculum?' you may very well ask. Recognising the signs and patterns (Criterion B!) of burnout is vital. Exhaustion and imbalance have such an impact on, initially, the delivered curriculum, then the assessed curriculum and finally, if you leave, the whole curriculum is impacted. The IB is a high-energy, demanding set of programmes, which can yield incredible results if implemented well. Unfortunately, we lose many good, potentially excellent, teachers due to these imbalances in work–life happiness calculus.

Is it possible to achieve balance between preparation and variation?

'... to achieve well-being for ourselves and others ...'

Can we balance routine and randomness? Schools are like a living organism – systems are in operation and yet much variation and mutation exists. It can drive teachers to distraction. There are predictable patterns and yet the most reliable pattern in a school is chaos! (Whether chaos is truly a pattern is a powerful debateable question to consider in MYP Mathematics too!)

It is also important to remind yourself, when you are in the first five years or so and it feels that the workload will never slow down, that this is the most intense period of investment in your career. You put a great deal of time into familiarising yourself with the curriculum, making resources, learning from positive and negative experiences. I spent all my twenties 'paying into' my bank of professional experience and, in my thirties, I could make withdrawals from the bank, allowing me to expand into more advanced aspects of curriculum development and writing. These investments allowed me later to apply this knowledge in thought leadership and expertise. None of this would have been possible without the hard yards of the first years, and the stress and effort they required.

There will be disruption and interruption that cannot be planned for. In data and statistics, variation is viewed as an annoyance, but in probability it is perceived to be an inevitable randomness. This is precisely how I view it in class too. Fire alarms, illnesses or an unannounced basketball tournament will disturb the best-laid plans. There are also times that you can predict it will be necessary to introduce variation, such as the lesson after an examination or the day after an open evening, when you're tired and listless. Friday fatigue (or Thursday torpor, depending on your school week) is a very real phenomenon, especially painful if you have grade 6 or grade 12 last period. Can forethought and preparation help us achieve or improve our wellbeing?

For me, things finally shifted when I started to accept these facts and plan accordingly. If I knew I would be tired, grumpy or busy I would pay careful attention to whether I would accept a meeting, plan an assessment or go wild with an inquiry circuit. Planning my energy balance, and knowing what would annoy or deplete me, meant that I knew if it was time for a quiet skills and drills class, the perfect time to give a little extra research time for students' projects, and so on. Understanding that giving the maximum isn't possible every day, that it was still possible to keeping going without letting standards slip was eye-opening. Where possible, I now plan for the unplannable. You might have just returned from a school trip and are expected to be back at work the next morning. Or you've had an unpleasant meeting and you cannot focus fully on the task at hand. I have a core group of activities and learning engagements designed to suit most such scenarios. These lessons, or parts of lessons, I then put into action to allow students to be productive and learning relevant material, even when out of sequence.

Remember, too, that timing and competition can raise anxiety in some students. It helps if you know your group and if they are 'competers' or 'completers'. I regularly used competition and speed as motivations until one student told me how much she dreaded them. She explained that I was intimidating and excluding my more introverted and shy students, for whom processing time was a scarce resource. They were used to being ignored in this regard. I was blown away by her astuteness and her bravery in giving me that feedback. It helped reframe a lot of my thinking about these types of activities. This is particularly important to consider.

Plan for **scarcity**, whether is it energy scarcity, resource scarcity, or a paucity of patience and enthusiasm. Developing an emergency kit that suits your style and context is so important, making sure that it is fully curriculum-compliant and complaint-proof. No word searches! No random filler research – relevant and valid activities.

I have often made the mistake of thinking that a very active, inquiry-based lesson on a Friday was a good idea. I never seem to learn this is not the best activity for a last lesson before the weekend, as students will be loud, interactive and messy. When it is complete, they leave and you have a mess to deal with; your nerves are jangling and it feels the worst possible way to start the weekend. You may feel frustrated, and that there exists an inverse law of how tired you are to how loud or independent the activity was. You're definitely more exhausted than you were at lunchtime when you chose what you thought would be a fun end to the class. I've learned to plan these types of activities for earlier in the week, when I can be guaranteed an energy level to match that of the students

That's all well and good, says you, but where do I start with balance of routine and variation? See the appendix for a comprehensive list of fillers and emergency ideas that are either suitable for most units or content-agnostic.

Here are some of my favourites, from filling five minutes while the whiteboard is logging in to half-lesson activities that work when most of the class is missing for a dress rehearsal or swimming gala. Consider a few for your own emergency toolkit: start with five favourites and add a new one per term. Identify which for you are high impact/low commitment and bring educational value to your teaching and learning.

Friday fillers	How does it work?	Good activity for:	How is it curriculum secure?
Spotify playlists	I show the students some humorous examples of how people have created playlists within Spotify, where the title of each song forms part of a mathematical equation. There are lots of examples of these playlists, and students enjoy the creativity.	If independent work is needed, developing ATL skills of creative thinking.	While independent of a particular branch of reasoning, this fun activity makes students aware of songs with mathematical connections and their equation-building is fostered. The task is differentiated by outcome as I have seen some excellent equations I could never have created myself.
They did the math	Again, making use of nerdiness online. This appeals to many students who like to argue, debate and correct you when they get the chance.	A lesson when your energy levels are low and you have a need for quiet research or an afternoon for fact-checking.	This is independent of any unit and it is fun to create long chains of calculations. The numbers get large quickly and are fun to work with. The sense of achievement when students prove the statement wrong is very enjoyable. Finding the 'right' answer builds their understanding of accuracy and limitations.
TrashGPT (AI fails)	Creating questions and answers in AI models where the answers are incorrect, invalid or hallucinating.	This is a good activity to do with students to help them understand how to start creating prompts and evaluating outputs.	I usually commend them for the most hilarious fails and testing the limit of the mathematical formulation in an LLM. As a media literacy and critical thinking activity, it is very powerful.

Friday fillers	How does it work?	Good activity for:	How is it curriculum secure?
Stained-glass windows	I keep a set of blank templates which have large images with multiple sections. Students must create a key or legend that has a fixed set of answers.	In each section students must create a series of problems with answers that result in specific colours. They then exchange their worksheets and complete them. It creates a great deal of variation and variety, which we can discuss mathematically too, identifying patterns in colour and question complexity.	The teacher can determine the level of open-endedness. I usually constrain the questions to the current unit only, but you can integrate a few questions from previous units too. Beware: geometric colouring for mindfulness can be popular with students but, without a curriculum focus, it has a law of diminishing returns. It will be seen, fairly, as busy work without merit. Much like word searches.
Cover page filler	At the beginning of each unit, when I am introducing the statement of inquiry, the concepts and the global context, I ask the students to create a cover page in their notebooks for this unit. We add to this throughout the unit.	It helps to break up the notebook, allowing students to see progression, and makes revision easier. It also allows them to identify the most important elements, equations, symbols or processes to add, and how to represent them.	This gives an interesting insight into what students are taking from the unit and how they perceive the relative importance. Some prefer to feature images, others write out problems. Some groups may need more direction, others can apply critical thinking. Remember to scan, photo or copy the best ones for displays or for the following year. Creative and conceptual.
Geometry Snacks	A wonderful book by Vincent Pantaloni and Ed Southall (2018).	Perfect for students who enjoy lateral thinking.	Supports spatial reasoning, logic and transfer skills in geometry and generally.

Friday fillers	How does it work?	Good activity for:	How is it curriculum secure?
Which One Doesn't Belong?	There are lots of resources for this – see, for example, https://wodb.ca/	Can be as long or as short as the time you need to fill.	Students must identify different groupings or exclusion reasons. Any one of the four images provided could be the one that doesn't belong and the power is seeing students apply different conceptual understandings to make their argument. Great as a warm-up or to encourage debate.
Mega City One	This is a great activity, which you can find in the *MYP by Concept* book (Bateson and Amlin, 2018) or by searching online for Nigel Aughterlaunie + Mega City One – for example, https://x.com/spleenal/status/830185752910774272?lang=en	It involves creating a 3D representation of geometric shapes by first photographing an assembly of random items.	Students use these images and refine and draw on them until they have created a futuristic cityscape. This develops their spatial awareness and dimensional analysis. This can be used once a year at the most!
Algebra with Pizzazz	This is an older book series, from the 1970s, packed full of algebra puzzles, all of which are a key to some pun or joke.	This is ideal for grades 6 to 8, who love to predict what the terrible joke answer might be and then race to find it. And groan at it.	The activities are not random, rather the book indicates which skill or procedural knowledge is fostered in the activity. It looks and feels dated, but the mathematics is sound and the jokes laughably bad!

Friday fillers	How does it work?	Good activity for:	How is it curriculum secure?
Chris Moyles' Musical Maths Shed	This is a set of videos from several years ago. Chris Moyles, a British DJ and TV presenter, used to ask celebrity guests to carry out musical mathematical challenges in real time. Visit The Mathematics Shed here: www.mathematicshed.com/chris-moyles-musical-maths-shed.html	This is fun, as it features some celebrities and songs the students are likely to be familiar with, and can also encourage them to make up their own problems using more recent hit songs.	The questions are sung to the tune of an already famous song and calculated in order by the guests. The students really enjoy comparing the answer provided versus what it should be if the correct order of operations is applied.

It is best if you choose activities that suit your interests for these low-energy, low-resource lessons. A few caveats ... Make sure students are not doing 'meet a mathematician' projects in every year of the MYP. Another valuable unit is on history of mathematics. While it is fascinating for us, twice in the MYP at the very most will suffice. And there must be a gap of at least three years between the incidence of this project, as the learning would naturally progress. It is preferable to do this larger timeline work when students are sufficiently familiar with the four branches. It is better still if they have seen sufficient mathematics to get excited about more modern mathematics such as Big Data, Mersenne primes, the infinite hotel paradox, fractals and the other fun stuff that exists. They need to have the cognitive ability and maturity to at least access these concepts. I find grade 8 an ideal grade for this. It is funny to note students' surprise at the relative youth of mathematical symbols and operations that they have just assumed have been around for ever. The fact that zero is so young also blows their minds, if they are appropriately engaged.

There are other activities that are similarly engaging but are a one-trick pony, such as Möbius strip cutting or pull-up nets, and these are better saved for an appropriate time in the curriculum. Don't let the urgent be the enemy of the important here, and hold them in reserve for the right time.

An interesting extension when discussing the development of number is to ask students how numbers could be represented in any other way. Some will suggest finger-counting or tallies and dots. Others find it incomprehensible that numbers could be any other way than their most familiar form. With the exception of some very specific culture families (e.g. Arabic speaking), students cannot separate the idea of the number from the symbols we use daily.

Speaking of Arabic numbers, one of my very favourite inquiry objects was a clock I bought in a souk in Saudi Arabia many years ago. I revelled in the questions from students when they would finally ask me, at least once a week, 'Miss, what is wrong with your clock?' It would always open an enriching conversation about the development of numbers and the historic contribution of Arabic mathematicians. But beware bringing your favourite objects to school! One day I came back to class and the bin was filled with glass and the clock face. I fished it out and started a furious hunt for the culprit. It turned out the PHE teacher said it fell off the wall and she simply had not realised the significance. I'm certainly not bitter!

There are some games I have had reason to retire. I used to use arithmagons a lot, but I found that students lost interest quickly if they were not immediately successful. Sudoku was also popular for a while, but interest waned over time due to overexposure. I also found it hard to connect to a part of the curriculum in which it would help students build valuable skills. I have tried other games from time to time and like to add to the repertoire. For more on resources for the curriculum, for any time or needs, see the appendix.

'We recognize our interdependence with … the world …'

Key feature: Resource signpost

- Save: templegrandin.com.
- Spend: https://www.youtube.com/watch?v=WlxH06IMHJo.
- Splurge: Splurge – Visual Thinking by Temple Grandin

Key feature: Anecdotal counterexample

Over the years, I have seen the introduction of therapy dogs in schools. The research on the benefit of therapy animals is positive and it is a lovely idea to have them in schools. Personally, I'm highly allergic and I find it a distraction. My own sister is a crazy bird lady who will have her primary students in a classroom while parrots or parakeets are sharing the same airspace. I appreciate the argument, but I cannot get on board with that. Another school I visited started with a therapy dog and then introduced some therapy chickens. Bear in mind this was not a primary school where they would learn from the fascinating hatching process. The school then moved on to a care goat! I rather agreed with the student who grumbled, 'It's like a flipping zoo in this place!' Management simply had not considered that the dog would cause anxiety for some, not to mention the smells!

How do we balance different student needs?

The IB identifies the following four essential principles in approaching differentiated learning. These should build opportunities for students and meet their needs by pursuing appropriate personal learning and achievement goals.

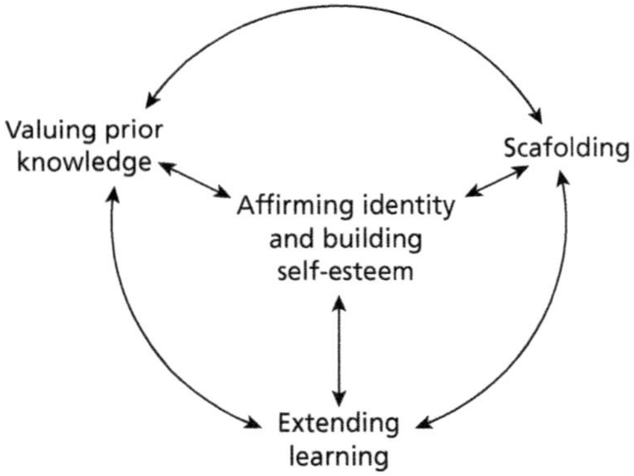

Principles of good practice for differentiated learning

Key feature: Resource signpost

Useful IB publications include:

- *Learning Diversity in the International Baccalaureate Programmes* (2010)
- *Language and Learning in IB Programmes* (2011)
- *Access and Inclusion Policy* (2022).

These publications refer to differentiation within the delivered and assessed curriculum in the following ways: 'Universal design for learning also provides a set of principles for curriculum development that gives all individuals equal opportunities to learn' and 'In these publications, the IB refers to differentiation in the following way - Teaching and learning should be personalised to the maximum feasible extent.' There is also a big distinction between differentiation and accommodations in the IB too.

Teaching and learning that takes place in MYP classrooms can be differentiated in various ways:

- exemplifying work by showing and sharing samples
- discussions of the achievement levels within the assessment criteria
- reviewing the structure and purpose of task-specific clarifications of assessments
- providing opportunities to work in pairs or groups
- giving structures and scaffolding in the form of graphic organisers and writing frames
- providing shorter deadlines and check-in opportunities
- adjusting the pace of learning experiences and activities.

Often students can be directly affected by their language profile, although mathematics can be a source of self-esteem for these transitioning students. Anecdotally, teachers report that they can often recognise more of the delivered curriculum in mathematics than other subjects, due to their language constraints and the (sometimes) ubiquitous nature of mathematical communication or notation.

In MYP Mathematics, the curricular goal is to reach all students where they are, whether they are mathematically curious or anxious. From our unique mathematical perspective, differentiation is understood by us mathematics teachers differently. For us, it is bound inevitably to think of difference in relation to the rate of change! As such, we can consider the valuing of prior knowledge as the constant term that can be analysed or addressed, but ultimately the main action is elsewhere. I see the scaffolding as an analogy for the gradient of learning required and the understanding of the limits of the situation to ensure successful learning while building self-esteem. For the students who are experiencing an educational lag, whether due to the pandemic or for other reasons, this prior learning piece is even more important.

Consider designing a diagnostic assessment for grade levels where you or your department can agree on expected prior knowledge. If time or resources are a challenge, create a diagnostic from the last three Criterion A assessments in the previous grade level. This can provide a baseline of expectations, which can help unpick student blind spots. Other diagnostics are available, such as CAT4 or MAP testing, which can assess student understanding by skills, although their association/correlation with the MYP mathematics framework is not yet fully developed.

'... balancing different aspects of our lives – ... emotional ...'

Other situations where differentiation may be required, or foresight can improve the balance of student needs with curricular outcomes, might include:

Student need	Consideration for mathematical activities planning
Physical limitations	I had a grade 6 class who regularly needed more physically active engagement. Their demeanour was perfectly described by a former colleague, Michel deBier, as 'those grade 6s are like putting popcorn in a microwave'. To counter this, I made sure to build in high-energy competitive mathematics, particularly last period on a Friday afternoon. What I overlooked, though, was that my student with global delay and another with a diagnosis of haemophilia were then virtually excluded from the engagements. We changed the focus from relay games, where pushing and shoving seems to happen, to a 'round the world' focus, which allowed physical space while keeping the competitive element. Students starting at different stations, with more stations than required, meant there was a buffer built in.
Cultural expectations	During Ramadan, Lent and any other religious observances that include elements of fasting, I always encourage my teachers to avoid units that require proportional reasoning, as the discussion will often lead to food or drink consumption. Likewise, activities involving cooking to test quantities in fractions or ratios are better left to the end of the week and not used during the aforementioned periods.
Sensory issues	There have often been sensitivities expressed by students, which I have learned to heed over time. To ignore them is to show a lack of regard to any learning blocks they are experiencing. These include students expressing perfume allergies or dislike of air fresheners. Students can have noise sensitivities to board wiping or chair scuffing. For autistic students, I have kept ear defenders in my room for fire drills. Similarly, a student with a stammer or one who is particularly introverted can suffer when pressured to answer or contribute beyond their comfort zone; I have sought excellent advice online about how to get the best out of these students, meeting them where they are.

'… balancing different aspects of our lives – … physical …'

If you know you have a student with a particular physical or medical **sensitivity**, the best thing is to read their notes fully and carefully, and discuss with their parents or caregivers. Once appropriate, I always speak to the student too, when the time is right. Typically, this conversation includes questions such as 'I noticed that your file mentions you xxxx ... What kind of things happen in class that might bother you?' or 'What do you wish all your teachers knew?' and 'If you were in charge of the school, what would be the first thing you would change?' It may have the positive impact, once they work through all the impossible asks, of something that would allow them greater access to the mathematics curriculum, either emotionally or physically. These types of conversations have resulted in speedy changes, such as 'I wish I could choose my own early departure partner', 'I wish I had a lift pass', 'I wish the teacher asked [or didn't ask] me about my levels', 'I wish I could sit away from the air freshener, window, etc.'

It should be mentioned that one of the main pressure points in an international school can be the high level of expectations of fee-paying parents. They often have a greater level of access to teachers than they would in a different type of school, and they feel very invested in the school relationship to help their child excel in their chosen focus areas. Before you make any commitments, consider whether the parents are looking for a curriculum partner or an accountability partner? Now is the time to take a balanced approach to making any judgement: 'Is what is being asked of me reasonable?' If it is a low-effort request, involving a small or short time commitment I usually say yes; if things are quiet and it is a request I could honour more than once, also yes. Otherwise, sorry, no.

Earlier in my career I felt beholden to find the websites, make recommendations and purchase study guides or exam papers to help them. Only when I moved my own child from one system to another did I feel very differently about the expectations. For the first time I appreciated that this is part of the cost–benefit analysis you make with regard to your child's education. As a parent I wouldn't expect the teacher to do my homework for me, so I do the research and make the commitments to plug the gaps myself. This has made me more insightful and empathetic with these families, and in particular what parents or carers are going through, while providing an *appropriate* level of guidance or assistance. If you want to go above and beyond, please don't let me stop you! All I would suggest is, ensure that you are not setting a precedent to becoming the go-to person for all future requests, of this repeating and annual nature.

Beware recommending Khan Academy, NRICH or IXL unless you have checked them first. Alignment with the US is the first priority of so many websites that you need to review them for usefulness. Alternatively, you may want to use some of the ideas or provocations for possible investigations in class. Check out a few websites that you feel comfortable with. I have my favourites for grades 6/7 and another groups of recommendations specific to grade 8 to 10. When the query arises, when the family is returning 'home' and they are worried their child will fall behind, I direct them to crosswalks or textbooks from their home syllabus. I never address the gaps with them, as that is a family responsibility.

In addition, since the pandemic the majority of tutoring has moved online, so it is much easier for families to source their own ACT or PSAT tutor. If the family has access to technology at home, they could be encouraged to experiment with using AI to differentiate and tutor to address any particular needs. Prompts such as 'Take on the persona of an experienced MYP teacher, helping out a student who is struggling with [concept, skill or topic]. Ask me questions until you have enough information about my knowledge now to help me progress my understanding in this area.' Encourage them to be 'mathematical risk-takers' with technology! Many families have not yet considered this as a support option.

I do offer to do a curriculum comparison if families can provide me with the home curriculum, at any point throughout the year. I leave it with them and often only hear back at the end of the year when preparations to return home have begun in earnest. If you are considering doing this for a family, before you start mapping, consider the direction of travel – it is usually more helpful for the families to move the MYP content and conceptual objectives to match where they are going to next. Consider each of the branches and where it matches or maps to the other curriculum, in the following order:

1. Begin with *numerical and algebraic reasoning*: these make up a large section of most international curriculums and this is something the next teacher will appreciate. Indicate what has been 'covered' to date and what has not, from which the family or school can generate a gap analysis.
2. Next, complete *the spatial reasoning branch*. Repeat the procedure but pay particular attention to trigonometry as the age group where this is introduced can move and shift throughout curriculums globally.
3. Continue the mapping for *reasoning with data*. Many systems have a lesser focus on statistics and data than the MYP, with a greater emphasis on algebra, for example. Students may find they are significantly ahead in S&P but behind in pre-calculus algebra in some cases.
4. Lastly, ensure that all of the framework points for reasoning with models have been reflected and matched where possible. If you are not seeing a direct match, consider alternative wording, such as functions or relationships. This is often integrated into algebra, or parts thereof, so can be mapped with this branch of reasoning also.

There are no opportunities to map the development of ATLs, such as thinking skills, and transfer to a similar idea in other systems – so it is often helpful for the next school to have a brief paragraph outlining this skill development. I often use a summary of any information I have shared with parents through reports or meetings, and capture it in the curriculum mapping to give greater insight.

We should not aim for a fully personalised and differentiated curriculum yet – there must remain a commonality to the experience or students could all stay at home and complete the work in splendid isolation. So this is not a counsel of despair, rather a profound gratitude that we are not obsolete. At least, not yet. There is a depth to any learning when it is shared and achieved together. The pandemic did more to illuminate this to families, as I think teachers were always aware of the need for personal care and interaction. For students, memories are formed and relationships strengthened. If the students are learning, and we are thriving through efficiencies and healthy limits, then balance is achieved.

Self-assessment

Complete the reflection:

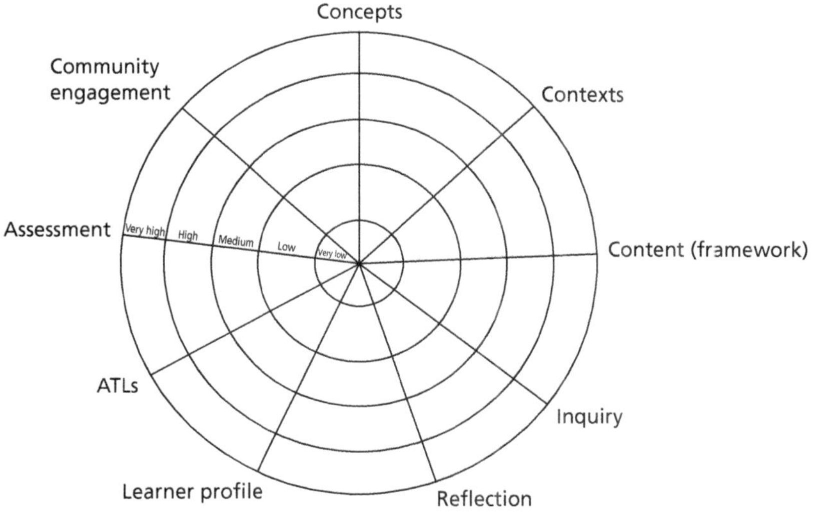

Shade in your knowledge level from low to high as you feel your comfort level lies.

Glossary

Adversarial Competitive.

Burnout A state of emotional, physical and mental exhaustion caused by excessive and prolonged stress. It typically results from being overwhelmed, overworked or feeling undervalued, and leads to reduced productivity, loss of motivation and feelings of ineffectiveness.

Collegial A relationship characterised by shared responsibility, authority and a spirit of cooperation among colleagues, typically within a workplace or professional setting. It emphasises mutual respect and equality among peers.

Congenial A colleague or atmosphere that is pleasant, friendly and agreeable in nature, creating a comfortable and enjoyable working relationship.

Curriculum security Stability in educational offerings, and the guarantee that all students can access the educational resources necessary to achieve academic success and personal growth.

Scarcity A situation where educational resources, opportunities or access are limited. This can include shortages of qualified teachers, insufficient academic materials, lack of funding for schools, limited access to advanced courses or technology, and overcrowded classrooms.

Sensitivity The quality or condition of being easily affected, influenced, or harmed by external factors or stimuli.

None of the above are official IB definitions.

CHAPTER 9
CARING

We show empathy, compassion and respect. We have a commitment to service, and we act to make a positive difference in the lives of others and in the world around us.

Key thinking points

In this chapter, there are explanations/discussions of:

- the reasons for choosing Caring as the learner profile attribute for this chapter
- suggestions for applying a sensitivity reading process to curriculum
- provocations to consider where diversity, equity, inclusion, belonging and ideas of justice can be applied to mathematics
- analyses of particular student or parent/carer needs, and how we can care for them
- contemplations on how we should care for mathematics itself.

Why choose Caring as the learner profile attribute for this chapter?

Caring in education can make all the difference between a robotic, impersonal experience at school and a life-changing one. The MYP years are particularly challenging for adolescents' development as they forge their sense of self and identity. As a result, we often need to practise empathy and compassion for ourselves, our students, and the wider family and school community. By committing to this caring approach, we truly can make a positive difference in their experience with mathematics. This chapter is devoted to ways to show that caring, in a practical and tangible way.

Who is this chapter useful for?

This is a good chapter for teachers in schools with diverse populations, whether inclusive schools or selective, also schools with high needs or high expectations. It is an important chapter for coordinators, heads of department and PTAs, as well as marketing departments, as caring for all the stakeholders is a tall order. This chapter is also helpful for anyone focused on increasing diversity, equity, inclusion, justice and belonging (DEIJB) in their curriculum.

First and foremost, we care for the students.

How can we demonstrate caring for students?

'We show … compassion …'

Showing care and compassion for our students may not always happen in real time. We have opportunities to care for them before and after our teaching and learning time, as much as we do during it. In this section, we will discuss one way that students can feel cared for, in **representation** and thoughtfulness by applying a sensitivity reading process to our curriculum throughout.

Sensitivity reading and DEIJB focus

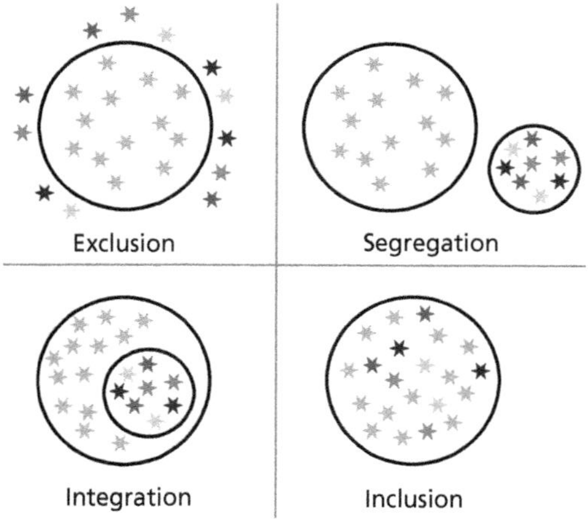

Source: https://www.readingrockets.org/inclusive-classroom-books-educators

General considerations for teachers and leaders

What is sensitivity reading? A sensitivity reader, or DEIJB (diversity, equity, inclusion, justice and belonging) consultant, serves an important function in educational contexts. By applying a deep understanding of various cultures, identities and experiences, they can help ensure that written content is respectful, accurate and inclusive. A sensitivity reader can identify potential issues related to representation, stereotypes and **bias**. They can alert the writer to oversights, bias or inaccuracies that may occur regarding race, ethnicity, gender, sexuality, religion, neurodivergence and **disability**, among other factors.

In this way, unintended or unintentionally harmful representations can be avoided. Sensitivity reading is typically applied to narrative or descriptive text, but the ideas can be transferred into general instruction, from classroom culture to assessment inclusion. It can be helpful, too, to know if your school/audience has policies or standards regarding sensitive issues? Have these been cross-referenced?

Try to ensure you are familiar with a wide range of cultures, identities and experiences, including those outside your own lived experiences. Reading, viewing and listening widely can be beneficial in this regard – researching further is always recommended. Librarians, trusted colleagues and parents can be a source of review or approval.

Remember that societal norms and understandings evolve. Sensitivity filters should be applied sparingly in the analysis of historical or contemporary texts, to avoid revisionist history or retconning. Recognise also that no one can be an expert in all areas, and listen to voices that might alert you to your own 'blind spots' or bias. Recognise where your scope of experience begins and ends. Try not to let potential insensitivities block or destroy the author's creative intent or voice. Look for minor adjustments over radical removals.

'Deep transformational change around diversity, equity, inclusion, and belonging can't just be transactional. It has to be relational.'

– Aiko Bethea, leader, builder & connector

Here are some factors to consider in all aspects of your planned, delivered and assessed curriculum:

- Stereotypical portrayals: avoid characters defined solely by a single characteristic, such as race, gender, disability or sexual orientation, without depth or complexity. Make sure writing avoids clichés that reinforce harmful stereotypes. These vary dramatically from context to context, culture to culture.

Where possible, avoid associating or overusing certain pronouns with certain occupations, making assumptions about rationality or emotions correlating to gender stereotypes (e.g. male engineer, women are overly emotional).

Stereotypical portrayals of family life can also cause some sensitivity among students, where assumptions of a certain type of family structure or heteronormativity are made. Exercises involving family trees, genetic legacies and suchlike can prove more challenging for students who are adopted, those from family conflicts or divorce, or who have experienced the loss of family members. Representations of family structures beyond the nuclear family with traditional gender roles can be considered. Community maps can be an inclusive alternative in these situations.

- *Cultural appropriation and misrepresentation:* depicting a culture inaccurately or in a way that trivialises its depth and significance. Authors using elements of a culture for aesthetic or thematic purposes without understanding their meaning or respecting their origin.
- *Insensitive language and terminology:* using outdated or offensive terms to describe racial, ethnic, sexual or disability-related identities, or employing language that is derogatory or dismissive of mental health issues, body shapes or gender identities.
- *Overlooking socioeconomic diversity:* ignoring the complexities and nuances of socioeconomic status and class, leading to a one-dimensional portrayal of poverty or wealth. This can be a potent block to assessments especially (e.g. assuming that students will understand that in golf it is desirable to achieve a lower score rather than a higher one). Likewise, using financial frameworks or quantities that are wildly out of kilter with the audience's lived experience or expectations (see triggers, below) – for example, a problem based on activities like sailing, which may not be familiar or accessible to students from landlocked regions, can be confusing.
- *Representation – inclusive examples:* suggesting the revision of questions or scenarios that inadvertently perpetuate stereotypes or exclude certain cultures. For instance, if a mathematics problem includes only names and contexts typical of a single culture, a sensitivity reader might recommend incorporating a diverse set of names and culturally varied scenarios to reflect a broader spectrum of student backgrounds.

- *Tokenism:* this is hugely important to get right when increasing **diversity** in representation, as discussed above. Inclusion without depth or belonging can lead to an 'othering' or 'fetishisation' effect. Where changes are made and diversity increased, ensure that characters or characteristics from a marginalised group have a meaningful role within the situation. Scenarios and representations in education should reflect the widest possible range of experiences and backgrounds, presenting them in a positive, respectful manner.

  Often, diverse roles or representations can be made submissive to the stories or needs of the more dominant group. The goal is not to 'claim' diversity by paying lip service to it. Ensure representation of a wide range of identities and experiences, including different races, genders, disabilities and socioeconomic backgrounds. This ensures all students can see themselves reflected in the material and understand the application of concepts in diverse contexts.
- *Historical representation:* take care when referring to historical facts or figures that consideration has been given, in a balanced or thoughtful way, to oppression, colonisation or injustice, especially in relation to the impact on marginalised communities. One example I have seen in class was a deep-seated and contextually appropriate objection to the game 'hangman'.
- *Representation of illness, divergence or disabilities:* a sensitivity concern can arise from an inaccurate representation of all of these. Take care not to treat an illness, divergence or disability as something that needs to be endured, overcome or triumphed over. Pay attention to those communities that have a diversity of thought on their self-identity (e.g. the deaf community or children with diabetes).
- *Sensitivity to potentially distressing content (triggers):* there is a division of opinion regarding the effectiveness of **trigger** or content warnings. There is a growing body of evidence to suggest that they do not lessen anxiety and may increase distress or anticipation. That being said, each curriculum developer and teacher will know their audiences best and an awareness of the triggers is beneficial at the very least.

  Highlighting content that could be distressing or triggering for some students without educational justification, such as unnecessary references to violence, abuse or **discrimination**, should be avoided. These are sometimes called triggers, and you may notice the media can sometimes give a trigger or content warning before a broadcast to allow viewers a choice. In assessments, no such choice is possible, so it is imperative to consider the choice of prompts carefully. Possible prompts to consider may be:

- *Violence and abuse:* apply a high standard of sensitivity, especially in matters of consent and/or violence. Consider the impact on students of failing to handle the topic with the sensitivity it demands. Even in abstract subjects, references to conflict, violence or disasters (even if used metaphorically or hypothetically) can be distressing to students who have experienced trauma related to these issues.
- *Socioeconomic assumptions:* scenarios involving expensive vacations, luxury items or even assumptions about home life, can alienate or upset students from different economic backgrounds and make accessing questions more difficult. Attempt to use a variety of contexts for word problems that don't presume specific economic advantages. Including scenarios that are universally accessible or abstract can help avoid these triggers. Students who experience economic hardship, poverty, financial instability or food insecurity may be more sensitive to questions of a monetary nature (budgeting, taxation, payday loans, etc.). Those from an affluent background may have had limited experience of payment, budgeting or resource allocation, and may not have the assumed background knowledge required to access financial questions (e.g. price comparisons or making savings).
- *Body image:* scenarios focusing on calorie counting, food tracking, weight loss, weight gain, body measurement or exercise might be sensitive for students dealing with disordered eating, body dysmorphia or body image issues. Choose health-neutral metrics, or questions without the need to track or measure, unless the data are relevant and the concept well articulated.
- *Medical, health and wellbeing-related content:* this may be an area of trauma for some students who have personal or family experiences with these conditions – for example, questions of cancer, death or mental instability should be addressed, not avoided, but with the correct supports and classroom culture in place. Using diseases or medical conditions as contexts for statistical problems, such as calculating the spread of a virus or the effectiveness of a treatment, can be appropriate with the correct supports in place. Questions that directly reference mental health issues such as depression, anxiety, suicide or self-harm can be particularly sensitive. While it's important to educate about mental health, care must be taken not to trigger students who might be personally affected.

- *Religious beliefs:* guidance regarding usury, gambling, controlled substances or sexuality may not be an appropriate avenue for inquiry in certain contexts. Similarly, directly questioning students on sensitive issues (such as political beliefs or religious practices) in a test setting might cause anxiety or discomfort, especially if the students feel their personal views could be judged. The IB has clear guidance regarding evolution and climate change, and teaching and learning should reflect this correctly. Where discussions such as these can intersect with religious beliefs, it's essential to navigate these topics with care, and communication with the home may be advisable. For example, when designing a chance carnival, all parents should be informed in advance regarding the study of risk and fairness, to allow full understanding and to permit adaptations where necessary.
- *Discrimination:* questions that touch on experiences of racism, sexism, homophobia, transphobia or any form of discrimination can be triggering, especially for students who have faced such issues directly.
- *Substance abuse, addiction and illegality:* some students may have personal or family experiences with substance abuse. These questions can evoke emotional responses or bring up difficult memories. Questions should be worded carefully to minimise bias, judgement or personal disclosure.
- *Disaster or tragedy:* problems that involve calculating the aftermath of natural disasters (e.g. death tolls, destruction costs) or outcomes of violent events can be traumatic for students who have lived through disasters or tragedy. Examples of this can be seen in the development of IB questions over the years where questions involving the collision of boats or aircraft or people modelling projectiles from a height have been avoided over time, for good reason.
- *Foods:* word problems involving the preparation or consumption of foods that are forbidden in some religions or cultures can be avoided by choosing generic or universally acceptable foods and scenarios that do not single out or potentially disrespect any religious dietary restrictions. Some examples are questions that might include beef, pork or dairy constituents.

If a student is triggered by something in the planned, delivered or assessed curriculum

Offer support and resources for students who might be affected by content, including counselling services or discussion forums to process any discomfort experienced. This support should be provided by a qualified, trained professional and any incident of this nature should be reported immediately to the relevant staff in school.

Remember to seek and take feedback from students and colleagues on the inclusivity and sensitivity of assessment materials, and be willing to make adjustments based on that feedback. The goal is not to avoid complex themes or issues, or to reduce resilience in our students, but to ensure that potentially sensitive content is essential for achieving the learning objective. We aim to broaden the scope of our students' representation and experience, and create an inclusive, respectful learning environment for all.

By being proactive and thoughtful in test design, educators can minimise potential triggers and support a more inclusive and emotionally safe learning environment for all students. Foster an environment where students feel comfortable discussing their needs and concerns regarding curriculum content that intersects with their religious beliefs. Implement a feedback mechanism where students can express concerns about test content. This can help identify unforeseen issues and inform future test design.

Sensitivity and inclusion in the classroom

Be mindful of gendered language when speaking with groups: 'guys', 'lads', 'mankind', 'manpower' are all terms that place men at the centre or in a place of dominance within conversation. Consider different terms when addressing groups.

When giving generic references, consider adding more dimensions – for example, I recently heard a presenter talk about Joe and Jane Bloggs, and I reflected how easy it would have been for the speaker to add another example to be more non-binary inclusive, such as Joe, Jane and Jay Bloggs. American educators seem to have a preference for little 'Billy' and 'Susie' or 'Janey', and similar expansion could be easy to integrate.

Always ensure classroom content and discussions are age and/or developmentally appropriate. Is the maturity level respected while appropriately challenged?

In conversation with students I have made more than my fair share of blunders. When I left Ireland, divorce was not only non-existent but illegal. Subsequently it didn't really feature in my mind. After several corrections when I'd said, 'Ask your mum and dad', I learned not to assume that parents lived together. And so I began to say what I thought was more progressive, 'Who do you live with, mum or dad?', as few seemed to mind correcting me with a surprised 'Both!' and others could answer freely one or the other. I thought I had cracked it!

One day, I was reprimanding a student, getting ready to follow up with a 'and how are they going to feel when I contact them about this?' when I asked my usual question, 'Who do you live with, mum or dad?' The student looked me straight in the eyes, waited a few seconds and then said, 'Well, I live with both my mums.' A lesson well learned about my implicit bias, how heteronormative I had been, and I endeavoured to be more thoughtful in my references to home from then on.

Sensitivity and inclusion in the curriculum

Do source choices promote international-mindedness and offer a global perspective? Are the themes relevant and engaging to the target age group? Does the content promote ethical reflection and the development of personal values?

Many Jehovah's Witness families, and other specific sects or orthodox branches of different religions, object to the use of *Harry Potter* references, or similar mentions of magic-making or superstition. This can have an unexpected impact on 'magic trick' examples in mathematics, such as a magic mind-reading algorithm or other so-called magic tricks within algebra.

Sensitivity and inclusion in assessments

When reviewing assessments, we are aiming to enhance their fairness, inclusivity and educational value:

- Are there opportunities for variety within the question contexts, or prompts to promote international-mindedness or inclusion? Have you made use of opportunities to feature the host country in an international school context?
- Is the assessment readily available in different formats to meet a variety of learning needs? Large text, supplementary materials and other accommodations are crucial for inclusion within assessment.
- Ensure that questions require an appropriate level of disclosure or information. Students might feel uncomfortable answering questions that ask them to share personal experiences or opinions on topics they may not feel comfortable discussing in an academic setting, especially if the content touches on identity, personal beliefs or private life.
- The use of measurement units (like miles, kilometres or any imperial unit) or currency (dollars vs. other currencies) specific to particular regions can disadvantage those students unfamiliar with them. Try to align with IB expectations and symbols where possible; likewise use the command terms in assessments to reinforce their meaning and rigour.

- Ensure that the language used in problems is clear, concise and free of colloquialisms or culturally specific references that could confuse students from diverse backgrounds.

Inspired by these principles, I applied them to a set of end-of-unit assessments across subjects. When analysed, it showed that almost 92% of images used in the assessments, when depicting a human, featured a middle-aged European or American male, either present day or historical. This was particularly noticeable in PHE, as the images were not of historical figures or sportspeople but served to represent a pose or skill. The teachers were admirably open to replacing them with a more diverse representation, and it did not impact the rigour but modelled inclusivity for our students.

In a similar vein, I saw recently that a similar audit of journalists' quotations and experts in the *Financial Times* gave such shocking results in favour of male voices that it has introduced a bot in writing that will alert the author if their sources become unbalanced or unrepresentative. A useful bot indeed!

Sensitivity and inclusion in communications

Ensure that language in emails, newsletters and reports or feedback is clear and concise. The simplification of language should not compromise content quality but should ensure it is understandable by parents, carers and students for whom English might be an additional language. This might include avoiding idiomatic expressions or culturally specific references that could confuse non-native speakers.

Addressing communications to parents/carers/loved ones can be made more inclusive. Likewise, some choose to use their email signature to identify their chosen pronouns or name pronunciation, using tools such as namecoach.com.

Extending your inclusivity – how to take a more active role in this space

In assessment, review any prompts or scenarios to add in diversity. Do you include only capital cities, for example? Are your questions often referring to the same countries or scenarios? Can variation be introduced here?

Is it possible to elevate the minor? Meaning is there a way of amplifying quieter voices? Who is usually not consulted or represented in this type of thinking? Consider the prevalence or occurrence of the following in your planned, delivered or assessed curriculum:

- First Nations and Indigenous peoples

- Roma, Romany or Travelling Communities
- representations of older adults, a variety of ages or future generations
- displaced peoples
- the balance between male and female representation.

An interesting example

In New Zealand, the Wellbeing Lab acknowledges and respects the Elders and Aboriginals.

The New Zealand curriculum has reviewed and consulted widely to ensure that it incorporates the entirety of the country's history and culture: 'From 2023, Te Takanga o Te Wā and Aotearoa New Zealand's histories will be part of all kura and schools' marau ā-kura and local curriculum' (Tui Tuia | Learning Circle, n.d.).

Look for teaching resources that allow localisation or personalisation. For example, experiment with PhET simulations (see, for example, https://phet.colorado.edu/sims/html/number-line-distance/latest/number-line-distance_all.html). These allow variety within the portrayal of people, place or objects in various simulations. PhET is careful to say that the images are not intended to 'represent the entire diversity of a region or culture'.

Specific to mathematics, try to expand your repertoire of **ethnomathematics** as much as you can. Islamic geometric patterns are beautiful and powerful, but why not simultaneously discuss the geometry of the Tartan clans, the shuka of the Maasai, Amish quilts and Japanese sangaku?

Using Microsoft Word Editor

One of the useful tools within the Editor function in some versions of Microsoft Word (e.g. Word 365 for Windows) is the feedback it gives on written content. (Google Docs has something similar, as do many AI models.) This will provide suggestions or corrections to be considered for the following scenarios, among others:

- sensitive geopolitical references – promotes using official or neutral names and phrases
- Editor recommends avoiding words that are specific to a US region – for example, it will suggest replacing *bubbler* with *water fountain*
- biased terms – it will suggest replacements for geopolitical terms that may imply bias, such as to replace *Orient* with *East Asia*
- current names for places whose names have changed over time (e.g. *GDR*, *Leningrad*)

- using modern transliterations, such as *Chongqing* instead of *Chungking*
- using official names of languages, such as *Persian* rather than *Farsi, or European Spanish/Spanish* over *standard Spanish*.

Advanced consideration

Intersectionality is a framework that recognises how various aspects of a person's identity – such as race, gender, class, sexuality and disability – interact in complex ways to shape their experiences and the ways they may face discrimination or privilege. In the context of the MYP, applying an intersectional approach to curriculum development can help educators create content that acknowledges and respects the multifaceted identities of their students, ensuring that the curriculum is inclusive and reflective of the complexities of student identities and social contexts. The goal is to apply a caring approach to all of the ideas above and to integrate these self-checks into our curriculum appropriately.

Key feature: Resource signpost

- Audiobook and book: *Demystifying Disability: What to Know, What to Say and How to Be an Ally*, by Emily Ladau (2021)
- Podcast and book: *The Authority Gap*, by Mary Ann Seighart (2021)

Now that we have looked at how we can be more caring of the different identities in our communities, let us look at how we apply the learner profile attribute of Caring to students in their uniqueness. It is not long into a teaching career when teachers discover that groups of students can have a personality unique to themselves. One of the skills that an experienced teacher will value is how to integrate that nature into their planning. Is it a group that relishes competition? Are they a class that needs time and space to process concepts?

'... we act to make a positive difference in the lives of others ...'

Does their particular group temperament impact your choices of inquiry? It can be nice to integrate their interests, and AI models can make suggestions for this. There is a very small window, too, where a fad can be embedded: using bottle flipping, Pokémon, dank memes, fidget spinners, TikTok videos and suchlike. These have a very short shelf life, but their use can be powerful if timed well. Beware, though: as soon as you reference something like this, it will become uncool. Students secretly appreciate the effort nonetheless.

'We show empathy ...'

How can we demonstrate caring for parents?

In the Communicators chapter (chapter 7), we consider supporting students in their various feelings and experiences with mathematics. We then develop this idea in the Balanced chapter (chapter 8) to consider how to balance their needs and expectations with our own. In terms of the delivered and assessed curriculum, another key stakeholder to consider is the family, typically with one point of contact (most frequently a mother or father) who communicates with the school. There is an argument to be made that we should show empathy and be caring with parents to, and to ourselves when those interactions are challenging.

Some parents or caregivers want more information than others, some press for a faster or slower pace, less or more homework, or explanations of grades, and some would prefer never to hear from you! There are those who are keen, clueless, involved or less so. As previously posited, mathematics seems to hold a much larger part of the educational psyche in parents than you would expect. Our conferences and meetings are often overbooked, and head teachers frequently report that dealing with parents takes up a disproportional amount of their time. This has been the pattern in school and after school, and it shows no sign of abating. Could it be that parents and caregivers are transferring too?

We should recall that in the context of many MYP schools, these are private or international schools, which can correlate to high expectations. Once I was teaching a grade 7 class and the door opened and in walked a mother of one of the students. She sauntered breezily in and sat down. Funnily enough, she did not sit next to her own child but chose a seat elsewhere, reached out and started to flip through the work of another student in the class! She stayed for the entire lesson and in my naivety and shock I didn't ask her to leave. I wish I had. The closest thing to brave I did that lesson was involve her in the questioning and put her on the spot for responses. At the end, she thanked me for the interesting lesson and reminded me to keep it up as her son would one day be attorney general and needed to excel. I was speechless (and couldn't wait to get to the staffroom to tell everyone!).

It alerted me to the privilege that some parents experience in that they feel free to assess and judge our curriculum in a myriad of ways, and empowered enough to bring that to our attention.

There will always be parents who want more or feel they might have an insight into mathematics. They might consider that the student needs extension or support, and they turn to you. How can this be managed reasonably within the curriculum?

For supportive parents looking to integrate mathematics into their daily lives, conversations and even viewing habits, please see the list of ideas and recommendations in the appendix. These can be useful at parent teacher conferences, as social media content or part of a newsletter/update communication. Some families may still have residual trauma from lockdown home-schooling experiences, so use these judiciously and match them to an appropriate unit so the link is authentic. Important, too, is that it is optional – it is impossible to try to reach into the home and impose anything on an environment with students of this age and the various relationships going on in this developmental stage. We are simply laying breadcrumbs for those interested parents, which can be ignored by time-poor or less interested families.

During protest marches, it is a known phenomenon that peaceful actions can be hijacked by 'bad actors' who are more interested in chaos or looting. Organisers talk about the importance of policing their boundaries and maintaining the focus. If you have followed protocols and been really professional, what can you do about a parent or carer who, like my classroom visitor, breaches your boundaries?

Tips on caring for parents regarding the planned, delivered and assessed curriculum

In order of frequency, you will hear from parents about assessments, then delivered curriculum (usually teaching style) and planned curriculum (usually content), and in that order. Treat each concern with care and use a different approach for each.

Assessed curriculum

- Mark quickly and often. Once I sought out comprehensive feedback from a group of students and the major theme was their frustration that it would take me a week or more to return an assessment. From then on, I always tried to stagger my assessments so that I had no more than two to correct at any given time and always marked them by the next class. I know that sounds unrealistic, but the boost it gives students and the trust it engenders in families is so valuable.
- Always give the relevant criteria on the assessment, with or without task-specific clarifications as it can bring home to families that there is no direct percentage or letter grade equivalent, and that the marking is transparent and linked to the competencies demonstrated.
- Never leave anything as a surprise for parents or caregivers. Be proactive and communicative by notifying them when a piece of work or achievement level is out of character, good or bad. This makes meetings smoother and

gives them very little chance to suggest that they have been blindsided, which means that the student gets the care they need from all angles.

- If a parent is challenging a grade or the validity of an assessment, make sure to include your head of department or coordinator in any communications. Consider using AI to add diplomatic language to your true feelings. These conversations can get heated and usually escalate quickly.

  It takes a great deal of empathy and compassion to understand that the criticism may be as a result of lack of education about the MYP and can be rooted in their own fears, either for their child or from their own experiences with mathematics. Did they struggle with the subject themselves, or is it because they are highly successful and attribute some part of their success to excellence in mathematics and other subjects? Note, too, the prevalence in IB schools of families with parents working in a corporate, educational or professional setting, and how this impacts their scrutiny of mathematics. It can feel exhausting and unfair. I choose now to see it as an opportunity to harness their interest to increase support at home, but it took years for me to have the experience and confidence to shift that focus.

Delivered curriculum

- Let's talk about the one who always wants more! While we are striving for a realistic and sustainable level of support, refer to the Balanced chapter (chapter 8). You are not the tutor or the organiser of their home activities, even if some parents might hope that you are. Ensure that you are meeting the needs of the students in a **reasonable** way and look at chapter 8 for suggestions on how to prioritise commitments and kindness to ensure that families, students, you and mathematics are all properly cared for.
- Many IB schools are private or fee-paying, and have expectations on your workload that may take you aback. Determine what you and cannot provide, when it is appropriate to refer onwards or refuse to support. There might be an expectation to give up your lunchtimes and break-times or other calls on your time. Take care not to take on a parental responsibility for extending or supporting a child beyond what is reasonable. Your role in this instance is to act as a signposter or a conduit to weekend and evening opportunities.
- You may decide that you would love to enrich the programme or the students' experience, and more power to you if you can! You might, at certain points in your career, decide that you'd like to accompany them. You might even feel that it would be beneficial to be seen to add value.

Consider carefully several factors, as I have seen the cycle of enchantment to disenchantment play out many times:

- Is it an activity you enjoy?
- What are the opportunity costs?
- How much does the time allocated benefit the students or you in your curriculum?
- What will happen when it is a time dedication you cannot afford?
- Do you love the activity, or do you have a connection with these particular students or cohort?
- Is it a self-sustaining thing? Something the PTA could support? Something that brings funding or prestige to the school?
- Will it impact on your home life?

If you can feel comfortable with your answers, then make the commitment to show caring in this way.

- Assume good intentions. We have to be mindful that we might not like or agree with their parenting choices or occasional apparent lack of interest, but ours is not the role of parent nor personal tutor. If they do ask you to help support their tutor, proceed with caution. Remember that there is no way to quality-assure external help, and you don't want to engage with the idea that the student is not getting adequate support or learning opportunities in your class.

Key feature: Who to follow

Brené Brown has lots of good guidance on parenting that might help reframe interactions with a 'difficult' parent. For example:

- podcast – https://brenebrown.com/podcasts/
- quotes – https://www.goodreads.com/quotes/9856333-assuming-positive-intent-does-not-mean-that-we-stop-helping

Planned curriculum

- One way we can show caring and empathy to parents is when they have questions or concerns about the planned curriculum. A frequent one might be that they have come from or are returning to a different system and perceive that their child is behind or ahead – or will be so when they get back. They can misinterpret the out-of-sequence nature of the move. They may insist on your cross-referencing or ensuring that gaps are addressed. This is a huge amount of work in many instances and the most caring, and efficient, thing to do is to direct them to, or provide them with, the multiple crosswalks online. There are state standards matching documents, lots of IB publications and, if all else fails, they can contact IB Answers themselves. Your responsibility is to deliver the MYP to the best of your ability and ensure that students are fully challenged within your school environs.

What about caring for mathematics?

'We have a commitment to service …'

In a curriculum review meeting during the development of the 'new' DP courses for Mathematics there was some time dedicated to talking about parts of the programme that might be overlooked in the excitement of playing with the content and concepts. There is a risk that such conversations could be perfunctory or tokenistic. Alternatively, someone will drop something that can have profoundly lasting effects that might change the course of the curriculum. The meeting was deftly led by Deb Sutch, and the participants got really stuck in with discussions of ATLs in the Diploma (still relatively new at the time) and the learner profile attributes.

We were in the middle of such a conversation about how we could see the different learner profile attributes manifesting in DP Mathematics and we were on 'Caring'. Unsurprisingly, most examples rallied around using data to help with **equity** and **inclusion**, or using trigonometry to make spaces accessible, when one participant blew my mind with his contribution. His name was Caspar and he simply said, 'But what about caring for mathematics too? Don't we have a responsibility to care for our subject itself?'

That simple comment has rolled around my brain like a marble for years. I love this idea that reminds us that the subject itself deserves the care and attention to do justice to it. Up to that point I thought mathematics should be used as a utility subject to help make the world a better place. This was a reminder that we can demonstrate caring to mathematics itself by advocacy of our subject. It was a cri de coeur that care can be shown by using correct mathematical communication or in a commitment to accuracy to the real world showing truth and validity. It was such a profound statement.

As the watch company once claimed, 'You never actually own a Patek Philippe. You merely look after it for the next generation.' This is how we can view our work – we aren't teaching mathematics, we are keeping it safe so we can transfer it to the next generation, in a long, almost continuous chain through the generations.

Self-assessment

Complete the reflection:

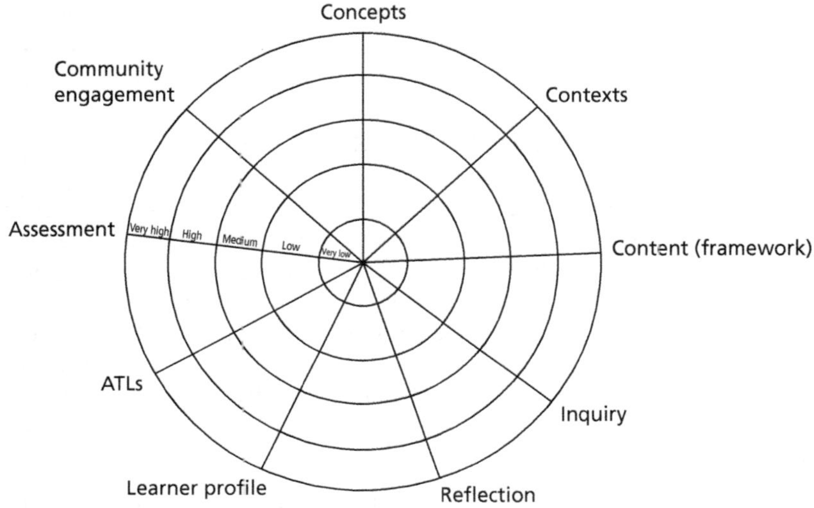

Shade in your knowledge level from low to high as you feel your comfort level lies.

Glossary

Bias Where a defined group (that is, racial or ethnic group or gender) performs differently on a specific question or task than the average for a reason other than ability in the trait that is being assessed.

Disability Refers to any physical or mental factor that complicates an individual's ability to perform specific activities and engage with their environment.*

Discrimination Unfair or unequal treatment of different categories of people based on specific characteristics shared by those categories.*

Diversity Refers to difference and uniqueness. Valuing diversity is about acceptance and recognition.

Equity As defined by the OECD, 'Equity in education has two dimensions. The first is fairness, which basically means making sure that personal and social circumstances – for example gender, socioeconomic status or ethnic origin – should not be an obstacle to achieving educational potential. The second is inclusion, in other words ensuring a basic minimum standard of education for all – for example that everyone should be able to read, write and do simple arithmetic. The two dimensions are closely intertwined: tackling access to and failure to achieve school outcomes helps to overcome the effects of social deprivation which often causes lack of access and quality outcomes.'

Ethnomathematics In educational mathematics, ethnomathematics explores the connection between mathematics and culture.*

Inclusion An ongoing process that aims to increase access to and engagement in learning for all students by identifying and removing barriers.

Reasonable adjustments Changes or additional conditions to the assessment process, which may not be standard and not covered in the list of inclusive access arrangements. They are unique to a student based on their requirements.

Representation The manner in which something is presented.

Trigger Something that initiates or causes a specific reaction or process to start.*

* *Not an official IB definition.*

CHAPTER 10
THINKERS

We use critical and creative thinking skills to analyse and take responsible action on complex problems. We exercise initiative in making reasoned, ethical decisions.

Key thinking points

In this chapter, there are explanations/discussions of:

- the reasons for choosing Thinkers as a learner profile attribute for the chapter on approaches to learning (ATLs) and community engagement (service)
- the mind in the MYP; ATL skills
- ATLs in mathematics
- the heart of the MYP – creativity; how to decorate our world with mathematics
- looking up, down and all around
- the hands of the MYP – service and community engagement; how to serve the world using mathematics.

DNA model – If ATLs are skills, how do they interact with content and skills, cracking the code of the DNA? Is this the last internal part of the DNA?

Why choose Thinkers as the learner profile attribute for this chapter?

The learner profile attribute Thinkers is a perfect match for this chapter as we consider aspects of curriculum development that engage the head, the heart and the hands. Reading the definition of 'critical and creative thinking', I think of some of the approaches to learning (ATLs) skills. When we see that students should 'take **responsible action**' we think of **service** learning, **service as action** and all the various forms of community engagement in the IB. When schools allow their students and teachers to exercise initiative, they can harness or ignite the creativity within.

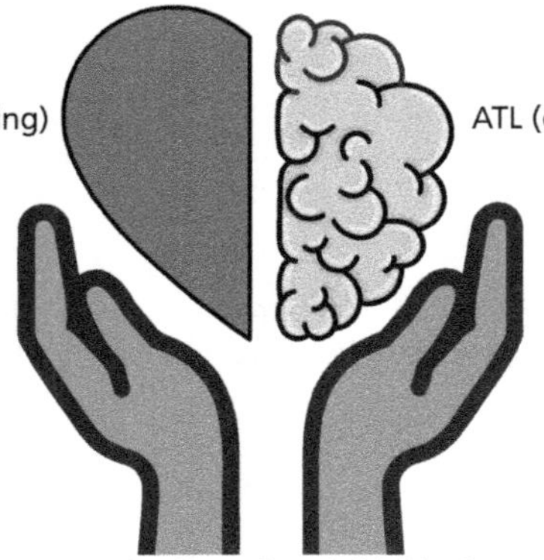

Mathematics can appear in the unlikeliest of places and, if we allow it, it can decorate time and space. All this thinking should give us answers to the ultimate MYP question: How can I use what I have to make the world a better place or myself a better person?

Who is this chapter useful for?

This chapter is intended for classroom teachers who feel their lessons are a tiny bit flat or are looking for inspiration. These teachers are likely to be confident and competent in their classroom delivery but looking for another challenge. It is for those who want to try out some of the cool stuff they see on Instagram or TikTok but are not sure when, where or how it is possible. It may be helpful for those with responsibility, such as service learning or ATL coordinators who keep trying to break into the mathematics curriculum but are struggling.

This chapter will suit MYP coordinators who recognise that mathematics needs love too, even when colleagues seem resistant. I hope they find ideas within to better connect with those who are hesitant or change-resistant. For more experienced teachers, who are confident in delivery, it may just take them to the next level of creativity. And for anyone anywhere in their career path, it may nudge them into re-evaluating their surroundings and mathifying them a little bit more than they currently are. My hope is that, by the end of it, you will be like my creative friend So-Shan, who complained, jokingly, that I was making her see mathematics everywhere. Lastly, it is a chapter for those special individuals in a school, the community-builders and magic-makers!

What are the IB approaches to learning (ATLs)?

'We use critical ... thinking skills ...'

If we return to the Middle Years Programme model (see the IB website), we can see the importance of thinking in the innermost ring, indicated by 'Approaches to learning' and 'Approaches to teaching'.

What are the skills that the IB considers most important to create a successful learner?

The focus of ATLs in the MYP is on helping students to develop everything they could possibly need to enjoy a lifetime of learning, be it skills, knowledge or insight gained from self-reflection. It helps them to understand how humans learn and how to judge what is most effective for them personally. The focus on **metacognition** (learning how to learn and thinking about thinking) and the tools for learning apply to all subjects and disciplines in the MYP.

ATL skills can be learned and taught, identified or improved with practice and developed incrementally. They provide a solid foundation for learning independently and with others. They provide a common language that students and teachers can use to reflect on, and articulate on, the process of learning.

IBO (2014)

Why do we give such emphasis to learning skills? Beyond factual knowledge, we are aiming for the holistic development of the student and providing them with the key competencies that will prepare them for life. Their ability to learn independently and **autonomously** is widely considered to be an important strategy to prepare for the changing world they will inhabit in the workplace. When many jobs have been replaced or adapted, skills-based competence is surely to be prized, and hopefully irreplaceable.

What competencies am I trying to develop in my learners?

This approach to learning helps students in a variety of ways – they learn to reflect with purpose, providing evidence for their reflections. They understand the diverse needs and strengths of human psychology and learning. It places an important emphasis on their role in creating productive, collaborative learning experiences. These ATLs give them an ideal preparation for later life, where they have a variety of strategies for both study and collaboration. Our intention should be to weave them seamlessly into our teaching and learning for students, without creating an additional cognitive load for them or any superfluous workload for teachers.

Over time, students can identify their competence in any learning strategy using terms like those shown in the accompanying image.

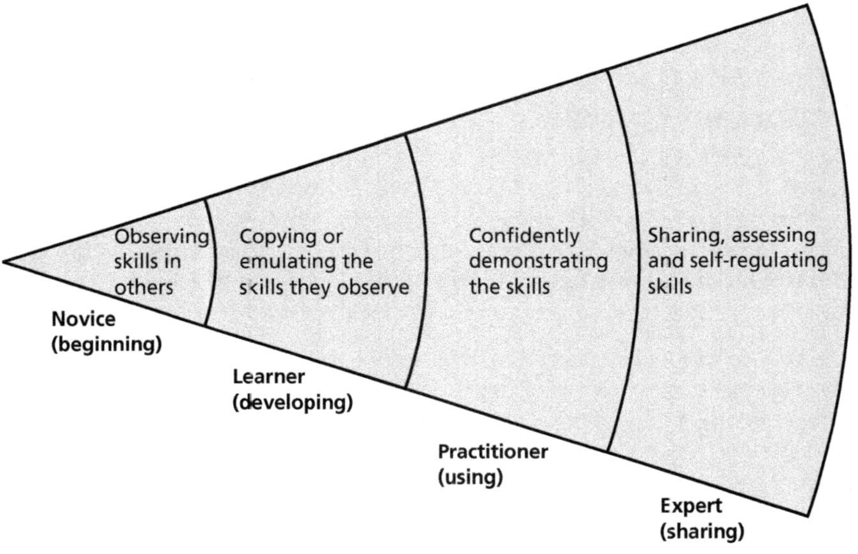

This means that students move from observing the skills in others, to copying or emulating the skills they observe, to confidently demonstrating the skills, to sharing, assessing and self-regulating skills.

What are these approaches to learning in the MYP, exactly?

IB programmes identify five ATL skill categories across all IB programmes, but these five categories expand to make room for 10 skill 'clusters'. These give more depth and specifics to the skills needed to make us better learners, in a developmentally appropriate way. How did we end up with different levels or taxonomies? These expanded categories were developed during the MYP curriculum review. It transpired that the Middle Years Programme wanted more detail, while other programmes did not. And so, we have the table below. For even more detail, there is an extremely long list at the end of *From Principles into Practice* (IBO, 2014), giving examples of these skills in a variety of ways. ATL skills should be focused on empowering students to succeed in both the MYP as well as their DP studies.

The alignment of the five categories with the 10 clusters is as follows:

ATL skill categories	MYP ATL skill clusters
Communication	I. Communication
Social	II. Collaboration
Self-management	III. Organization IV. Affective V. Reflection
Research	VI. Information literacy VII. Media literacy
Thinking	VIII. Critical thinking IX. Creative thinking X. Transfer

In order to develop ATL skills, students need models, clear expectations, developmental benchmarks (or targets) and multiple opportunities to practise.

IBO (2014)

While ATL skills are not formally assessed in the MYP (not *assessed* but *addressed*), some schools still experience the overwhelming urge to measure them. This measurement usually manifests on the report card, often quantitatively or semi-quantitatively, or is referenced in teacher comments. Teachers should make sure to provide regular and explicit feedback to students about the ATL skills.

There have been many discussions on skills that have not been included and maybe should be. During my time at the IB we had vociferous discussions about whether the time students spend online nowadays made a strong argument that *curation* skills should be included, in the wake of Pinterest, Twitter (X), LinkedIn and Instagram. More recently, it could be argued that now the most valuable skills when dealing with AI content and generation will be *discernment*, *evaluation* and *authentication* skills. There is a lot of exciting thinking to do in keeping our ATLs as relevant as possible to our students.

Summary

A well-designed and delivered curriculum should use ATL skills to develop stronger, more self-regulated learners, whose confidence leads to a love of learning and success. Using content, concepts, contexts and skills enforcement allows them to be excellent *knowers* as well as *thinkers*. Remember to set goals that are challenging as well as realistic.

How can we support ATLs in MYP Mathematics?

When considering ATL choices for each unit, ask yourself are you teaching for mastery or exposure? Will students develop these skills or practise them?

Table of possible curriculum links by ATL skill cluster

	Numerical and abstract reasoning	Thinking with models	Reasoning with data	Spatial reasoning
I. Communication	Use intercultural understanding to interpret differences in time zones, schedules and calendars.	Make efficient summary notes for different quadratic functions as models.	Structure data correctly, confidently and concisely in summaries and reports.	Use appropriate forms and units for angles (degrees and radians) in different contexts.
II. Collaboration	Use ratios to practise empathy.	Build consensus in network design tasks.	Give and receive meaningful feedback in statistical investigation tasks.	Encourage others to contribute in group tessellation design tasks.
III. Organization	Select and use appropriate technology to represent numerical and algebraic symbols correctly, e.g. exponents, surds and variables.	Use appropriate strategies to organise complex composite functions.	Use appropriate strategies to organise, and use, large datasets.	Bring construction and measurement instruments to class for task completion.
IV. Affective	Demonstrate persistence in calculating and representing compound inequalities.	Deal with failure when choosing possible factors for solving quadratic solutions.	Analyse and attribute causes of failure in theoretical compared to experimental probabilities.	Practise focus and concentration in composite area and volume calculations.

	Numerical and abstract reasoning	**Thinking with models**	**Reasoning with data**	**Spatial reasoning**
V. Reflection	Identify strengths in proportional reasoning investigations with Criterion D.	Reflect on the composition and application of Pascal's triangle in so many fields of mathematics.	Understand simultaneous change as a covariance.	Demonstrate flexibility in selecting and using volume compared to capacity in spatial reasoning.
VI. Information literacy	Use critical literacy skills to interpret terms and conditions (small print) in financial communication.	Evaluate digital tools for modelling functions effectively and easily.	Understand the limitations of sensory learning and input when considering probabilistic literacy, e.g. recency, superstition.	Use long-term memory techniques to conceptualise and recall linear equation: $y = mx + c$ or $y = mx + b$
VII. Media literacy	Understand the impact of media representation of units and scale in reporting.	Communicate simultaneous equations/systems of equations information effectively.	Communicate ideas of correlation versus causation effectively and ethically.	Demonstrate transformations of shapes in space using different media.
VIII. Critical thinking	Make informed choices, appreciating the nature of errors and margin of error in polling.	Identify obstacles when representing functions, including asymptotes, domain, range and scaling.	Recognise unstated or inbuilt bias in sampling or questionnaire design.	Draw reasonable conclusions about trigonometric relationships and identities in inquiries.
IX. Creative thinking	Apply existing understanding of number systems to create new operators or representations.	Design improvements to algorithms based on evidence and outcome improvement.	Make unexpected data representations or visualisations.	Ask 'what if' questions about polar coordinates.
X. Transfer	Make connections between sequences and financial contexts.	Make connections between transformations and works of art.	Apply probability skills in unfamiliar situations to ease decision-making.	Inquire into vectors to understand air travel better.

What role does creativity play in the MYP Mathematics curriculum?

'Art is how we decorate space; music is how we decorate time.'

Jean Michel Basquiat

Let's consider this quotation by Basquiat and co-opt it for our own purposes. We could consider 'mathematics is how we understand space' or 'mathematics is how we control time.' Alternatively, we could consider mathematics as a means for decorating time and space. In this section we will look at possible ways to creatively extend mathematics outside the classroom, allowing us to 'mathify' our surroundings.

Decorating space

'We use ... creative thinking skills ...'

To do this, we need to see the world around us in a renewed mathematical way. In some systems, this is referred to as having 'mathematical eyes' or a filter or lens. It distorts our vision to show us what we have not seen before. Giving the students a superimposition of mathematical concepts onto their world can be massively rewarding, as well as entertaining. Encourage them to use these mathematical filters/lenses/eyes daily.

Viewing the world from a mathematical perspective allows students to see examples of number sense, or to recognise connections and interdependencies such as cause-and-effect relationships. They will hone their ability to identify visual images, and to link mathematical knowledge and skills to real-world, immediate surroundings.

You may wish to start off with the immediate mathematics vicinity. Consider switching out standard text for something more mathematical, as a low-cost, low-energy start. This could include class names, room numbers or signage in general.

Once you've completed your corridor audit, extend your field of vision beyond the classroom. There are so many ways for us to extend mathematics creatively within or beyond our walls. Consider where your limitations are: budget? Time? Ideas? Power to implement? Let us look at some simple ideas that can help you decorate both time and space mathematically:

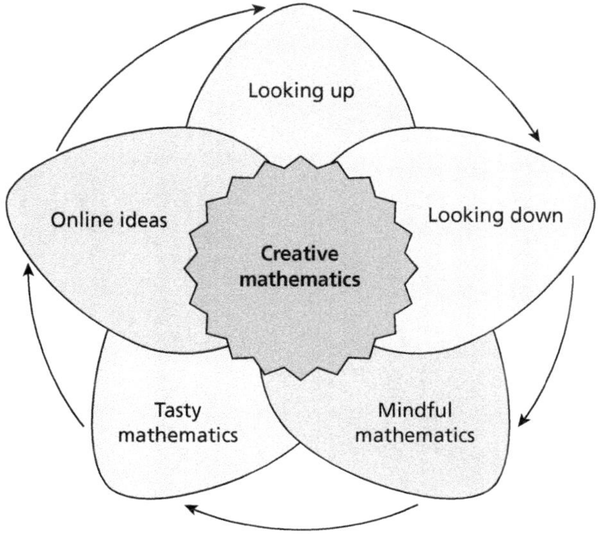

Maybe you are exceptional at harnessing the zeitgeist? Can you instantly find thee mathematically relevant connections between the fad of the day and your lesson planning? Over the years I have seen attempts at 'popmath', with different levels of success. Whether fidget spinners, bottle flipping, Pokémon, ASMR, duetting or the latest online challenge, beware tenuous links. This may be an excellent outlet for your creativity, or may be a chance to encourage students to make those external connections themselves, without putting pressure on yourself to remain 'online' and up to date on the ever-changing interests of middle years aged students! Mindful colouring seems to be past the peak of its popularity, but many teachers still use geometric colouring books to embed a sense of creative spatial reasoning when in need of a mindful, calming activity that has curricular connections.

What could 'next level creativity' look like?

Given all these stimuli, what can this next level creativity look like? If you have space and time, why not consider some more ambitious projects with students or staff? Here is a selection of ideas from the Mathematikum in Germany, which I have seen emulated in different schools globally in different ways.

Let us use the language of ATLs to imagine what a progression of creativity might look like in your classroom or school:

- **Novice:** to get started, consider what small creative additions you could make to bring mathematics to the community's attention.

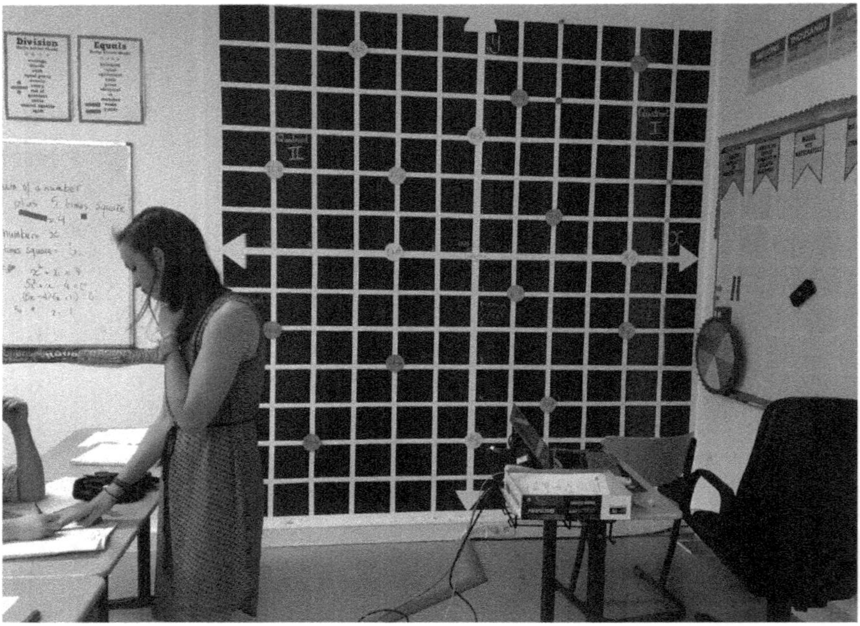

The large Cartesian grid pictured here is an excellent addition to a classroom, it has high impact but requires little financial outlay. One unexpected side effect was that there was an optical illusion effect at the boundaries of the black paint with the white walls. If a permanent change is not permitted in your school, a patterned shower curtain can serve almost the same purpose. Students then have a visual reminder of Cartesian grids and there are a variety of manipulatives you can use with this. It adds scale and movement to your lesson, and gives students an opportunity to apply their modelling quickly when technology is unavailable or inappropriate to the task. Make sure to measure and mark well for this one as it can be a permanent distraction if painted erroneously.

- **Learner:** the image shows an idea that requires more advanced ATLs in students wishing to mathify their surroundings.

- **Practitioner:** here is an idea that could be implemented, but not without a financial or spatial commitment. It is visually stimulating and mathematically rich but would require some planning and purpose. Who doesn't love a swing, though?

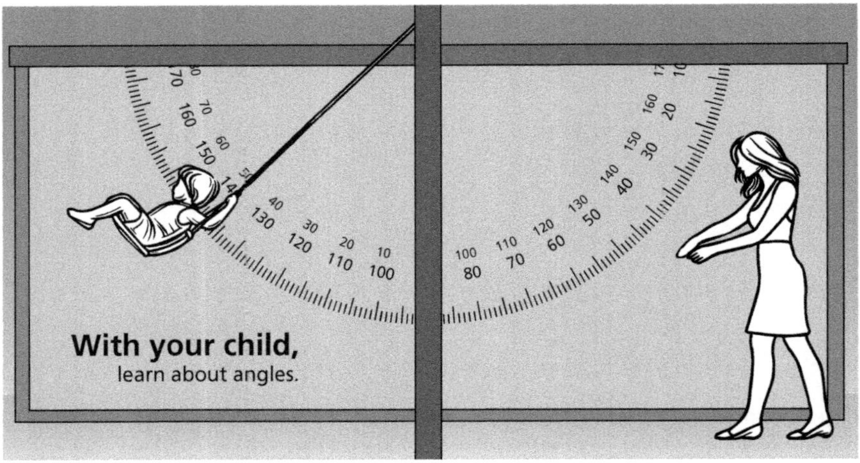

- **Expert:** The ultimate mathematics clock:

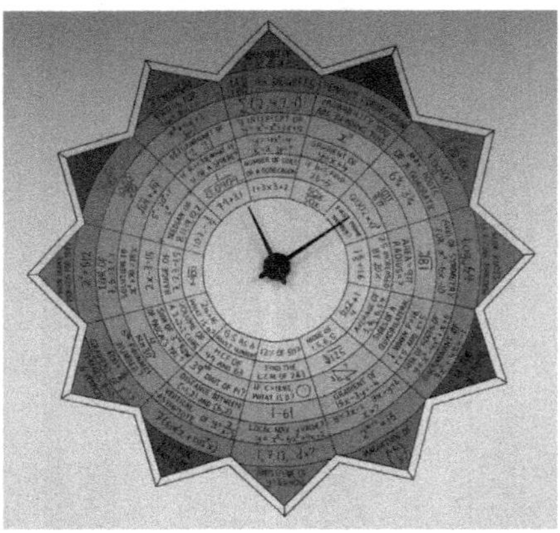

The mathematical clock pictured here was designed by students and teachers, and completed painstakingly by Michael Sweerts, a teacher at the school. Each question gave the answer to the time (in hours) but the rings of the clock corresponded to curriculum from the year group. So, for instance, the innermost ring should be answered by grade 6s, sampling from the curriculum across the different branches. Each ring increases in difficulty, leading to a variety of DP-level questions. If I were to instigate this project again, I would love to try it for a continuum school, including PYP Mathematics at the centre.

You may be surprised where you can find the inspiration once you make yourself open to it. I encourage students to remember to 'look up' as well as 'look down', to notice the often overlooked. In this way we have found examples of geometry in manhole covers, architectural treasures above shop fronts and fractals in clouds. Encourage students to seek out fresh perspectives, and do the same in your planning. Drone photography, Google Earth images and the new drone 'firework' displays can be employed for teaching about anything from vectors to distances to conversion in a visually appealing way. How can you use your local resources for your mathematical understanding and planning?

As I walked underneath the canopies pictured here, at a school I visited recently, I remarked to the mathematics teacher how this would make an excellent Criterion D. He seemed surprised, until I explained how in an area unit, this could be an interesting investigation into *Area* = ½ *ab sin C*. I could already imagine students with chalk and measuring devices engaging in an activity of physical measurement and estimation. I could then see a natural extension into discussions about accuracy, given the droop, shadow and movement, etc.

This surprised the teacher, who honestly acknowledged that he doesn't see the world that way, but he would endeavour to do so. Remember to look for opportunities for spatial reasoning in the buildings and grounds of the school environs.

Investigations that allow students to take mathematics literally out of the classroom give an authenticity to the subject and make for lasting memories, especially helpful if they are low cost in time or resources and can be implemented easily without taking time from normal teaching and learning routines.

When I am introducing students to this idea of extended mathematical vision (or training them, some might say!) I encourage them to apply it to online experiences too. Although students have to endure so many ads, banners and popups that they become blind to them, many of these can encourage positive mathematical talk. Often, students start taking screenshots, which they show me excitedly in the next class.

Sometimes it may not have a connection, and they save and share it just because it 'felt mathsy'. There can be no greater satisfaction than seeing the student move from mathematically hesitant to curious.

Using what you have

It is possible to build a world-class mathematics programme sustainably. Consider what you have in abundance in your environment, both physical and educational. I have seen excellent creativity in action in schools that had other contexts that could be connected to mathematics – for example, schools with a 'singing school culture' using this to amplify mathematical songs. Other schools, which follow an Ocean Schools or Forest Schools philosophy, can make use of these natural resources for data exploration, representation and relationship modelling that supports these programmes. In schools with a performing arts commitment, such as Juilliard, mathematics can be used to nurture ideas of algorithms, sequences and symmetry. Wherever possible, consider the local environment and knowledge economy to mathify your surroundings with meaning.

Decorating time

Throughout the year, there are a variety of national and international days that are connected to our subject. Some of these are celebrations, days that give an opportunity to play with mathematics – for example, days such as 100 Day or Pi Day. These days can be linked to a variety of topics or themes, and can manifest in highly creative ways.

Other celebration days can act as stand-alone activity generators that can be included in teaching and learning on that day, without requiring massive investment or resourcing. These are also less likely to distract from the sequence of learning. Days such as Palindrome Day can fit well when students are already in a unit of numerical reasoning. On Huntrodds Day, for example, probability can be highlighted and developed at a variety of levels, while Pythagorean Day would provide a good springboard for activities in a geometric reasoning unit.

Here are some fun, and interesting, fixed points in the year that can lend some creativity or depth to the delivered curriculum:

- **Huntrodds' Day** – 'Francis Huntrodds and his wife Mary, buried together in Whitby [North Yorkshire], died within five hours of one another on their 80th birthday – their joint 80th birthday. They were both born on September 19th 1600, and both died on September 19th 1680. And, for completeness, got married on September 19th too' (source: www.huntrodds.com).
- **Pi Day**, also known as **International Mathematics Day**. Pedants can make sure to celebrate at increasingly precise times, representing the continuing digits of pi. It was an extra special celebration in 2015: 3.1415 (14 March 15, with celebrations at 9.26 am 53 seconds!).
- **100 Day**, a popular occasion where the school celebrates reaching 100 days of classes in the academic year. Especially so in primary schools, when if lucky it can coincide with Pi Day or Valentine's Day for September-start schools.
- **Tau Day**. This a special day that is celebrated every year on June 28th to the number τ (tau). τ is a constant that is equal to 2π and so is recognised on 6.28 every year. Like Pi Day, the day can also be celebrated with increasing precision.
- **Earth Hour**, 28 March. Many international recognition days, which may at first appear scientific, can also lend themselves to mathematical inquiry.
- **Earth Day**, 22 April. As with Earth Hour, Earth Day gives many opportunities for data reasoning, modelling and quantifying, with some lovely activities to use these practically.
- **Women in Maths Day**, 12 May. This day has been chosen to recognise two influential and inspiring female mathematicians: Maryam Mirzakhani and Florence Nightingale.
- **Perfect Number Day**. On this day students can investigate perfect numbers as they might appear in the date. Perfect numbers are defined as positive integers that are equal to the sum of all their positive divisors except themselves, e.g. $6 = 1 + 2 + 3$ and $28 = 1 + 2 + 4 + 7 + 14$.
- **Origami Day**, 11 November (see the 'Who to follow' box).
- **Ada Lovelace Day**, 10 December.
- **International Day of Girls in Science and Mathematics**, 11 February.

Key feature: Who to follow

Search 'Matt Parker origami' or 'Alex Bellos origami' online for inspiring activities to teach mathematical principles using origami.

- **International Day of Women and Girls in Science**, 11 February.
- **E-Day** (Euler's number). This happens on February 7th (2.7) and can be tied in with logarithms and related topics.
- **Fibonacci Day**, 23 November: 1, 1, 23.
- **National Mathematics Day**, 22 December. This national celebration in India was chosen to honour mathematician Srinivasa Ramunajan's birthday.
- **December Hour of Code**, varying dates.
- **Palindrome Day**. An example palindromic day might be 4/20/24. Students can calculate more.
- **Metric System Day**, 7 April. Celebrates the adoption of the metric system.
- **Pythagorean Theorem Day**. Celebrated for the famous theorem of geometry, when the sum of the squares of the first two digits in a date equals the square of the last digit in the date, e.g. July 24, 2025: $7^2 + 24^2 = 25^2$. Students can use Pythagorean triples to discover the next ones.
- **Square Root Day** is an unofficial holiday observed on dates when the day and the month are both the square root of the last two digits of the year. Created by American high school teacher Ron Gordon, the first celebration took place on 9 September 1981.
- **Math 2.0 Day**, 8 July. A day that brings together mathematics and technology, and celebrates how they have advanced our lives.
- **Number Day**, February. Launched by the NSPCC, with a focus on improving children's attitudes to being numerically literate.
- **World Town Planning Day**, 8 November. This is an example of an interdisciplinary day where we can use the context to develop transfer of understanding. During this celebration of good urban design, we can introduce the students to deeper spatial reasoning through form and function.
- On 5 April, **Read a Road Map Day** can be a useful introduction into scale and proportional reasoning, with some spatial reasoning thrown in for good measure.
- **National Scavenger Hunt Day**, 24 May. This fun activity can be co-opted by mathematics using a variety of mathematical clues, images or objects.

- **Perihelion Day**. The day when the Earth is closest to the Sun.
- **World Braille Day**, 4 January. An insight into a mathematical application and an abstraction of patterns to communicate. Students will examine how the raised dots enable people with visual impairments to read in a different way.
- **National Learn Your Name in Morse Code Day**, 11 January. A fun way to understand the dying skill of encoding and decoding Morse Code.
- **National Opposite Day**, 25 January. This is a source of great mirth in class, where students revel in responding in a negative way. From a mathematical perspective it is a valuable day to deepen students' knowledge of inversing and opposition in mathematics. I like to connect the order of operations and solving linear equations as it shows them the direction of each.
- **Leap Day**, 29 February.
- **Lego Day**, 28 January.
- **History of National Measure Your Feet Day**, 23 January. An unusual one! I'm not sure how much I believe this one but it definitely intrigues students and gives us a lively debate each time. 'The story behind National Measure Your Feet Day originates from ancient Icelanders who spent most of their free time participating in activities that involved their feet, and when spring, a time that is known for extreme rainstorms in Iceland came, the natives would run into their huts and celebrate the rain by measuring their feet. This was a traditional way to celebrate the rainstorms' (source: daysofhteyear.com). Although the logic doesn't stand up, students enjoy this whimsical celebration. It is a free source of data and a handy insight into distribution of results.

Key feature: Resource signpost

Other useful sources of links to mathematics-related calendar days, national and international days include:

- Important Days in Mathematics Celebrated in the World, https://mathsquery.com/knowledge/history/important-days-in-math/
- World Maths Day, https://www.daysoftheyear.com/days/world-maths-day/

If it is culturally appropriate, it can be highly engaging to tie in subject content or inquiry to the time of year or season. For example, in Germany my trusty department engaged in several themed investigations, including one on a 3D polyhedral, which we made a key focus of our Christmas preparations.

Similarly, in the run-up to Halloween, we created a Criterion D assessment investigating surface area of different composite shapes for witch and wizard hats.

There was a fun designing element but most importantly, students had valid insights into optimising surface area and minimising waste. These assessments have valuable student progress data but also mathified our spaces beyond the usual.

In another school, which may have a different context, an investigation into where on Earth has the longest Ramadan fasting day might be more engaging. Allowing students to investigate and then represent their findings in different visualisations fulfils the same need for creativity and decorating both time and space.

What about community engagement?

'... take responsible action on complex problems ...'

Over the past few years in the IB world, we have had a vast array of terms for engaging in the community in a useful and meaningful way. There has been a, frankly confusing, distinction between service learning, CAS (creativity, activity, service and service as action, with overtones of **agency**. As we now move into a more harmonised world of **community engagement** as an overarching term, I think the distinction of personal, local and global will resonate much more with students and teacher alike. In this section we will look at opportunities to create meaningful connections for mathematics curriculum into the planned and delivered curriculum, with some lesson learned to help you on your way.

If we return to our definition of 'Thinkers' at the start of the chapter, we note the call for 'reasoned ethical decisions' and 'responsible action', and we will allow this to frame all our considerations for community engagement in MYP Mathematics.

What could be meant by responsible **action** and reasoned decisions? Responsible action relates to service arising authentically from the curriculum or school context. More often than not, it can be reasonably integrated into teaching and learning without any negative impact on curriculum development. Reasonable ethical decisions can be an outcome of engaging with service in the curriculum. Can students think deeply about a problem within a certain context and make ethical and measured decisions, thanks to their mathematical understanding?

Curriculum should give rise to authentic and student-centred action. Where can we provide a springboard or these ideas?

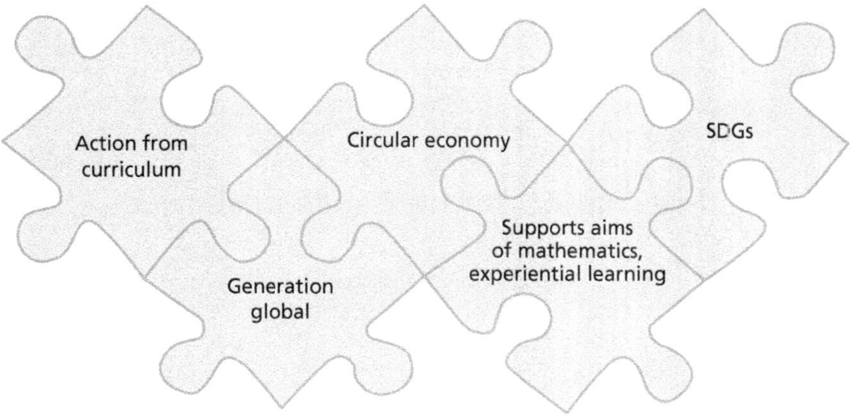

Before we look at personal, local and global engagement in more detail, let us consider some helpful principles and processes to have in place, to give your service learning contributions both direction and lasting effect. One excellent foundation piece is to have a clear channel of communication and information between home and school. If this exists, amplify the voices coming from mathematics. This can be micro, such as notifications from Toddle or posts on the school's social media feed, or more macro by direct mailing parents. If the school does not have specific, strict guidelines around contact or content, consider starting a newsletter or communication culture to encourage critical and creative thinking at home. When I have implemented these in schools, I found that parents who wish to engage are very forthcoming. It opens up an alternative way to appeal for speakers or resources, or to provide additional ideas for home, for which some parents seem to have an insatiable need. It provides a powerful, optional, conduit from the mathematics department to home, and raises the profile of the teachers and the subject in a powerful way.

One final consideration before we look at specific ways in which mathematics can connect to community engagement is to understand that the meaning and intent of charity has become much more complex in recent years. There are now so many more things to think about and discuss with students when engaging in charitable acts. When I started teaching, there was no discussion of concepts such as 'beyond the bake sale' or 'white saviour syndrome', but I think they are worthy conversations to have with students. How do we introduce them to ideas such as universal credit? Can they engage with the positives and negatives of interventions? The idea of vacationing in someone else's misery, or a 'poverty safari', is really important to acknowledge with a community that can be privileged and well intentioned. International school students can often be relatively better served than their community, and it is important to make sure that they do not exist in an expat bubble, treating the local community as an 'Other'. Co-opting culture, or cultural appropriation, can also be a factor in students engaging with the local community, and should be treated with great care. These are complex, but important, ideas – for them and for us.

What is the role of mathematics in service learning ?

'... making reasoned, ethical decisions ...'

Mathematics has a vital role to play in supporting student development of service learning and community engagement. We want students to take mathematics out of the classroom, and for the real world to inspire their journey with mathematics in return.

Here are 10 provocations that can allow mathematics to support authentic service learning:

1. Data
2. Visibility
3. Awareness raising
4. **Advocacy**
5. Environment
6. Citizen science
7. Peer education
8. Aesthetics
9. Equity and access
10. Mathematics as a service subject for other disciplines (leading to academic success across the board).

This last one is contentious. A moaning, but timely, reminder that sometimes we are rehabilitating the reputation of mathematics or mathematics teachers in the eyes of the families.

Move carefully and don't break things! I realise this is the opposite philosophy to the tech world's bravado of 'Move quickly and break things', beloved of disruptors. My position would be that the opposite approach should apply to community engagement and service learning. Take reasoned decisions about changes to your programme. Determine which charity events or beliefs align with your values and simultaneously support the curriculum. Ask questions like: 'Is it relevant to the cohort or community?' and 'Is this mathematically meaningful?'

Community engagement can happen at a personal, local or global level, where local could be both the immediate school community and wider community. It connects clearly to the transfer of ideas, central to the definition of a 'Thinker'. Here are some ideas and examples for engagement in different categories of community.

Personal engagement

- Making positive lifestyle changes in response to learning.
- Addressing issues around consumer activism and corporate ethics.
- Representing the school by participating in mathematics competitions, scholarships, extension programmes such as CTY or MIT, or local equivalents.
- Combining creativity and service by entering mathematical interpretations in other competitions, e.g. songwriting or poetry competitions with mathematically influenced entries.
- Using the library to develop a love of mathematical casual reading (see the appendix for suggestions of suitable texts to suggest).
- Personal project: engage in a mathematically related theme or topic. Personal projects in the MYP are sustained inquiry but, more practically, they foster sustained independence for students.
- Completing work experience or job shadowing in a mathematical field.

Local engagement

- Donating to a recycling drive and tracking contributions.
- Donating to a community fundraising initiative and calculating proportional impact.
- Donating resources to a disaster relief situation.
- Getting involved in class, school and community projects.
- Representing a collective voice in class or school meetings.
- Taking on the role of student or school ambassador or representative at a variety of levels.
- Considering consumption of materials, energy, food and water in the school setting.
- Advocating for fair trade or other ethical considerations in school events or dining options.
- **Community project**: students can use mathematics in their sustained collaborative project in MYP 3.

- Considering ethical action for school trips or excursions, e.g. carbon offsetting or Pack for a Purpose.
- Mentoring or tutoring a younger student.
- Volunteering for parent evenings, open days or mathematics games night/ family fun showcases.

Remember, if you are leveraging the local or parent community for speakers, make sure to build your archive. They may not have the time or availability to come in every year. Can you capture their session? If a speaker comes, record it, generate social media content, display it, have a visitor wall. Too many great sessions or visitors disappear without a trace over time and institutional memory is a valuable thing.

Global engagement

- Considering, and acting on, positive changes in issues of equality and equity.
- Advocating for human rights globally, contributing to letter writing campaigns.
- Being aware of democratic processes and taking part in decision-making, following campaigns and elections critically.
- Participating in a campaign for social change.
- Contributing to data collection for citizen science projects, e.g. the Great Butterfly Hunt, Star Count or NASA Heliophysics.

Key feature: Resource signpost

One fulfilling personal service learning opportunity I have done for a few years uses an app called Be Your Eyes. This app connects users who are blind or have a visual impairment with sighted people, to assist them. If I receive a phone call, the camera will display the user's field of vision and then I can assist them in their query. Current curriculum manager Lenny Dutton initially brought this to my attention and I have found it a lovely experience. Interestingly enough, many of the queries I have received via the app have been numerical in nature, such as, what is the expiration date on this milk? How long will this train journey take? What time is my movie starting? There are age and safeguarding considerations for this app, but I would strongly encourage you to test it out, and search for similar ways to make volunteering as easy as possible and technologically enabled.

Key feature: Case study

When we first opened an IB school in Dublin, we had the opportunity to make every school decision with intention and with fidelity to the IB philosophy. With this in mind, in the dining facilities there was a weighing scale beneath the bin for food waste. As students emptied their plates into the trash can, they would see the weight increase. Each day the head chef would then create a new entry for her continuous bar chart. It helped her get feedback on the popularity of certain menus, but for students it nudged them to reconsider their portions and waste.

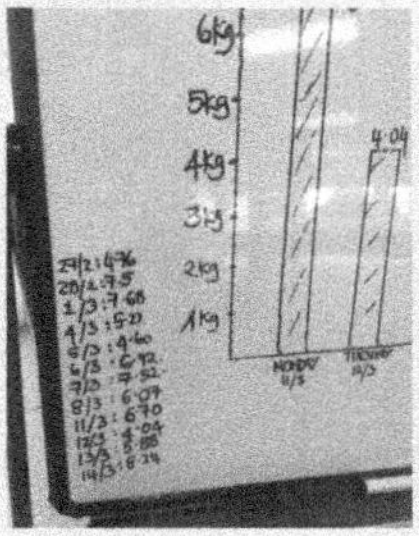

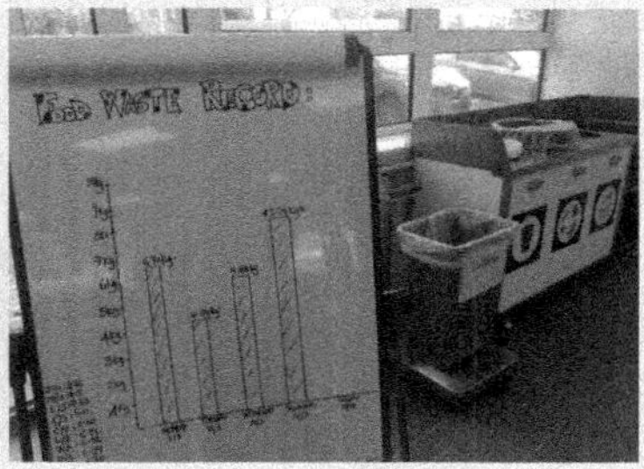

No matter the initiative or commitment, remember that it will place strain on your planned and delivered curriculum, even when righteous in intent. These activities offer a means to transfer our values and integrity, but they are not the sole aim of our mathematics classes. Be on the lookout for scope creep, where the number of ideas or expectations on the curriculum goes far beyond what can be managed. Say no sometimes if you feel that something is not sustainable or relevant to the subject. Always start a new project with a trial period, with the expectation for students that it will only last for the promised period, and commit to that period. Service is not for ever! Good intentions will not compensate for their disappointment if you move on or find there is no space for the commitment with your new roles or responsibilities over time. Plan for this, and build honest and open expectations of experiments.

For example, when all grade 8 mathematics classes were invited to participate in a beach clean-up, we were assured that there would be meaningful mathematical connections. I had hoped for measures of spread and tendency, picturing valuable data analysis on the nature of the recyclables or the distribution of rubbish, leading to meaningful change. When it turned out that the mathematical connection was limited to counting and weighing the bags of trash collected, I learned to proceed with caution when giving up learning time to certain projects. I think it is really important that students engage with these activities in their community – but with the right format and intent. Also, ensure that you're not the 'mathematics won't work with anyone ever' brigade – you still need to be a team player but a discerning one ...

Research shows that connection to community is a massive indicator of happiness and longevity. These are the benefits we want for our students. They will begin to understand that time and freedom are precious resources, as is access to darkness or silence. And their compassion and empathy for others will be better for it. If their surroundings have opportunities for creative and critical thinking, and they can develop the ability to transfer ideas to make change, we are creating the most optimal Thinkers we possibly can.

Self-assessment

Complete the reflection:

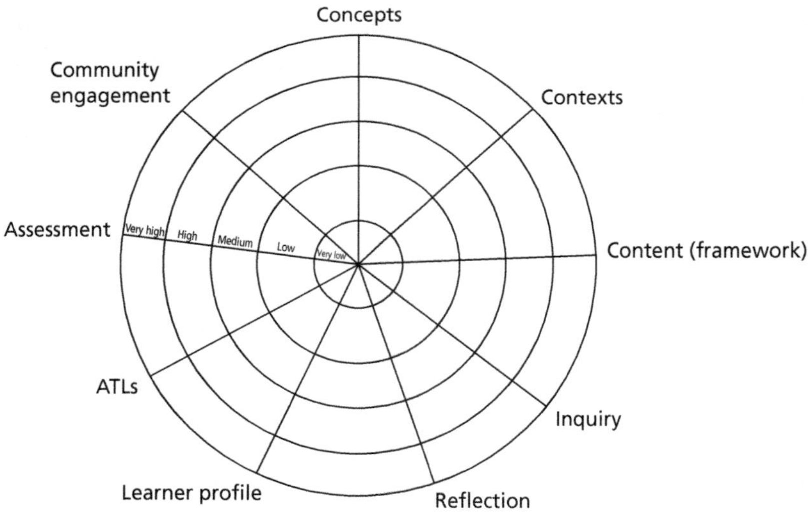

Shade in your knowledge level from low to high as you feel your comfort level lies.

Glossary

Action The act of engaging individually and/or collaboratively with local, national and global challenges and opportunities.

Advocacy Supporting and committing to action for positive change for oneself and others.

Agency A philosophical, sociological and psychological idea that acknowledges humans as active participants in their own lives with the capacity to initiate intentional action.

Community engagement A variety of ways to engage in service learning, including personal, local and global opportunities .*

Community project Focuses on community and service, encouraging students to explore their right and responsibility to implement service as action in the community. The project gives students an opportunity to develop awareness of needs in various communities and to address those needs through service learning.

* *Not an official IB definition.*

Metacognition Thinking about thinking. It is the ability to be aware of, reflect on and understand one's own thought processes.

Responsible action Taking action that is informed, responsible and ethical.

Service A shared value of the IB community. IB learners strive to be caring members of the community who demonstrate a personal commitment to service, and act to make a positive difference to the lives of others and to the environment.

Service as action With appropriate guidance and support, MYP students should, through their engagement with service as one of the significant forms of action, meet the learning outcomes to develop the skills and attributes of an IB learner. IB World Schools value service with others as an important way to engage in principled action across a range of overlapping local and global communities.

CHAPTER 11
PRINCIPLED

We act with integrity and honesty, with a strong sense of fairness and justice, and with respect for the dignity and rights of people everywhere. We take responsibility for our actions and their consequences.

Key thinking points

In this chapter, there are explanations/discussions of:

- how the Principled learner profile attribute applies to the assessment and objectives of MYP Mathematics
- the four prescribed assessment criteria and the differentiated levels
- appropriate and inappropriate grading practices
- the most important assessment principles
- MYP assessment in practice
- opportunities and challenges in MYP Mathematics assessment
- the recording and reporting of criteria achievement levels and final grades.

Why choose Principled as the learner profile attribute for this chapter?

Assessment can be one of the most challenging areas for teachers new to the MYP or the IB. In the absence of a clear philosophy and practice of assessment, it is possible for corners to be cut, misunderstanding to affect teaching and learning, and in the worst version, **grades** to be inflated, deflated or invented. Many teachers attending workshops express that their priority is clarity on how to write, grade or scaffold assessments correctly. It is sadly not uncommon for students to have such a variety of experiences that one year they are flying high in **achievement levels** and the next they come crashing down. While this cannot be linked solely to teacher understanding of the criteria, it certainly has a marked effect. If we approach assessment in a principled way, we can discuss the various challenges openly and honestly, and move the fairness of the application of these complex criteria to the advantage of the learning happening in classrooms.

Ensuring principled assessment is an end unto itself. We as teachers take responsibility for setting the standard, being transparent about the expectations, and then applying this standard equitably and consistently. You might think this is an accepted truth, but the reality is that there is a long way to go in this regard in many situations. I have heard teachers exclaim such worrying statements, from 'I don't give anyone higher than a 4, so they have room to grow' to 'Just give them a 6, not too high but also the parents won't complain!' These are genuine comments and reinforced in me a belief in the power and principle of **criterion-related assessment** as a way to refute these malpractices.

Who is this chapter useful for?

Mathematics assessment in the MYP can be an area of frequent questions, so this chapter serves as an introduction to them, in their ideation as well as applying them. It is designed to meet the needs of teachers new to the MYP, to instruct what the most suitable types of assessments might be in each criterion but also to inform of the most frequent challenges. It can also give experienced teachers an extra insight into the current version of the criteria and how to ensure assessment is carried out in schools in the most principled way, ensuring the dignity and integrity of teachers and students in the learning process.

What does assessment look like in MYP Mathematics?

Mathematics assessment in the MYP is direct statement of what is valued and promoted in our classrooms. When we address them in class they are referred to as the 'objectives'; the same language is used as an **assessment tool**. These are then called 'criteria', which are used to 'assess'. It is a distinction, without being a major difference, but you will notice the change in language when planning units in Toddle or ManageBac, for example – objectives/address and criteria/assess.

The objectives/assessment requirements are composed of four, equally weighted and equally important, domains of mathematical knowledge, which are:

1. Criterion A: Knowing and understanding
2. Criterion B: Investigating patterns

3. Criterion C: Communicating
4. Criterion D: Applying mathematics in real-life contexts.

The criteria are prescribed and *must* be applied to assessments at least twice per criterion in every year of the programme. Each criterion has level **descriptors** to distinguish students' achievement relative to these descriptions. They increase in complexity and mathematical confidence and are banded as well as differentiated by different year groups across the programme. We will discuss each criterion in turn, looking at how we can distinguish between them, the aims, success and frustrations of each. Our discussion will then turn to how we can ensure there is a common, rigorous standard applied to assessments in our MYP classrooms and how we can communicate this to our whole school community.

Many other curriculums or systems will focus on knowing, understanding and communicating in mathematics (Criteria A and C). I am extremely proud, some might say tribal, about the additional objectives and **assessment criteria** in MYP Mathematics, namely pattern-spotting and real-world contexts (Criteria B and D), as they really reflect the IB's commitment to life-worthy learning.

For a detailed explanation of the principles of assessment in the MYP, consult *From Principles into Practice* (IBO, 2014), where you will see that the IB's philosophy is that assessment is integral to all teaching and learning. This document is the most essential reading for MYP philosophy.

Also important are the following key ideas for MYP assessment development as part of the assessed curriculum.

MYP assessment:

- must allow students chances to achieve at all possible levels of achievement; a badly designed assessment will not give the possibility to demonstrate learning at each level individually
- allows for the highest level of achievement (7–8); these should be provided by rigorously designed but accessible challenges – 8 should not be impossible, nor should it come easily; in practice not many students in each class will be able to access this level, and they should feel no shame in this; too many teachers explain this away to students saying, 'It's not possible to get an 8, you have to be a genius' (see the comments below on Criterion A specifically for this)
- allows for the lowest level of achievement (1–2) by reflecting an 'entry level' of knowledge, building a student's confidence or recognising what they can do if their ability or knowledge is limited; it should be hard to

achieve a 0 (failure to demonstrate any understanding), as every student knows something about the topic, if even from prior learning

- is founded in disciplinary understanding
- must be aligned with the objectives and criteria, reflected in some supporting tools, e.g. rubric, task-specific clarification or mark scheme
- encourages creative and clear design of **assessment tasks** and opportunities to demonstrate learning
- must be age-appropriate and aligned with a school's specific context
- can be seen in action in the Teacher Support Material (TSM) in the Programme Resource Centre on the My IB website; this gives many examples of student work, with and without annotations as well as assessment feedback; some of these are quite old now, but there are still useful articulations of different ideas therein
- provides different versions of the criteria to show the development over the years of the programme specific to Years 1, 3 and 5 of the programme
- means that each unit must have a **summative assessment** and should have **formative assessment** opportunities.

MYP assessment does not:

- have to take place at the end of a unit or learning period only; summative assessment may be most appropriate as the end of a unit but can also be a culminating demonstration of a section of learning within a longer unit
- prescribe any content for tests or assessments
- use only recall of factual information
- apply percentages, ever
- translate into another system by a direct conversation; I have heard it explained away by teachers that parents can consider an 8 to be an A+, 7 an A, 6 a B+, and so on; this is not only untrue but also unfair on both systems as it gives families and schools a false equivalence, so avoid this practice at all costs!
- prevent the use of marks, however these should be used sparingly and only really recommended as a transitioning mechanism to prepare students for DP marking; you may see this in the philosophy behind on-screen assessments – here the mark schemes will show how questions on-screen have been designed with marks, to ensure validity and reliability of marking but coming from a criterion based and conceptual understanding to support MYP philosophy, balanced with examination demands; this is a contentious and live area of debate in the MYP community – some feel it

goes entirely against the philosophy of holistic grading; I can definitely see merit on both sides of the argument

- demonstrate the highest level achievable – you will notice this particularly with the TSM on My IB; I asked why this was the case, why not set a high standard and model for teachers, how far a teacher and student could go with an investigation; I was told that this then sets a limit or ceiling for teachers, beyond which they might not go, and would remove the flexibility prized by so many schools.

Further discussion of inappropriate grading practices

The following grading practices are inappropriate and are counter to MYP assessment principles:

- determining grades using a proportion of scores for classwork, homework and tests
- determining grades by averaging summative performance scores over the year
- ensuring that grades are equally or normally distributed, relative to one another
- using single pieces of work to determine final grades
- reducing the content or standards to accommodate individual student needs, to the detriment or advantage of that student over others
- using group work as individual achievement level.

This causes the most headaches for teachers and coordinators especially. Consistent misunderstandings on this require significant parent education in the community. Leadership, too, sometimes as it is often too granular for them to engage with.

How do we distinguish between formative, diagnostic and summative assessments?

Formative assessment is like the changes in tactics and players during a sports match, while summative assessment is the final score plus rating of team performance. If we seek out a non-sporting example, is it a dress rehearsal before a performance when there is time to make changes and tweak the ideas, given feedback. They are the axioms before the theorem.

Formative assessments should support and encourage student learning, and can have a motivating effect. They can enhance teaching, too, as it gives you instant feedback about what is working for your students and where their needs are unmet. It can also be a strong indicator of when their efforts in or outside class are falling below expectations. Introducing students to the assessment expectations through classroom activities and home learning can support their ability to then transfer their knowledge into a successful demonstration of understanding in a summative assessment.

By far my most hated phrase to hear during my time at the IB was 'positive backwash'. This was often used by the Assessment division to explain how the IB could model or shape expectations as a driver to improve teaching and learning at a distance. Despite my personal, visceral, aversion to this phrase, it is a powerful idea and reflects what is happening when we create rich, engaging formative assessments for students too.

If formative assessments are a practice or rehearsal, and summative assessments the performance, then there is still a place for diagnostic assessments where we can analyse skills and prior knowledge. To further our analogy, this may be running lines, playing scales or practising certain drills as fundamental parts of our learning process. Diagnostics can be used differently by schools, from entrance exams to cognitive testing such as CAT4 or MAPS, to see different aspects of students' learning. Diagnostic assessment can also be used to dive deeper into students' mathematical anxiety or as an indicator for dyscalculia, etc.

What are the most important principles to have in place for assessment?

'We take responsibility for our actions and their consequences'

Assessment practices in the MYP can sometimes represent significant challenges to existing school practices, in their initial introduction but also later in their consistent use, with staff and student turnover married to curriculum development. It is so incredibly important that all staff teaching mathematics really understand how MYP assessment works. They must understand what is mandated and what is not, and to rely on published guidance for clarity. Too often schools get an idea of what would be 'frowned upon', but it isn't always accurate!

The MYP places an emphasis on assessment processes that involve the gathering and analysis of information about student performance, and that provide timely feedback to students on their performance. MYP assessment plays a significant role in the development of ATL skills, especially those that are closely related to subject-group objectives, which in the case of mathematics can be virtually all of them. The MYP approach to assessment recognises the importance of assessing not only the products, but also the process, of learning. A key feature of the MYP is that tasks are designed or created by teachers in their schools and not provided by the IB directly, which is intended to support the professional **judgement** of teachers who know their students and school best. *From Principles into Practice* (IBO, 2014) does insist that assessment is done regularly and consistently, and that meaningful feedback must be given, as this should be the best model to help students improve their understanding and performance.

If you are establishing a department understanding, or renewing and refocusing your assessments, here are the most important principles to have in place:

- Ensure all teachers have read the *MYP Mathematics Guide* (IBO, 2020) and the *FPIP* (IBO, 2014) references above.
- Make collaborative working time available to discuss and develop ideas.
- Practise standardising and discussing assessments, both before and after they are carried out.
- Share the load in designing assessments, bringing new ideas and modelling best practice.
- Consider collaborative marking, or levelling synchronously to find an agreed level of expectation for students.
- Craft some assessment design guidance for teachers, to ensure a common basis or 'family resemblance' for assessment. Some schools have a shared assessment cover sheet or a determined font and layout. Decide what is best for your particular context and consider the environmental impact thereof. For example, if you have a cover page, a page for each criterion and then a two-page **assessment rubric**, you might turn a four-page test into a 10-page booklet!
- With regards to font, there are interesting discussions online and in staffrooms regarding the best practice here. Some recommend Comic Sans, some Aptos, others believe Bionic Reading is the future. Discuss this and come to a school-based judgement.
    - It is interesting to consider a study from Song and Schwartz (2010), where identical tasks were given but in different fonts. Participants were asked to rate how easy or hard the tasks would be. The tasks in the easier-to-read font were rated as easier to perform. If we contrast this to other studies which suggest knowledge that is harder to acquire is embedded deeper, then we must decide which is the most suitable and accessible font, and by extension layout, for our assessments.

- Make sure there is a common agreement, or better yet a policy, on how you will handle common situations where the IB does not give guidance. You will see more of these frequently occurring discussion points in the practices section later in this chapter.
- Do not give a direct grade equivalent to students or families – never, ever suggest that an 8 is equal to an A+, for example.
- Take time for discussion in your school, team or own mind. What do you feel is the purpose of assessment? How and when is there a limit to what can and should be assessed? Is there a value in making learner profile attributes explicit in assessments? Same questions for ATLs?
- Sufficiency of evidence: to determine these achievement levels, teachers must gather sufficient evidence of achievement from a range of learning experiences and assessments. (How do we determine or define for ourselves what is sufficient evidence? What do we owe the students in terms of opportunities to perform?) Teachers need to ensure that this evidence comes from the performance of the student over the duration of the unit(s) taught.
- Discuss carefully what you will say to the student who performs inconsistently across a test – for example, achieving in the higher-level questions but not on the lower end of the achievement-level descriptors.

Key feature: Anecdotal evidence

I have had this challenge many times over the years, where inconsistent performance on a test makes for difficult levelling. I had one particularly vociferous student, let's call him Frederick, who would skip right to the end and complete the most challenging questions only. He argued, cogently and increasingly loudly, that by completing the level 7–8 he had implicitly demonstrated that he had mastered all the other skills and abilities. His sincere conviction was that this implied everything I needed to award him the highest level. He had successfully argued this with other teachers and he saw no reason why I should be any different. My position was, and remains, that implying is not enough. As his teacher, and a professional, I need verifiable evidence for each of the levels, and he had put me in the unenviable position of not knowing if he had blind spots in any areas or deficiencies of communication. I'm sure, if he thinks of me at all, it is not fondly, but he certainly conceded and ensured that he completed all questions on the next assessment. He achieved a 6, indicating that his time management was a factor and helped him understand the need.

The guidance states that subject groups must address all strands of all four objectives at least twice in each year of the MYP. The emphasis should be on 'at least' and best practice is to apply the criteria wherever appropriate to a unit. Each unit should have at least one criterion, and two wherever possible.

If you are working alone, such as in a department of one, or would prefer to develop your understanding independently (perhaps working in a non-collaborative or resistant context), follow the steps above but apply them in a solo setting.

How do the MYP Mathematics criteria work?

'We act with integrity and honesty ...'

As outlined earlier in the chapter, there are four mandated criteria of equal weight, two of which are very familiar to mathematics teachers and two that give a lot of practitioners a degree of discomfort. Each of the four criteria progresses in complexity over the MYP years, with differentiated level descriptors to show development from Year 1 to Year 3 to Year 5. Each descriptor gives a narrower range of student achievement, to give detail and granularity so teachers can use their professional judgement and place the student's work at the lower or higher end of the descriptor. There are no differentiated criteria provided for Years 2 or 4. This can generate many questions from teachers and schools as to what to use in those transitioning years. Here are three possible models, any of which is acceptable, depending on the school context.

1. Ambitious model: As soon as students enter MYP Year 2 they begin using Year 3 criteria. Likewise, teachers immediately apply Year 5 criteria once assessment of learning begins in Year 4. This raises students' game and keeps standards high, according to those who use this option. Students can experience an initial dip in achievement, but this is usually resolved before long. It can also increase mathematics or test anxiety in those who are prone to it.
2. Personalised model: Students begin Year 2 with the past year's criteria and in Year 4 they continue with Year 3, until the teacher feels they are ready for the next jump up. The benefit of this system is that students transition when they are ready and experience less disorientation. Negatively however, this is difficult to implement when there are multiple classes at the same level, and unless it is synchronised there will be an unfairness built into the comparative assessment levels.
3. Slow-release model: Teachers keep all students on Year 1 criteria for the first and second year, transitioning to Year 3 criteria only at the start of the actual Year 3. To ensure equity, they then keep Year 4 on Year 3 levels until

they transition temporally and academically to Year 5. This supports the mathematically anxious students but does not always meet the needs of the more mathematically capable or curious learners. These students may crave challenge and if they feel they are 'maxing out' on the levels already can conversely lead to disaffection.

The *MYP Mathematics Guide* (IBO, 2020) provides a useful table of comparison to illustrate the progression of learning from Year 1 to Year 3, and then on to the expected levels for Year 5 and transition to the Diploma Programme. The difficulty (or sophistication) of the mathematics encountered must increase across the years in line with the table.

Objective A: Knowing and understanding

Year 1	Year 3	Year 5
In order to reach the aims of mathematics, students should be able to:		
i. select appropriate mathematics when solving problems in both familiar and unfamiliar situations ii. apply the selected mathematics successfully when solving problems iii. solve problems correctly in a variety of contexts.	i. select appropriate mathematics when solving problems in both familiar and unfamiliar situations ii. apply the selected mathematics successfully when solving problems iii. solve problems correctly in a variety of contexts.	i. select appropriate mathematics when solving problems in both familiar and unfamiliar situations ii. apply the selected mathematics successfully when solving problems iii. solve problems correctly in a variety of contexts.

Source: IBO (2020)

Criterion A is best suited to classroom tests, timed assessments and independent work. There are no apparent changes between the years, which implies that the nature and complexity of the familiar and unfamiliar problems must be increasing year on year. This should coincide with students' ability to transfer knowledge and demonstrate their reasoning in all branches of the framework.

This could be coarsely translated as '(i) get started, (ii) do the mathematics, (iii) get it right'. This may be why teachers find it so familiar, and students too – it is a comforting criterion in a way, where little subjectivity is required and less in-depth reading, compared to Criteria B and D.

Strengths and opportunities of this criterion

It pairs well with Criterion C! The lines of reasoning required in solving problems at all levels give ample opportunity to assess communication simultaneously. Make sure to include questions that involve lines of reasoning, units, and so on. See the list for Communicating, below, to maximise the demonstration of learning.

If questions of increasing complexity are asked, or better still the level of the question is indicated explicitly, students experience less anxiety. They are less suspicious around what the question is asking, and this gives them a clear indication of where they are and what is still needed to progress to the next level. When they accept that the later questions are intentionally much more challenging, they often report less intimidation. I take this to mean that they don't feel bad about not managing them and it does not dominate their assessment experience. When they do 'conquer the evil questions' they are often over the moon.

Some teachers choose to use Criterion A with Criterion B, but it can be very difficult to clearly define where the two criteria will be delineated and how they will be applied in unison. It is challenging to design an assessment that requires a fresh pattern to discover as well as familiar contexts to apply knowledge. The advice given in the guide for this unorthodox pairing is to ensure that 'the task is rigorous enough to allow students to achieve the highest levels of both criteria'. Best to be avoided.

Cautions and challenges for this criterion

How should we distinguish between the levels: simple – complex – challenging – unfamiliar?

Test layouts can make marking this criterion needlessly complex. As indicated above, my preferred layout is a clearly indicated set of questions for level 1–2, usually two to three if time allows and with multiple opportunities to show learning. I then progress to level 3–4, giving slightly more questions than in level 1–2.

I give a similar number for level 5–6, as most students will be in the range of 3–6 and I need a solid body of evidence to see where they sit in these bands. For level 7–8 questions I give two to three too, to keep it symmetrical with level 1–2. This also helps because these questions are more challenging to write. Students must be creative in the application of their knowledge but in a way that has not been seen in class. I make sure to hold back some ideas for this, beyond just using worded problems.

Remember: 'Unfamiliar' problems in level 7–8 refers to the situation being unfamiliar, not the mathematics. I have seen examples of tests where a brand-new piece of mathematics was suddenly introduced in the last question and students naturally had no chance to access or understand it. For example, a test of Venn diagrams and sets that suddenly introduced Boolean algebra as an unfamiliar question.

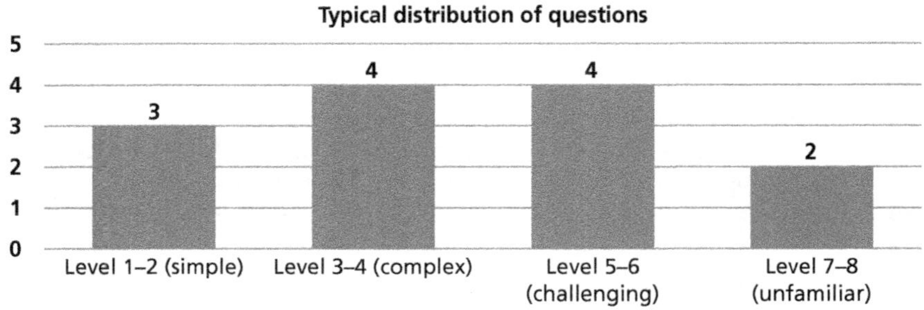

A typical distribution might look like that in the image here. Experiment with this, bearing in mind the access level of each question, the time available and the speed of marking. Criterion A can be a very efficient process, and is affectionately called 'tick and flick'. My rule of thumb is to sit the test myself, once I am happy with the layout, and time the process. I then multiply the time by three, or four if the test is especially challenging, to see how long it should take the students. I do this to ensure the test is approximately the correct length, and to gain insight into things I may have overlooked when I wrote or adapted a question from elsewhere. Similarly, I will always complete a worksheet or assessment I have found elsewhere, as I have been burned before. It may seem like a beautiful worksheet, which on first glance meets your needs exactly, but as soon as the students are working on it, there will inevitably be something 'untaught' in there (e.g. truncation instead of rounding). I also scan worded problems for ambiguities or unfamiliar language, to ensure I have removed any additional language blocks or confusion (e.g. slope versus gradient, imperial versus metric, or zeros, intercepts and roots confusion).

Speaking of worded problems, try to use them liberally throughout the levels of questions. It is true that they make accessing the information harder, so may not be appropriate for level 1–2, but do not always leave them for level 7–8 as this may give students the mistaken impression that putting mathematics into words is a higher-order transfer skill. We want them all to be able to translate everyday situations into mathematics in their heads, regardless of difficulty level.

In many curriculums this accounts for a much larger proportion of the syllabus and assessment. You may be tempted to use Criterion A as your go-to assessment, so make sure to balance its use and importance with the other three criteria. Within this criterion, gather examples of how questions can be assessed and how you can move the expected levels to suit your cohort. What is considered simple, challenging, complex or unfamiliar for this group and in your school? These are school-based discussions and most successful if task design is completed collaboratively. The second-best time to have these types of discussions is when moderating or standardising levels as a group. This aligns everyone's expectations of the standard required and will inform changes to the level of questions for next use. Typical discussions may lead to comments such as, 'I thought this one would be really hard, but they found it easy so I'd probably move to a level 3–4 next time, while in the one I thought was easy they really struggled with units and rounding.'

Objective B: Investigating patterns

Year 1	Year 3	Year 5
In order to reach the aims of mathematics, students should be able to:		
i. apply mathematical problem-solving techniques to recognise patterns ii. describe patterns as relationships or general rules consistent with findings iii. verify whether the pattern works for other examples.	i. select and apply mathematical problem-solving techniques to discover complex patterns ii. describe patterns as relationships and/or general rules consistent with findings iii. verify and justify relationships and/or general rules.	i. select and apply mathematical problem-solving techniques to discover complex patterns ii. describe patterns as general rules consistent with findings iii. prove, or verify and justify, general rules.

Source: IBO (2020)

Pure mathematics is, in its way, the poetry of logical ideas.

Albert Einstein

Criterion B is best suited to immiserating the mathematically anxious. It also generates the highest degree of insecurity in teachers. It is designed to be an investigation, an opportunity to place with numbers, or to guide students, through inquiry to a recognised pattern (i.e. formula). Students must have sufficient freedom to choose their own techniques to identify patterns and how to describe them. The investigation must be achievable in the time provided and allow for simple or complex patterns to be identified, giving every student at least the chance to begin to investigate.

Strengths and opportunities of this criterion

I'm sad to say that this is one of the least loved criteria. The benefit of pursuing it nevertheless is that it moves students from pattern spotting to generating general rules over time. It is typically not enjoyed by students due to the rigorous nature of abstraction and, to be honest, I hear a lot of teachers querying the value of embedding patterns into curriculum and endowing it with 25% of the criteria assessments. I wholeheartedly disagree with this perspective. Mathematics is nothing if not pattern spotting and the brain is often described as a pattern-processing machine.

An excellent Criterion B investigation will have short, well-structured scaffolded questions, allowing students to still achieve the lowest levels. This means they can identify simple patterns, perhaps in words, if not fully mathematically communicated. Our goal is to encourage them to identify these patterns, explain their observations and justify them mathematically. Not all students achieve at all levels, but we can foster a sense of independence, agency and interest in patterns. It is often the case that students can see the pattern but not how to express it in anything other than words. Maybe Criterion B is the *pons asincrum* of the MYP world? I find this ironic given how good humans are at pattern finding, adolescents in particular. They can triangulate drama at the speed of light and can identify which teachers will tolerate what, in fine detail. They can extend a pattern and express their shock or dismay when you deviate from your usual routines. Yet they baulk when we ask them to express it using letters and variables.

The criterion achievement levels can be crudely translated as:

- Complete the scaffolding questions to get to the pattern, use a table if you need to
- Describe the pattern and then generalise (abstract it)
- Check your rule with the given data
- Try it in a new situation
- Understand the power of 'general rules'.

How to distinguish between the levels

The beginner level is effectively 'needs teacher support to get started'. Students who require help to begin, when they don't see a pattern at all, are likely to score poorly from then on, expressing rules in words only. Simple patterns achieve a level 3–4, while 5–6 is the threshold for complex patterns. There is no distinguisher for level 7–8, so reference the other strands to effectively place an investigation.

There is a clear incline in complexity from 'state predictions' to 'suggest general rules' to 'describe patterns as general rules', which must be consistent (valid, if not correct) with the highest level, 'describe patterns with correct findings'. This makes it clear that a full description, correctly identifying the pattern, is necessary for a 7–8. For those who score below this level, it feels somehow unsatisfying. This makes it very different to Criterion A, where students feel only a little more knowledge is lacking. Failing to achieve higher levels in Criterion B seems to them that they are lacking a skill rather than knowledge, leading to their displeasure with the experience. To offset this, I make sure to model several examples per year and encourage their understanding of the difference between levels.

The most important clarification I can give for this criterion is the importance of understanding the ideas of proof, verification and justification. Make repeated reference to these definitions to clarify the difference for students, who are used to using these terms interchangeably in everyday language. It helps to have the definitions from the guide, and available in the Glossary, on display in the classroom. Between the three **command terms**, I tend to use 'verify' as a synonym for 'check', giving the example often seen online, 'verifying that you are human'. This allows us to expand the justify conversation to model checking beyond the dataset provided and using the rule with a number outside the dataset. We came to this understanding after a lively discussion in the first rounds of the eAssessment online examinations. This verify and justify means that students should predict a term outside the set, by drawing or calculating, and then compare their result with the general rule. The students who do succeed in this find it immensely satisfying that 'their rule' can be seen to work. Encourage this feeling and it will inspire breakthroughs with their more resistant peers.

Cautions and challenges for this criterion

If an investigation is too guided, then the maximum level that can be awarded is a level 4 in MYP 5. This is unlikely to be imposed by the author of the assessment, but it may come to light with an external reviewer or moderator. Similarly, if a student finds a rule based on incorrect findings but describes the rule well and it is of equal complexity, they can still achieve a maximum of level 6. Criterion B is unique in this regard as it also allows for teacher support but with a limiting achievement level of 2.

There is also a frequent problem with Criterion B where it arrives as a stand-alone assessment, for the sake of it, to meet the requirement in time for a reporting season. In this case it comes out of the blue for students and doesn't seem to fit in with the learning, because it genuinely doesn't. If it does not support, reinforce or apply, or transfer the learning from the learning period then it is not a valid performance of understanding. Many of the branches of reasoning lend themselves especially well to Criterion B, such as geometrical formulae or algebraic relationships.

Sadly, students in general do not enjoy Criterion B. They can often be heard to exclaim, 'But I just don't see it!' or 'Can't we just have test questions to solve?' I have to assume that it is the process of abstraction, or a mental block about the mechanics of algebra, that lies at the heart of this dislike. Encourage students to make liberal use of the tables provided and to create their own, if none is given. This will begin to train them to look for patterns horizontally and not just from term to term, as they are inclined to do.

Mark with Criterion c as often as possible, and make sure to include questions that involve lines of reasoning, units, etc. See the list for Communicating, below, to maximise the demonstration of learning.

Remember: Make sure to try to do formative Criterion B assessments to increase students' understanding of what is required at each level. Practice may indeed make possible. If time permits, have students create their own, given strict parameters, and discuss what makes a valid pattern different to a correct one. Demonstrate for them the progression from simple patterns described in words, to abstracted and generalised rules.

Objective C: Communicating

Year 1	Year 3	Year 5
In order to reach the aims of mathematics, students should be able to:		
i. use appropriate mathematical language (notation, symbols and terminology) in both oral and written statements ii. use appropriate forms of mathematical representation to present information iii. (not demonstrated at this level) iv. communicate coherent mathematical lines of reasoning v. organize information using a logical structure.	i. use appropriate mathematical language (notation, symbols and terminology) in both oral and written explanations ii. use appropriate forms of mathematical representation to present information iii. move between different forms of mathematical representation iv. communicate complete and coherent mathematical lines of reasoning v. organize information using a logical structure.	i. use appropriate mathematical language (notation, symbols and terminology) in both oral and written explanations ii. use appropriate forms of mathematical representation to present information iii. move between different forms of mathematical representation iv. communicate complete, coherent and concise mathematical lines of reasoning v. organize information using a logical structure.

Source: IBO (2020)

Criterion C is best suited to everything, everywhere, in my humble opinion. When completing assessments, it is virtually impossible not to communicate. I love it. I add it to everything, like hot sauce. Test? Communication. Poster? Communication! Investigation into a real-life problem? So much communication! Many of the command terms in this criterion are also heavily dependent on ATL skills: organise in a logical structure, communicate clearly and coherently, being sufficiently informationally literate to use and move between forms of representations.

If you wish to use Criterion C independently, it could be used for reports or projects that explain how certain mathematical domains are carried out. Any assessment of this type, such as 'Meet a Mathematician' or 'The History of Units', would have to be scaffolded in a way that ensure students would have to employ a logical structure and be required to communicate using different forms of representation. To write about mathematics would not be sufficient to show achievement at each level – they would have to present in a variety of ways and forms to show that they understand thoroughly.

Communication is such a vital element in mathematics. This criterion can help students become confident consumers and creators of mathematics. When they progress to the Diploma Programme, if they have been immersed in a vibrant MYP they can wonder where the relative importance of each skill went. They see marks only as correlating to Criterion A. I find it very helpful to share examples of DP mark schemes with them, to see how this criterion especially has been transferred there. Their skills developed throughout the MYP put them in the best position for their clear, concise and correct communication marks throughout. It is a much easier criterion to evidence than the more abstract examples of where patterns and real-life contexts go in grade 11/IB1.

Strengths and opportunities of this criterion

This is a wonderful criterion to encourage correctness and accuracy in students' working. It allows the opportunity to have conversations about the importance of using the right symbol and how mathematical notation has a very exact and unique meaning, which allows us to communicate very effectively and efficiently. It provides a springboard to distinguish between mathematical notation and calculator notation, and how each is different (and when not to use calculator notation).

An opportunity when designing assessments that assess this criterion is those that will develop students' understanding of technology too, labelling graphs made by technology or learning to use MathType or Equation Editing, as examples. We must repeat, ad nauseam, the importance of remembering headings, labels on axes, units, etc., but a low Criterion C grade is often a much more effective way for them to accept its importance. See the IB guidance on preferred symbols and notations in the MYP, aligned to best preparation for DP or higher-level mathematics. There is no danger of over-assessing it, as we have already seen the relative importance of communication in the IB overall (learner profile, ATLs, criterion and concept).

Cautions for this criterion

This criterion is also an excellent training ground for the Diploma Programme in that it rewards, or enforces – depending on your point of view – the importance of laying out lines of reasoning that are easy to follow. It makes our lives easier when marking and it puts students in a better position when sitting DP exams. The biggest challenge with the criterion, ironically, can be our high-fliers. They may resent the need to lay out every single step, which they find to be self-evident or a waste of time. They may just 'see' the answer, or find capturing the steps to be facile. We must encourage them to persist, not only due to the need for an external reader to understand their thinking but also as a caring act for the mathematics itself and as a preparation for the time when the topics covered will not come so easily to them to keep it all in their heads.

Teachers frequently ask for clarity on what is meant by 'moving between forms of representation'. This can be adapted to the age and challenge level of classes and topics. It can cover all manner of conversions, be they standard form or changing from representations such as forms of equations. This could be moving between fractions, decimals and ratios, or changing units or approximations.

How to distinguish between the levels in each strand

- (i) limited – some appropriate – usually use – consistently use. The level of expectation of accuracy and precision here is to be determined by the teacher, and it is helpful to model for yourself what 'some' might look like or how 'usually' might look different to 'consistently'.
- (iv) If work is difficult to interpret, it automatically limits students and their achievement level. As also mentioned already, this provides an excellent opportunity to course-correct those students who rush to complete and make avoidable errors in that rush.

Another strength of this criterion is the proximity of the strands to one another. By this I mean the level displayed by individual students is rarely wildly different throughout the assessments from strand to strand. The strands work closely together and it would be unusual to have a student with a limited use of appropriate symbols and notation (i) but extremely coherent logical structure. They tend to demonstrate pretty consistently as the strands are interwoven and this makes assessing the holistic grade much easier for this criterion.

Objective D: Applying mathematics in real-life contexts

Year 1	Year 3	Year 5
In order to reach the aims of mathematics, students should be able to:		
i. identify relevant elements of authentic real-life situations ii. select appropriate mathematical strategies when solving authentic real-life situations iii. apply the selected mathematical strategies successfully to reach a solution iv. explain the degree of accuracy of a solution v. describe whether a solution makes sense in the context of the authentic real-life situation.	i. identify relevant elements of authentic real-life situations ii. select appropriate mathematical strategies when solving authentic real-life situations iii. apply the selected mathematical strategies successfully to reach a solution iv. explain the degree of accuracy of a solution v. explain whether a solution makes sense in the context of the authentic real-life situation.	i. identify relevant elements of authentic real-life situations ii. select appropriate mathematical strategies when solving authentic real-life situations iii. apply the selected mathematical strategies successfully to reach a solution iv. justify the degree of accuracy of a solution v. justify whether a solution makes sense in the context of the authentic real-life situation.

Source: IBO (2020)

Criterion D is best suited to introducing the ideas needed to transfer mathematical thinking outside the classroom and apply them to more concrete, less abstract problems. During early curriculum development the criterion referred to real-life problems but this was deemed too negative and narrow in scope. Thus, the idea of a real-life situation, and context, to which mathematics can be applied and made useful for insights or solutions, was developed. Criterion D required students to decipher a situation, extract what is important and relevant, and then model the situation to find a solution to a stated problem.

Strengths and opportunities of this criterion

In 1976, a British statistician named George Box wrote the famous line, 'All models are wrong, some are useful.' What a wonderful statement – it can shake our students' beliefs in the correctness of mathematics, but it opens their minds to the idea that we model to try to get as close to the truth of a complex situation as we can, and that we must also assess how far that model is from reality.

There is a very definite family resemblance between Criterion D and Criterion A (knowing and understanding) for the first three strands, as it could be roughly translated as '(i) dig out the information/figure out the right bits to use, (ii) do some mathematics on it and (iii) get an answer'. The levels increase in similar complexity to Criterion A, and some teachers make the distinction between them as A (pure mathematics) and D (applied mathematics). I don't fully agree with this interpretation, but I understand where they are coming from. I prefer to think of it as a difference in detail and scaffolding. Criterion A tests are sampling different topics and problem-solving skills, whereas Criterion D is assessing a student's interpretation, creative application and independence when faced with a realistic (or semi-realistic) situation to be analysed.

Where it differentiates massively is in the use and utility of the last two strands. Here we begin to reform how students think about answers and truth. Criterion D iv and v give us markers towards modelling in the most powerful way. Students begin to grasp the difference between a correct answer and a valid answer, and that while they can create a descriptive model, it may not make sense in reality. All models lie, but some are useful, or models are plausible but rarely true.

How to distinguish between the levels

- (i) Some elements, the right elements, relevant, then the same for 5–6, and 7–8.
- (ii) How accurate is it (only expected after level 4, and moves from explain to justify.
- How sensible is the answer? (Only expected to discuss at 3–4, then explain at 5–6 and then justify at 7–8.)

Sadly, level 1–2 are not expected to be able to question their own work. I do find they are good at lateral thinking as to how the answers may not be trustworthy or close to the truth. Closeness to truth being the biggest idea here, by which I mean they must learn how to interrogate numbers and apparent statements.

Cautions with this criterion

Mark all Criterion D assessments with Criterion C as often as possible, and make sure to include questions that involve lines of reasoning, units, etc., to maximise the demonstration of learning. This criterion was previously one of Reflection and a trace of this idea survives in the analysis and reflection on the accuracy and sense of solutions. I really appreciate the changed importance to include limitations of mathematics to fully answer every real-life situation and problem.

Over the years, I have found that students who enjoy a debate or challenging perceived wisdom do well at the last two strands of this criterion. Others find it very uncomfortable to critique either their answers or the mathematics used. Many can accept that they should consider the degree of accuracy in terms of rounding or estimation but struggle beyond that. Make it clear to them that 'I did all the calculations, therefore my answer is accurate' is not an appropriate answer here. Nor is it a science experiment, where it would be appropriate to suggest repeated calculations or wander into meaningless complexity. I find the question 'How close do you think your answer might be to the truth and what would make it different from the truth/true answer?' helps them to focus in on what is required here.

Remember: This criterion provides opportunities to use mathematical concepts to solve real-life problems, or as close to real life and relevant to their lives as you can get. Tasks have to be simplified somewhat to fit the needs of the unit specifically and students welcome the chance to 'undo' those simplifications. In a stadium sightlines assessment, once they have used trigonometry to find the appropriate levels for seating, they must then draw on their knowledge from elsewhere to discuss why their proposed solutions may or may not make sense in the context. I find the students who enjoy debating, or have broader life experience, do well in this criterion. They will be the ones who know about restricted views, or access for people with disabilities, or the drive to maximise seats to make profits, or the ability to charge differentiated prices for comfort, as an example.

The *MYP Mathematics Guide* gives the following advice for Criterion D: 'Mathematics can be used to model many situations (for example, painting a room, analysing mobile telephone tariff plans, triangulation, diet plans)' (IBO, 2020, p. 31). Beyond this, though, it can be an excellent place to embed other formats of assessing understanding, such as Dan Meyer's three-act problems (kylepearce3, 2012) or a high-ceiling, low-floor assessment. It allows us to bring in enthusiasms, fads and interests of the class or teacher in the form of a real-world scenario, requiring a solution. Criterion D can also be an excellent way to address the global context of a unit, asking a question of importance to humanity that mathematics can contribute to, as well as the UN Sustainable Development Goals (SDGs).

Criteria and objectives are subject to change and, as mentioned in chapter 1, a review is overdue. However, they are true at the time of publishing. There will naturally be changes and developments in 'enhancing the MYP', but the heart of the assessments will no doubt be transferable under any new requirements.

Key feature: Anecdotal example

Before the last curriculum review the criteria had developed semi-independently and bore very little family resemblance. As they piloted different forms, bands of three marks per band were trialled. Very quickly it was discovered that everyone tended towards the middle, safe ground and left the other bands uninhabited. The criteria were also originally conceived as a holistic judgement for all the strands in unison, without differentiation, as the best and closest descriptor of the work being assessed.

This has been a matter of heated debate in our home for more than a decade! My husband, as a past chief examiner for MYP Design, had a very clear approach where he, and his team, would grade per strand in Design and then find a best fit quantitatively. My perspective was always that the holistic nature of the strands and level descriptors in mathematics must be different, as it is perfectly appropriate, in an almost qualitative way, to find the most appropriate fit to all the strands on first read through. My husband disagrees with this 'vibes based' approach, and always has; which is why this argument has continued in our home for so many years!

While these four criteria work harmoniously in the MYP, students then progress to the DP and experience a slight shock that everything is marks and percentages. Where do the criteria go? We discuss this in their final year of the MYP in terms of how their important ideas and aims continue but their manifestation is quite different. I like to discuss with students where all four go to, in two different ways: those that dissolve into the curriculum and those that evaporate.

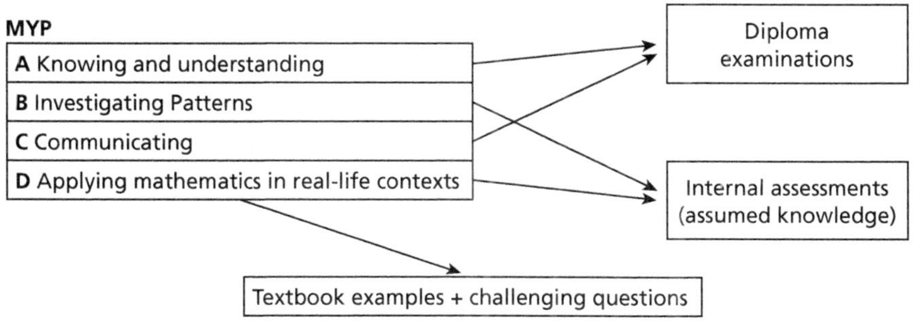

What does assessment look like in practice?

When we establish our assessment principles, we consider everything that is important and valid in assessment, and aim to set up the best possible teaching and learning for our students. Naturally, as we move from principles into practice, reality takes hold. Assessment practices give us direction and the understanding of how we prepare for, and manage, the unexpected.

Timing: how and when?

In chapter 8, Balanced, I outlined the importance of timing in assessments as a key driver for work–life balance, for you as well as the students. Leaving all assessments to the end of every semester or term creates an assessment logjam, coupled with high absence rates. Plan the dates of your assessments well, and build in buffer time in case of illness, absences or other typical school clashes. These can take the form of urgent test requirements or a sudden assembly, and cannot be avoided in school life.

Over time you may find certain patterns in the best timings for assessments, which lead to optimal results. You may choose to involve outside-class working time, but build in safeguards for academic honesty throughout. There may be a pattern which means that first period of the day is unsuitable for an assessment due to lates, and the last period of the day sees a decline in focus or behaviour in students. This cannot be avoided, but it is helpful to factor it into planning. For example, if I am coming to the end of a statistics unit and I know I have a Criterion D assessment with multiple valid answers, then I am less likely to worry about collusion and the assessment could span two lessons. With a Criterion B I would not make the same value judgement as I wouldn't want the students to share the correct pattern identification between sessions. If the volleyball trip is returning on Wednesday, I will not be scheduling a Criterion A test for that same week, as the students will not have had sufficient revision time, despite their assurances that they would keep up. And experience has taught me to expect a high degree of absence that week too. Given the weekend, though, I would certainly schedule it for the start of the following week to give them reasonable time to prepare. If you have this degree of schedule flexibility, as many MYP schools have, then it can be beneficial to assume there will be disruption to the assessment schedule

Now, given the impact of AI in the submissions of students, I would argue that in-class assessment for A, B and D continues to be the most appropriate. I have submitted lots of classic tasks to ChatGPT to see how it would compare to a typical grade 8 student. The results are mixed, with good Criterion A solutions but less ability to create independently. This is particularly obvious when a discussion of accuracy in Criterion D or verifying in Criterion B was required. With the new AI reasoning models this is much improved, particularly when I fed it the criteria, asked it to create its own rubric or mark scheme and then repeat the task. Much like the students, the machine only needed to know what I was looking for to make a vast improvement.

'... with a strong sense of fairness ...'

What is the process for applying the criteria?

Here we must again refer regularly to *From Principles into Practice* as the fountain of all assessment knowledge: 'At the end of a period of learning, teachers must make judgements on their students' achievement levels in each subject-group criterion' (IBO, 2014). Interesting to note here is the subtle language: 'At the end of a period of learning'. It does not have to be automatically at the end of a unit where students are assessed, but it must come at a natural break in a period of learning. This could apply to the middle of a lengthier unit or to assess skills worked on over two units consecutively.

The tasks are designed, or often inherited by, the teachers, and the chosen, mandated criterion assessed is clear and known to the students in advance. Once complete, teachers make decisions about student achievement against the defined criteria above by using their professional judgement. This assessment should be as precise and transparent as possible but will require the teacher to use a 'best fit' approach to find the final achievement level award.

The process of awarding the level is a complicated one, and while it is clearly defined in *FPIP*, teachers often require support 'reading between the lines', as they put it. This method of assessment is referred to as 'criterion-related approach', in contrast to 'norm-**referenced**' or 'criterion-referenced'. MYP assessment is definitively not norm-referenced as the students are never compared to one another to establish a normal distribution of grades or outcomes. As a teacher I really like this aspect, as it is easy to explain to students: 'Either you meet or demonstrate this skill or you don't, and it doesn't matter what anyone else does, you are only competing with your own previous performance.'

Neither is this model of assessment strictly criterion-referenced, where each level must be comprehensively fulfilled before progressing to the next. The flexibility to find the most appropriate match, once sufficient evidence exists, is termed the 'best-fit' approach. The procedure is best described as a bottom-up approach, where the teacher reads the descriptors from the first one onwards to see if the work has met, or exceeded, the level expected. This should continue until the teacher reads a descriptor that can no longer be said to match, or describe, the work seen. *FPIP* gives some guidance regarding the classic problem where a student has performed reasonably well, or partially well, in the lower levels but better in the harder questions or higher-level question. How do we handle this? 'In certain cases, it may appear that the student has not fulfilled all of the descriptors in a lower band but has fulfilled some in a higher band. In those cases, teachers must use their professional judgement in determining the descriptor that best fits the student's performance' (IBO, 2014). Namely, use your best judgement. Is this their usual standard? What are their formatives like? Was it a simple mistake in the lower levels? Did they deserve the 5? Does it feel more like a 6? These are the questions you start to hear when work is standardised, and it is a good indicator that the criteria are being correctly used and that learning, of teachers, is taking place.

I must acknowledge here that this drives some teachers up the wall! Their preference might be to have a globally defined standard for each, and a tick-box approach to each level and strand. This will never happen, so it is best to embrace the process of developing and refining your assessment practices and professional judgement as much as possible.

And so we now perceive the value of **standardisation** in this process. This is the time-consuming step, more so than even the marking, as it requires dialogue and agreement between professional opinions. To ensure there is no misunderstanding of process, or grade inflation or deflation creeping in, teachers should work together to establish common standards to evaluate each assessment holistically. This will involve disagreement, uncomfortable as that may be. Make time in collaborative planning or meetings to establish this process as one of the most valuable things you can do to build understanding, capacity and collegial support.

I would recommend implementing this even with teachers who may not be teaching the same year groups or exact courses, as it builds a knowledge base across the team of what is happening in other classes or years. It will increase the reliability of judgements and models for one another how we justify said judgements. It is also highly insightful into academic malpractice, if such exists. It brings misunderstandings to light in a less combative way. The more you can do this throughout the year, time permitting, the stronger your curriculum development will be.

Through this process I have refined both my personal preference and professional judgement throughout the year. In one school I was clearly the harshest marker, always arguing with colleagues that they were too generous. Later, in another context, expecting the same experience I found that I was suddenly considered more generous than others, giving too much benefit of the doubt to students.

These discussions are invaluable as I feel confident now that I balance both of these instincts in my judgements and am more self-aware as a marker.

Coming to an agreement and establishing the culture of expectation can rarely be done well without this. Sometimes a resolution will be needed if there is no final level determined, and the head of department or most experienced may pull rank, but the preceding discussion still has incredible value.

While we acknowledge that there is no expected normal distribution for application of criteria, it can still be used in analysis of outcomes over a longer period. When I was head of school, I could use the distribution of levels and grades to investigate possible grade inflation. This is where I first encountered the 'fear of parents leading to a safe middle ground' phenomenon. This was quickly revealed and corrected with support from the amazing MYP coordinator there.

As previously suggested, in the assessment principles advice (page 252), make sure there is agreement or, better yet, a policy on how you will handle common situations where the IB does not give guidance. These include:

- 'But it's two weeks late!!!' Timeliness. This is a bone of contention for many. As the criteria are so carefully designed and worded to be skills, there is nothing punitive relating to late entries. Schools must decide how to address this with deadline enforcement and external motivations, which must not impact the grade.
- 'They didn't even bother submitting it. I'm giving them a zero!' Zero versus N/A. You will see this debate rage online from time to time. When can you award a zero (failure to achieve any level described below) or when should it be N/A for not assessed? This can cause ructions in a department, too, so it's best to have a common understanding that still allows the requirement of at least two judgements for every strand of the criterion in the academic year. My personal opinion is that a zero is merited only when the student has had a chance to submit, albeit later. I do not use it as an instant punishment, only when the options have been exhausted and they still cannot demonstrate their learning.
- 'Are you asking me to make the test easier?' Accommodations. It can be really helpful, and healthy, to have a departmental or division approach to making changes or accommodations to assessments to meet students' needs. If there is a common language policy, for which there is guidance on the TSM section of My IB, then that is helpful. In Hamburg there was an extremely productive relationship between the mathematics and the EAL department, forged by the fact that one of the latter's number, Nisar, also

happened to be a mathematician. Nisar then acted as a bridge between the two departments, allowing us to create parallel assessments for mathematics but with fewer linguistic barriers. Over time, the principles of universal design took over and we found that if the language was clearer for non-native speakers, then it could be helpful or clearer for all.

- 'Why do you bother putting a smiley face on all your investigations?' To what extent do your teachers add personalisation to their assessments? Do they ask for feedback? Is any question not related to the task or assessment directly a distraction? Can images or design choices be justified?
- Extra credit or extension. I made this mistake early in my MYP career. I would add extra credit assignments that might 'bump them up' or keep them busy at the end of tests. Before long I realised that this was effectively creating a level 9–10 structure, as once they have demonstrated the highest levels, what am I asking them to actually do? It also reduced student motivation to perform on the first attempt, while simultaneously increasing workload – the dream combination! Once I was consistent and held students to their deadlines, within reason, this increased resilience and focus.
- Students who perform inconsistently across criteria. You will see, from time to time, students who perform radically differently depending on the criteria, who may excel at real-life situations but fall to pieces in a test. They may have overall levels of 2, 5, 5, 7 for Criteria A, B, C and D, respectively. While I am entirely comfortable reporting and recording those grades, I have known colleagues for whom this sits uneasily, asking questions like 'Is this person a good mathematician or not?' For a total of score of 19, this student would achieve a 5, which I feel is appropriate. Have these discussions when standardising and moderating to fine-tune everyone's understanding of the grading process, as well as typical student profiles.
- 'You want me to re-mark this?' There is no explicit information provided by the IB as to whether students can or should resubmit work for marking. I would be of the opinion that if a school allows this, it is an additional judgement and should not replace the original. I have heard of unethical practices where teachers' achievement levels or grades were influenced by administration or leadership. These include changes made to grades or an insistence that certain levels were impossible to achieve, such as giving students below a 4 for fear of parental pushback. My advice is to give honest, detailed feedback when returning assessments, and ensure that your own personal practices are as ethically sound as possible. The only thing a teacher can ensure, in an ethically compromised position such as this, is that no moral injury is done to them or their students in the process.

How should assessments be recorded or reported?

'... respect for the dignity and rights of people ...'

To be principled in our assessment of student achievement, it is important to pay attention to the most accurate demonstration of student performance. We cannot average the levels, nor simply take the most recent one. Some teachers will initially try to mechanically and uncritically average the achievement levels over given reporting periods, or they might attempt a similar process with individual strands. If we consider our motivation in assessing their work to require a strong sense of fairness and respect, then we must determine what is the most appropriate judgement for where the student is now in their understanding, given the evidence at hand.

How do we turn criteria into grades and how does this feed into the grade descriptors?

Final grade	Grade boundary	Descriptor
1	1–5	Produces work of very limited quality. Conveys many significant misunderstandings or lacks understanding of most concepts and contexts. Very rarely demonstrates critical or creative thinking. Very inflexible, rarely using knowledge or skills.
2	6–9	Produces work of limited quality. Expresses misunderstandings or significant gaps in understanding for many concepts and contexts. Infrequently demonstrates critical or creative thinking. Generally inflexible in the use of knowledge and skills, infrequently applying knowledge and skills.
3	10–14	Produces work of an acceptable quality. Communicates basic understanding of many concepts and contexts, with occasionally significant misunderstandings or gaps. Begins to demonstrate some basic critical and creative thinking. Is often inflexible in the use of knowledge and skills, requiring support even in familiar classroom situations.
4	15–18	Produces good-quality work. Communicates basic understanding of most concepts and contexts with few misunderstandings and minor gaps. Often demonstrates basic critical and creative thinking. Uses knowledge and skills with some flexibility in familiar classroom situations but requires support in unfamiliar situations.

Final grade	Grade boundary	Descriptor
5	19–23	Produces generally high-quality work. Communicates secure understanding of concepts and contexts. Demonstrates critical and creative thinking, sometimes with sophistication. Uses knowledge and skills in familiar classroom and real-world situations and, with support, some unfamiliar real-world situations.
6	24–27	Produces high-quality, occasionally innovative work. Communicates extensive understanding of concepts and contexts. Demonstrates critical and creative thinking, frequently with sophistication. Uses knowledge and skills in familiar and unfamiliar classroom and real-world situations, often with independence.
7	28–32	Produces high-quality, frequently innovative work. Communicates comprehensive, nuanced understanding of concepts and contexts. Consistently demonstrates sophisticated critical and creative thinking. Frequently transfers knowledge and skills with independence and expertise in a variety of complex classroom and real-world situations.

Source: IBO (2020)

This conversion table and grade descriptors show how the total of all four criteria judgements work together to make a final grade. When I was writing the descriptors it was important that they aligned not only with the contents of the individual criteria but also the DP grade descriptors, which had already been in existence for a long time. It was a challenging exercise, moving eight levels of differentiation into seven, while reflecting all four criteria in each grade. The distinguishers are very useful when comparing the totals to the students that you know well. If they get a 5 total, but you're not sure that they generally produce high-quality work, then perhaps it would be good to revisit those judgements. Does your student produce high-quality work but it is formulaic and rarely innovative? You won't be surprised then when they come out at the end of the semester with a 6 overall.

Key feature: Case study

One of the (valid) criticisms you might hear, or share, about the MYP is that it fails to give students experience in examinations, to prepare for Diploma examinations. I have had families who expressed concern that their children would get to 18 or 19 never having sat an official examination and may not have the skills to cope with that intimidating environment. Some even argue that, while eAssessment and online assessment are available for the MYP, until the DP follows suit students will still need strategies and techniques for high-stakes, paper examinations. While head of school, I introduced a model of high-stakes environment with low-stakes assessment to develop these skills and reduce test anxiety.

In this model, from grade 9 (MYP 4) onwards students would sit what felt like official examinations but counted as no more than a typical criterion assessment. In Mathematics this meant that they were engaging with a classic test but they had desk configurations, examination posters, even the script used during Diploma examinations, so all would be familiar. They were given a schedule, invigilators and study leave, to emulate the process. By having the low-stakes assessment attached they were free to focus on acclimatising to the systems, and pressures, of a high-stakes environment.

Self-assessment

Complete the reflection:

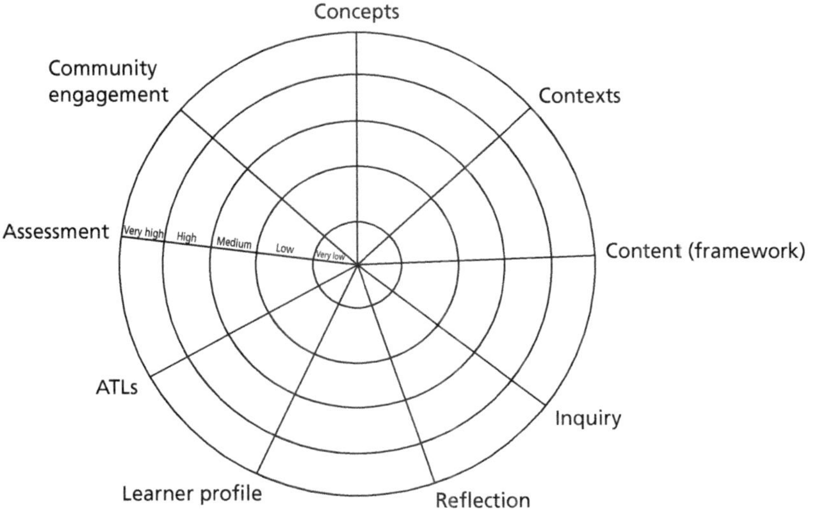

Shade in your knowledge level from low to high as you feel your comfort level lies.

Glossary

Achievement level The level given when the student work reflects the corresponding descriptor. Achievement levels are shown in the left-hand column of the assessment criteria.

Assessment criteria Criteria against which a student's performance is measured.

Assessment rubric The grid that connects levels and descriptors.

Assessment task An activity or series of activities with which students engage in order for assessment to take place.

Assessment tool A method of collecting information about a learner's performance and understanding.

Command term The word(s) in a question that explain the assessment objective that is being assessed.

Criterion-related assessment An assessment process based on determining levels of achievement against previously agreed criteria. The standard is therefore fixed rather than dependent on the achievement of the entire cohort of students.

Descriptors Achievement level descriptors describe the features of student work expected to be seen at each achievement level.

Formative assessment Ongoing assessment aimed at providing information to guide teaching and improve student performance.

Grade The description of student achievement. Final grades for student work range from 1 (lowest) to 7 (highest). The grade represents the IB's judgement on the overall qualities that the candidate has demonstrated, and is consistent between years and subjects.

Grade boundary The point at which candidate achievement moves from one grade to another. It is often used to indicate the lowest or highest criterion level totals that correspond to a particular grade.

Judgement The consideration of a candidate's work against an individual assessment criterion.

Summative assessment Assessment aimed at determining the competency or level of achievement of a student, generally at the end of a course of study or a unit of work.

GLOSSARY

** Asterisked entries below are not official IB definitions.*

Achievement level The level given when the student work reflects the corresponding descriptor. Achievement levels are shown in the left-hand column of the assessment criteria.

Action The act of engaging individually and/or collaboratively with local, national and global challenges and opportunities.

Adversarial Competitive.*

Advocacy Supporting and committing to action for positive change for oneself and others.

Agency A philosophical, sociological and psychological idea that acknowledges humans as active participants in their own lives with the capacity to initiate intentional action.

Alignment Agreement in principle and practice between shared values and aspirations for learning (designed/planned curriculum), how teachers actually work (delivered curriculum) and what students actually learn (assessed curriculum).

Anxiety A feeling of worry, nervousness or unease about something with an uncertain outcome.*

Approaches to learning Refers to a range of skills that help students guide, support and structure learning.

Assessed curriculum MYP assessment gives teachers and students reliable and valid information on student learning. Integrated with the designed/planned curriculum and delivered curriculum, the assessed curriculum is considered throughout the processes involved in planning for learning.

Assessment The collection of evidence in order to make judgements about teaching and learning.

Assessment criteria Criteria against which a student's performance is measured.

Assessment rubric The grid that connects levels and descriptors.

Assessment task An activity or series of activities with which students engage in order for assessment to take place.

Assessment tool A method of collecting information about a learner's performance and understanding.

Autonomy The freedom to decide for oneself and pursue a chosen course of action.

Bias Where a defined group (that is, racial or ethnic group or gender) performs differently on a specific question or task than the average for a reason other than ability in the trait that is being assessed.

Branches A division of the mathematical domain of knowledge, organised by types of reasoning featured within.*

Burnout A state of emotional, physical and mental exhaustion caused by excessive and prolonged stress. It typically results from being overwhelmed, overworked or feeling undervalued, and leads to reduced productivity, loss of motivation and feelings of ineffectiveness.*

Collegial A relationship characterised by shared responsibility, authority and a spirit of cooperation among colleagues, typically within a workplace or professional setting. It emphasises mutual respect and equality among peers.*

Command term The word(s) in a question that explain the assessment objective that is being assessed.

Community engagement A variety of ways to engage in service learning, including personal, local and global opportunities.*

Community project Focuses on community and service, encouraging students to explore their right and responsibility to implement service as action in the community. The project gives students an opportunity to develop awareness of needs in various communities and to address those needs through service learning.

Concept Conceptual learning focuses on powerful organising ideas that have relevance within and across subject groups.

Conceptual understanding When concepts are used to formulate the understandings that students should retain in the future; they become principles and generalisations that students can use to understand the world, and to succeed in further study and in life beyond school.

Congenial A colleague or atmosphere that is pleasant, friendly and agreeable in nature, creating a comfortable and enjoyable working relationship.*

Content An IB education encompasses disciplinary knowledge and understanding that meets international university standards for rigour in terms of depth and breadth, which content articulates.

Criterion-related assessment An assessment process based on determining levels of achievement against previously agreed criteria. The standard is therefore fixed rather than dependent on the achievement of the entire cohort of students.

Curriculum An overall plan for learning that is broad, balanced and coherent. It describes the entire learning experience in a school.

Curriculum security Stability in educational offerings, and the guarantee that all students can access the educational resources necessary to achieve academic success and personal growth.*

Delivered curriculum The construction of meaning so that students' learning will be purposeful in class. Previously called the taught curriculum.

Descriptors Achievement level descriptors describe the features of student work expected to be seen at each achievement level.

Differentiating Modifying teaching strategies to meet the needs of diverse learners, through varied content, process and products.

Disability Refers to any physical or mental factor that complicates an individual's ability to perform specific activities and engage with their environment.*

Discrimination Unfair or unequal treatment of different categories of people based on specific characteristics shared by those categories.*

Diversity Refers to difference and uniqueness. Valuing diversity is about acceptance and recognition.

eAssessment Assessment carried out on a computer or similar device.

Equity As defined by the OECD, 'Equity in education has two dimensions. The first is fairness, which basically means making sure that personal and social circumstances – for example gender, socioeconomic status or ethnic origin – should not be an obstacle to achieving educational potential. The second is inclusion, in other words ensuring a basic minimum standard of education for all – for example that everyone should be able to read, write and do simple arithmetic. The two dimensions are closely intertwined: tackling access to and failure to achieve school outcomes helps to overcome the effects of social deprivation which often causes lack of access and quality outcomes.'

Ethnomathematics In educational mathematics, ethnomathematics explores the connection between mathematics and culture.*

Evaluating Making an appraisal by weighing up the strengths and limitations.

Form 'The shape and underlying structure of an entity or piece of work, including its organisation, essential nature and external appearance. Form in MYP Mathematics refers to the understanding that the underlying structure and shape of an entity is distinguished by its properties. Form provides opportunities for students to appreciate the aesthetic nature of the constructs used in a discipline' (IBO, 2020).

Formative assessment Ongoing assessment aimed at providing information to guide teaching and improve student performance.

Framework The MYP framework provides a structure for organising parts of a curriculum and the relationships between them.

Global context A common language for powerful contextual learning, identifying specific settings, events or circumstances that provide more concrete perspectives for learning and teaching.

Grade The description of student achievement. Final grades for student work range from 1 (lowest) to 7 (highest). The grade represents the IB's judgement on the overall qualities that the candidate has demonstrated, and is consistent between years and subjects.

Grade boundary The point at which candidate achievement moves from one grade to another. It is often used to indicate the lowest or highest criterion level totals that correspond to a particular grade.

Horizontal planning/articulation Planning horizontally involves a team of teachers of the same grade level working together to plan for learning.

Inclusion An ongoing process that aims to increase access to and engagement in learning for all students by identifying and removing barriers.

Inquiry A perspective on learning, emphasising that meaning is actively constructed.

Judgement The consideration of a candidate's work against an individual assessment criterion.

Key concepts Broad, organising, powerful ideas that have relevance within and across subjects and disciplines, providing connections that can transfer across time and culture.

Logic A method of reasoning and a system of principles used to build arguments and reach conclusions. Logic in MYP Mathematics is used as a process in making decisions about numbers, shapes and variables. This system of reasoning provides students with a method for explaining the validity of their conclusions.

Mastery Deep understanding and proficient application of knowledge and skills in a subject area.*

Mathematics framework A detailed document showing the mathematical content suggested to schools and required by schools engaging with eAssessments.*

Metacognition Thinking about thinking. It is the ability to be aware of, reflect on and understand one's own thought processes.

Neurodivergence Variations in the human brain regarding sociability, learning, attention, mood and other mental functions. A term often used to describe individuals whose brain functions differ from what is considered typical or neurotypical.*

Neuroplasticity The brain's ability to reorganise itself by forming new neural connections.*

Objective One of a set of statements describing the skills, knowledge and understanding that will be assessed.

On-screen examination A formal, timed, externally produced, media-rich examination comprising a series of tasks related to the subject, designed to be answered in a secure exam environment.

Pedagogy The art and science of teaching (young people) as a professional practice.

Planned/designed curriculum A formal, comprehensive, school-wide set of documents written by the school, which describes what will be delivered in each subject to each age group. Previously called the written curriculum.

Prior learning The MYP mathematics framework is based on the expectation that students in MYP Year 1 have at least five years of prior mathematics experience and are familiar with the topics and skills, as outlined in the *MYP Mathematics Guide*.

Provocation An open-ended stimulus to engage student thinking.

Reasonable adjustments Changes or additional conditions to the assessment process, which may not be standard and not covered in the list of inclusive access arrangements. They are unique to a student based on their requirements.

Reflection A cognitive act that considers past experiences in order to improve, modify and plan for the future.

Related concepts Concepts that are grounded in specific disciplines and explore key concepts in greater detail, providing depth to the programme.

Relationships In MYP Mathematics this refers to the connections between quantities, properties or concepts, and these connections may be expressed as models, rules or statements.

Relationships provide opportunities for students to explore patterns in the world around them. Connections between the student and mathematics in the real world are important in developing deeper understanding.

Representation The manner in which something is presented.

Responsible action Taking action that is informed, responsible and ethical.

Rigour A thorough and robust understanding of subjects that prepares students for further education and lifelong learning.*

Scaffolding The use of a variety of teaching strategies and tools to support a student's progression in their learning. Scaffolding is temporary, appropriate and responsive.

Scarcity A situation where educational resources, opportunities or access are limited. This can include shortages of qualified teachers, insufficient academic materials, lack of funding for schools, limited access to advanced courses or technology, and overcrowded classrooms.*

Sensitivity The quality or condition of being easily affected, influenced, or harmed by external factors or stimuli.*

Service A shared value of the IB community. IB learners strive to be caring members of the community who demonstrate a personal commitment to service, and act to make a positive difference to the lives of others and to the environment.

Service as action With appropriate guidance and support, MYP students should, through their engagement with service as one of the significant forms of action, meet the learning outcomes to develop the skills and attributes of an IB learner. IB World Schools value service with others as an important way to engage in principled action across a range of overlapping local and global communities.

Skills The abilities we use to guide, support and structure learning.

Statement of inquiry This statement expresses the relationship between concepts and context; it represents a transferable idea supported by factual content.

Summative assessment Assessment aimed at determining the competency or level of achievement of a student, generally at the end of a course of study or a unit of work.

Synergistic thinking The interplay between factual and conceptual thinking.

Topic For the purpose of external assessment, the MYP identifies a range of subject-specific topics that constitute one of the variables that authors consider when they create on-screen examinations.

Trigger Something that initiates or causes a specific reaction or process to start.*

Unit In the context of the MYP curriculum, a unit can be defined as a period of study that concludes with a summative assessment. Also can be defined as a series of lessons, focused through a statement of inquiry and inquiry questions, designed to enable students to achieve some of the objectives of an MYP subject group summative assessment.

Vertical planning/articulation The goal of vertical planning is to sequence learning (in terms of subject-group objectives and ATLs) to ensure continuity and progression from Year 1 to Year 5.

APPENDICES

Here you will find a 'collection of collections', ideas for resources, both real and virtual. Many of these are cheap or free to implement, while others may require investment. Wherever possible, I encourage you to find resources from the circular economy. I often find rules, calculators and other mathematical items in charity or thrift shops. The school newsletter or social media channels can be used to appeal to families for donations such as Lego or board games, even eye masks! Before you purchase a new item, consider if there is an environmentally sustainable solution.

1. Inquiry box
2. Resources cabinet
    (a) Class sets
    (b) Bespoke items
    (c) Investment pieces
    (d) Consumables
    (e) Paper items
3. Games
4. Books
5. Interdisciplinary suggestions

1. Inquiry box

See chapter 5 for more about the role and purpose of an inquiry box. The box can be filled with a variety of objects, which usually transcend branches but all items feel inherently mathematical. Here is a small sample of the items in my collection.

An **old-fashioned calculator**, like a Walther vintage mechanical adding machine, is probably the most popular item in my inquiry box. I received it as a gift and it has been a profound source of inquiry ever since.

I never give students any instructions or direction, simply placing the very heavy object in the centre of their desk. They are intrigued, and several have figured out how to add or multiply. They are simply ecstatic when they finally solve the problem and close the curiosity gap.

This **calculating monkey** was another gift, from a student who wanted me to explain how it worked. The monkey's feet can be moved along the factor scale below and it automatically shows the product in the base of the arrow, between the monkey's hands.

The student was so intrigued that the second I had opened the gift, she snatched it back to show me and query the mechanics. It was another instant hit in the inquiry box. Another interesting provocation is that there is something I find unsettling about this. I cannot be sure whether it is about anthropomorphism or animal subjugation, or something even more sinister, but I often ask students if they like it. Some agree that they find it unsettling and I have also had a few students argue that it is subliminally racist. It creates great conversations and inquiry, while simultaneously testing students' multiplication prowess.

The simple child's toy shown in the accompanying image can be used in a variety of ways.

- I ask students to find out how many equations or inequalities are possible.
- Can they predict what is on the opposite, unseen side?
- Are there more true than untrue statements? How many turns will it take to change a true statement into an untrue one?
- How many combinations and permutations are possible?

I also collect mathematical items wherever I see them, often on holidays. These inquiry artefacts support international-mindedness and the transfer of mathematical understanding. Again, I give them no context and simply ask students, 'How is mathematics being used/communicated here?' I get some fascinating answers.

Other times, the task may be a creative one. In this case I give them a promotional bookmark from a bookstore and ask them to create a similar object but for our current unit. Given a very short time, they must synthesise the unit quickly and employ their creative thinking to make a finished product.

Alternatively, I will give them a tool such as the geometric template shown here and they must work collaboratively to create a specific design in the inquiry time. This may be used to create a recognisable figure or a tessellation, or during angle units. It is a helpful introduction to composite shapes but also useful during mensuration and conversion units.

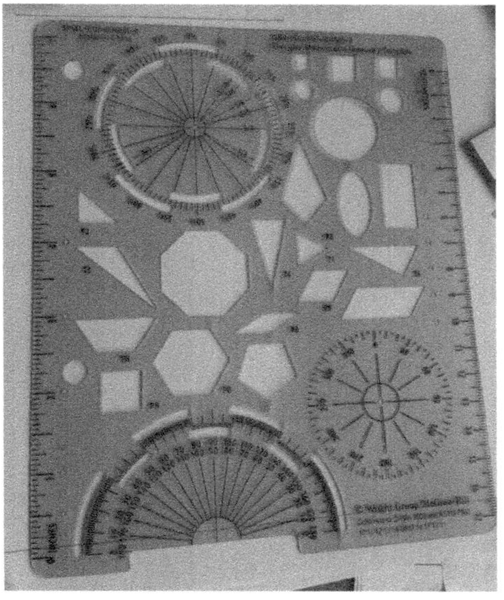

Discussion objects like the child's game of matching shapes and spaces pictured here can help develop students' critical thinking. A typical instruction I might give them for this would be, 'I hate this object, mathematically speaking. You have three minutes to figure out why.' Alternatively, I might ask them to compare the relative areas, perimeters or orientations, which leads to fruitful dialogue.

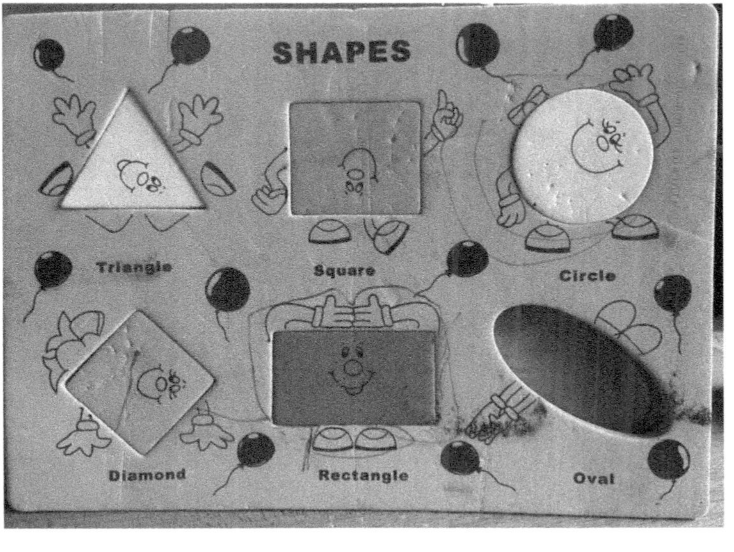

I quite often also give them a popular game with no instructions, time permitting – a game like Sum Fun – to see if they can pick it up within the time.

2. Resources cabinet

Let me help you spend your budget! You might not know this, but we mathematicians are renowned for asking for very little and sometimes failing to spend the entirety of the departmental allocation of budget. I can help with that!

a. Class sets

Try to have at least a full set of each of the following items (add 10% for breakages and losses):

- geo boards and rubber bands (I recommend 11 x 11 grids)
- dice (standard six-sided)
- counters, spinners
- dominoes
- algebra tiles
- mathematical snap cards (fractions, number sets), 'I have; who has?' card sets
- playing cards.

b. Bespoke items

The following are useful for demonstrations and explanations, as well as inquiry:

- A helix four-piece boxed set
- a few packs of giant playing cards
- a grid shower curtain, useful as a Cartesian grid
- four styrofoam cones, to show conic sections
- a 3D Pythagoras model
- a jumbo magnetic spinner
- a board geometry set
- spare calculator charger cables (always needed around exam time)
- a flipchart on a tripod (comes in useful much more often than you might think for collaborative and independent work)
- several blank clocks for project work
- examples of timetables

- calendars
- measurement tools, including scales, trundle wheels and counters (sweets, beans, plastic counters)
- sets of international stamps and coins
- a beach ball, globe or icosahedral model of planet Earth.

c. Investment pieces

These might include:

- a laser measurer
- a few magnetic board wipers (not necessarily an investment but valuable and they get stolen regularly)
- spirographs
- a Binostat or Plinko device
- an old-fashioned calculator.

d. Consumables

For instance:

- rubber bands
- Post-its
- window markers
- sidewalk/pavement chalk
- cardboard for nets and constructions
- batteries
- blank pre-cut puzzles
- masking or painters' tape.

e. Paper items

Such as:

- tracing paper
- isometric grid paper, different types
- graph paper, different grid sizes
- double-sided plastic mirror.

3. Games

Make sure to have a wide variety of games available for those post-assessment quiet times, or for celebration and reward. Where possible, choose a game to tie into the specific branch of reasoning – Othello is excellent for networks units, while Mancala helps with abstract reasoning, and so on.

Guess Who? is especially useful as, if you have several copies, some can be repurposed as 'Guess Which?' games, in which students can design their own 'characters', such as different polygons or polyhedra, and test their factual knowledge.

Here are some other games I have found helpful in developing numerical, spatial or abstract reasoning:

- Domino
- Timeline
- Tangram
- Abalone
- Sudoku
- Spirogram
- Kalaha
- Bloku
- Quoridor
- Prime Climb
- Battleship
- Scrabble
- Exploding Kittens
- Monopoly Deal
- 4 in a row/Connect 4
- Colour and number sudoku.

4. Books

- *Professor Stewart's Cabinet of Mathematical Curiosities*
- *Professor Stewart's Hoard of Mathematical Treasures*
- *Professor Stewart's Casebook of Mathematical Mysteries*
- *Learn to Read with Great Speed*
- *Professor Stewart's Incredible Numbers*

- *The Joy of X: A Guided Tour of Mathematics, from One to Infinity*
- *The Calculus Story: A Mathematical Adventure*
- *The GCHQ Puzzle Book*
- *Bletchley Park Brainteasers*
- *Alex's Adventures in Numberland*
- *Can You Solve My Problems? A Casebook of Ingenious, Perplexing and Totally Satisfying Puzzles*
- *Alex Through the Looking Glass: How Life Reflects Numbers, and Numbers Reflect Life*
- *The Original Area Mazes: 100 Addictive Puzzles to Solve with Simple Maths – and Clever Logic!*
- *Geometry Snacks: Bite Size Problems and Multiple Ways to Solve Them*
- *Sherlock: The Puzzle Book*
- *How Many Socks Make a Pair? Surprisingly Interesting Everyday Maths*
- *Fermat's Last Theorem*
- *The Simpsons and Their Mathematical Secrets*
- *The Code Book: The Secret History of Codes and Code-breaking*
- *Big Bang: The Most Important Scientific Discovery of All Time and Why You Need to Know About It*
- *The Music of the Primes: Why an Unsolved Problem in Mathematics Matters*
- *The Great Mathematical Problems: Marvels and Mysteries of Mathematics*
- *Seventeen Equations that Changed the World*
- *Things to Make and Do in the Fourth Dimension*
- *M.C. Escher Kaleidocycles: 17 Models of Escher's Graphics and the Story of How They Were Devised*
- *Kaleidocycles Paper Shapers* (craft).

5. Interdisciplinary suggestions

For the final set of resources, let us consider some ideas for interdisciplinary units between mathematics and other subjects.

Remember: Interdisciplinary work is a vital component of a broad and balanced MYP curriculum and schools are required to have at least one IDU peer academic year, across subject groups. We also hope to inspire this convergent thinking in our students to prepare them for a world with creative connections between sectors such as AI regulators, data historians, molecular artists and so many more jobs not yet created.

'Interdisciplinarity, as experienced in the MYP age group, should be purposeful and integrative,' says the IB. With willingness between departments, some of these activities can even become fixtures in the annual calendar – such as the collaboration between Mathematics and Design departments in a chance carnival. This is often scheduled for MYP3 around the personal project time, as parents can then visit both. Likewise, when Mathematics and I&S collaborate to create a UNESCO 'judging panel' this can feed into class trips and learning experiences outside the classroom.

With this in mind, here are 10 suggestions for meaningful interdisciplinary links:

1. Science – the mathematics of snow science (including the geometry of snowflakes etc., crystallised air, pressure bars for direct proportion)
2. Art – first nations' art and their use of ethnomathematics
3. I&S (business) – the mathematics of crypto, e.g. how can we use statistics from the past to predict the probabilities of the future of cryptocurrencies?
4. I&S (geography) – the fractal nature of coastlines
5. Dance – the mathematics of Samuel Beckett and his play, *Quad*
6. Design – the mathematics of everyday sexism in modern design (including the work of Caroline Criado Perez)
7. Language and literature – the mathematics of poetry, studying different forms and structures of poems that follow and break the conventions
8. PHE – the precision and accuracy of athletic performance, focusing on recording and reporting achievement
9. Language acquisition – the study of macaronic songs and the proportional analysis of the dominant versus other language
10. I&S (history) – the role of mathematics in folklore, sacred numbers and custom/traditions.

BIBLIOGRAPHY

Amlin, I. and Bateson, R. (2017) *MYP by Concept: Mathematics 1*. Hachette Learning.

Amlin, I. and Bateson, R. (2018) *MYP by Concept: Mathematics 2*. Hachette Learning.

Barton, C. (ongoing) *Mr Barton Maths Podcast*. Available online at: https://www.mrbartonmaths.com/blog/

Bateson, R. (2017) *MYP by Concept: Mathematics 4 & 5*. Hachette Learning.

Bateson, R. and Amlin, I. (2018) *MYP by Concept: Mathematics 3*. Hachette Learning.

Boaler, J. (2015a). *Mathematical Mindsets: Unleashing Students' Potential through Creative Math, Inspiring Messages and Innovative Teaching*. Jossey-Bass, Inc.

Boaler, J. (2015b). *What's Math Got to Do With It? How Teachers and Parents Can Transform Mathematics Learning and Inspire Success*. Penguin.

Box, G.E.P. (1976) 'Science and statistics', *Journal of the American Statistical Association*, 71(356): 791–799.

Castro J. (2024) 'How to make a map of smell', *Aeon*, 12 April. Available online at: https://aeon.co/essays/odours-have-a-complex-topography-and-its-been-mapped-by-ai

Delaney, S. (2016) *Become the Primary Teacher Everyone Wants to Have*. Routledge.

Dweck, C. (2013) *Mindset: The New Psychology of Success*. Ballantine (updated 2017).

Erickson, H.L. (2011) 'Synergistic thinking and conceptual understanding in the IB programmes', IB Symposium, The Hague, October. Available online at: https://www.ibo.org/contentassets/477a9bccb5794081a7bb8dd0ec5a4d17/lynnerickson_ib_kynote_hague_oct__2011.pdf

Forrest, J., Waldman, P., Chang Wathall, J., Doering, S., Harris, D. and Stoyanova Kennedy, N. (2019) *Oxford IB Diploma Programme. IB Mathematics: Applications and Interpretation*. Oxford University Press.

Gonzalez, J. (ongoing) *Cult of Pedagogy* [website]. Available online at: https://www.cultofpedagogy.com/

Gonzalez, J. (2013) 'Find your marigold: the one essential rule for new teachers', cultofpedagogy.com, 29 August. Available online at: https://www.cultofpedagogy.com/marigolds/

Ilaria, D. (2024) 'Stop using these four words in math class', middleweb.com, 29 January (updated 21 February). Available online at: https://www.middleweb.com/50208/stop-using-these-four-words-in-math-class/

IBO Community Blog (2014) 'Review process', 17 January. Available online at: https://blogs.ibo.org/sharingpyp/2014/01/17/2639/

International Baccalaureate Organization (IBO) (2010) *Learning Diversity in the International Baccalaureate Programmes*. IBO.

International Baccalaureate Organization (IBO) (2011) *Language and Learning in IB Programmes*. IBO.

International Baccalaureate Organization (IBO) (2014) *MYP: From Principles into Practice*. IBO.

International Baccalaureate Organization (IBO) (2019) 'Mathematics curriculum development report', January. Available online at: https://resources.ibo.org/myp/subject-group/Mathematics/resource/11162-54552/?lang=en (member-only content).

International Baccalaureate Organization (IBO) (2020) *MYP Mathematics Guide*. IBO.

International Baccalaureate Organization (IBO) (2022) *Access and Inclusion Policy*. IBO.

International Baccalaureate Organization (IBO) (2023) 'Our mission'. Available online at: www.ibo.org/about-the-ib/mission (updated 6 June).

Kunkel, T., Seiler, P.M., Torres-Skoumal, M. and Weber, D. (2014) *IB Skills: Mathematics – A Practical Guide*. Hachette Learning.

kylepearce3 (2012) 'Problem solving with Dan Meyer's three-act math stories', *Make Math Moments*, 22 October. Available online at: https://makemathmoments.com/dan-meyer-three-act-math-problem-solving

Ladau, E. (2021) *Demystifying Disability: What to Know, What to Say and How to Be an Ally*. Ten Speed Press (also available as an audiobook).

Liljedahl, P. (2020) *Building Thinking Classrooms in Mathematics, Grades K-12: 14 Teaching Practices for Enhancing Learning*. Corwin.

Morrison, T. (2000) Quoted on *The Oprah Winfrey Show*. Available online at: https://youtu.be/_HAFtuJEgKk

Nicolson, M. (2010) *History of the Middle Years Programme*. IBO.

O'Neil, C. (2016) *Weapons of Math Destruction*. Crown.

Pearcy, D. (2020) *Mathematical Beauty*. John Catt.

Seighart, M.A. (2021) *The Authority Gap*. Doubleday. Also available as a podcast at: https://www.maryannsieghart.com/the-authority-gap/

Song, H. and Schwartz, N. (2010) 'If it's easy to read, it's easy to do, pretty, good, and true', *The Psychologist*. British Psychological Society. Available online at: https://www.bps.org.uk/psychologist/if-its-easy-read-its-easy-do-pretty-good-and-true

Southall, E. and Pantaloni, V. (2018) *Geometry Snacks: Bite Size Problems and Multiple Ways to Solve Them*. Tarquin.

Tui Tuia | Learning Circle (n.d.) 'Aotearoa New Zealand's histories'. Available online at: https://www.learningcircle.co.nz/pld/aotearoa-new-zealands-histories#:~:text=From%202023%2C%20Te%20Takanga%20o,content%20from%20term%201%202023

United Nations (UN) (n.d.) 'The 17 goals'. Available online at: https://sdgs.un.org/goals

Vanderkam, L. (2024) 'Magic is just labor, hidden well', *Before Breakfast*, 19 February (podcast). Available online at: https://omny.fm/shows/before-breakfast/magic-is-just-labor-hidden-well#description

Watson, A., Jones, K. and Pratt, D. (2013) *Key Ideas in Teaching Mathematics*. Oxford University Press.

Wiggins, G. and McTighe, J. (1998) *Understanding by Design*. Association for Supervision and Curriculum Development.